KIEŚLOWSKI ON KIEŚ

Danusia Stok is a writer and translator. She has worked on numerous documentaries on Poland as translator or researcher and is the co-author of Jerzy Skolimowski's film *Moonlighting*. From 1976 to 1981 she lived in Poland, where she met a number of leading Polish film-makers, including Krzysztof Kieślowski. Now living permanently in England, Danusia Stok visits Poland regularly and maintains strong contacts with the film world in both countries.

KIEŚLOWSKI
ON
KIEŚLOWSKI

Edited by
DANUSIA STOK

faber and faber
LONDON BOSTON

First published in 1993 by
Faber and Faber Limited
3 Queen Square London WCIN 3AU
This paperback edition first published in 1995

Printed in England by Clays Ltd, St Ives plc

A CIP record of this book is available from the British Library.

ISBN 0 571 17328 4

6 8 10 9 7 5

Contents

List of Illustrations   vii

Acknowledgements   ix

Introduction by Danusia Stok   xiii

Epigraph   xxii

1 BACKGROUND

   Returning Home   1
   Film School   22

2 THE UNIQUE ROLE OF DOCUMENTARIES

   From the City of Łódź   44
   I Was a Soldier   54
   Workers '71   54
   Curriculum vitae   58
   First Love   63
   Hospital   68
   I Don't Know   73
   From a Night Porter's Point of View   75
   Station   79

3 THE FEATURE FILMS

   In Order to Learn: *Pedestrian Subway*   93
   A Metaphor for Life: *Personnel*   95
   A Flawed Script: *The Scar*   99
   A 'Period Piece': *The Calm*   106
   A Trap: *Camera Buff*   110
   Chance or Fate: *Blind Chance*   113
   The Communist Virus: *Short Working Day*   115
   We All Bowed Our Heads: *No End*   125
   The *Decalogue*   143

A Short Film about Killing   159
A Short Film about Love   166
Pure Emotions: *The Double Life of Véronique*   172

4 'I DON'T LIKE THE WORD "SUCCESS"'   204

5 THREE COLOURS   212

Notes   229

Filmography   237

Index   265

List of Illustrations

1   'My father was a very wise man but I couldn't make much use of his wisdom. It's only now that I can understand some of the things he did or said.' 3

2   'My father was more important to me than my mother because he died so young. But my mother was important too and one of the reasons I decided to go to film school.' 4

3   'My father had tuberculosis. He'd go to sanatoria and my mum, me and my sister, we'd follow him.' 4

4   'I was never a goody-goody or a swot. I got good marks but didn't make any special effort.' 11

5   'I used to go to sanatoria for children. The whole idea was to spend time in a good climate and to have healthy food.' 12

6   'My father eventually died of TB. He was forty-seven, younger than I am now.' 14

7   'Then, by chance, I got into a school in Warsaw which was an arts school. It was a fantastic school.' 17

8   'Later on, my mother lived in Warsaw. Life was very hard.' 19

9, 10   'I don't really talk to my daughter about important matters. I write her letters.' 21

11   'I was a complete idiot ... pretty naïve and not very bright.' 30

12–17   (Photographs by Krzysztof Kieślowski) 'Film School taught me how to look at the world.' 46–7

18   'I had already married Marysia, my present wife, when I was in my fourth and final year.' 50

19, 20   'I made two so-called commissioned films.' *Between Wrocław and Zielona Góra (Między Wrocławiem a Zieloną Górą)* ...   52

21, 22   ... and *The Principles of Safety and Hygiene in a Copper Mine (Podstawy BHP w Kopalni Miedzy).*   53

23, 24,   'Tomek Zygadło and I directed *Workers '71 (Robot-*
25   *nicy '71).'*   56

26   'Everything concerning the Party Board of Control in *Curriculum Vitae (Życiorys)* was real.'   61

27   'Whereas everything that the main character brings in is fictitious.'   61

28, 29   *Hospital (Szpital).* 'They worked their twenty-four hours then another seven, making it thirty-one hours non-stop.'   71

30   *Hospital.* 'We became such good friends.'   72

31, 32,   *From a Night Porter's Point of View (Z Punkta Wid-*
33   *zenia Nocnego Portiera).* 'The porter wasn't a bad man.'   76–7

34   *Station (Dworzec).* 'People looking for something.'   80

35   *Bricklayer (Murarz).*   82

36, 37   *Seven Women of Different Ages (Siedem Kobiet w Różnym Wieku).*   83

38, 39   *X-Ray (Prześwietlenie).*   84

40   *Refrain (Refren).*   85

         Tracking:

41   *Concert of Requests (Koncert Życzeń).*   87

42   With Jacek Petrycki during filming of *Before the Rally (Przed Rajdem).*   87

43   *The Calm (Spokój).*   88

Behind the camera:

44 *From the City of Łódź (Z Miasta Łodzi)*. © Piotr Jaxa-
    Kwiatkowski. 89

45 With Jacek Petrycki during filming of *First Love
    (Pierwsza Miłość)*. 90

46 With Witold Stok during filming of *Workers '71*. ©
    Andrzej Arwar. 90

47 *Workers '71*. © Andrzej Arwar. 91

48 *The Calm*. 91

49 With Krzysztof Pakulski during filming of *Short Work-
    ing Day (Krótki Dzień Pracy)*. 92

50 *No End (Bez Końca)*. 92

51–4 *The Scar (Blizna)*. 100–101

55, 56 Jerzy Stuhr in *The Calm (Spokój)*. 107

57 On set: *The Calm*. 109

58, 59 Jerzy Stuhr in *Camera Buff (Amator)*. 111

60, 61 Boguslaw Linde in *Blind Chance (Przypadek)*. 114

62 On set: *Short Working Day (Krótki Dzień Pracy)*. 117

63 Artur Barciś in *No End*. 132

64–6 Grażyna Szapołowska in *No End*. 132–3

67 With Sławomir Idziak and Agnieszka Holland in Can-
    nes, 1988. 139

68 With Edward Żebrowski in Switzerland. 139

69 *Decalogue I (Dekalog I)*. 147

70 *Decalogue II (Dekalog II)*. 148

71 *Decalogue IX (Dekalog IX)*. 148

72–6 Mirosław Baca in *A Short Film about Killing (Krótki
    Film o Zabijaniu)*. 163–5

77 Grażyna Szapołowska in *A Short Film about Love* (*Krótki Film o Miłości*). 167

78 Olaf Lubaszenko in *A Short Film about Love*. 167

79 G. Szapołowska and O. Lubaszenko in *A Short Film about Love*. 168

80 With Zbigniew Preisner in Paris. © Monika Jeziorowska. 178

81 Irène Jacob in *The Double Life of Véronique* (*La Double Vie de Véronique. Podwójne Życie Weroniki*). 183

82 Philippe Volter in *The Double Life of Véronique*. 183

83, 84 I. Jacob in *The Double Life of Véronique*. 184

85 Krzysztof Kieślowski with Krzysztof Piesiewcz. © Piotr Jaxa-Kwiatkowski. 214

86, 87 *Blue, Red*: liberty, fraternity. 219

Acknowledgements

Primarily, of course, I would like to thank Krzysztof Kieślowski who, tired as he was, agreed to let me interview him on numerous occasions and who let me rummage through his family and 'on set' photographs. This book is largely based on interviews recorded with Kieślowski in Paris in December 1991 and May 1992 when he was working on the scripts of the triptych *Three Colours*. A third set of interviews, covering the triptych, was recorded in Paris in the summer of 1993 once *Three Colours* had been shot.

There are a number of people whom I'd also like to thank for their support, assistance and encouragement: Witold Stok, Jacek Petrycki, Grażyna Petrycka, Marcel Łoziński, Ann Duruflé, Marysia Kieślowska, Tadeusz Żeńczykowski, Anna Pinter and, most certainly, Tracey Scoffield for her extremely helpful editorial assistance.

I would like to thank the British Film Institute for its permission to include quotations from the *Guardian* Lecture held with Krzysztof Kieślowski in April 1990.

Excerpts from Kieślowski's reflections written for the monthly cultural magazine *Du* (Zurich, Switzerland) have been worked into the text. The passages are my own direct translation of Kieślowski's original words.

Stills and photographs appear by courtesy of: Krzysztof Kieślowski as well as Andrzej Arwar, Piotr Jaxa-Kwiatkowski, Monika Jeziorowska, Jacek Petrycki, Archiwum Film Polski, Archiwum WFD, Gala Film Distributors, MK-2, TVP Archiwum Filmowe.

Introduction

Alongside Andrzej Wajda, Roman Polański, Jerzy Skolimowski and Krzysztof Zanussi – all from the Łódź Film School – Krzysztof Kieślowski has become one of the best known of Polish film-makers. Yet it took a while before his talent was recognized in the West. *Camera Buff* (*Amator*), made in 1979 and winner of the Grand Prix in Moscow, brought his name to the Western film buff's attention but it is only with *No End* (*Bez Końca*) and, more importantly, with the *Decalogue* (*Dekalog*), made in 1988–9, that his reputation has spread through the general – though not yet commercial – market. But by this time Kieślowski already had several feature films to his name, not to mention numerous award-winning documentaries.

In fact, it is with documentaries that Kieślowski's career started. And one kind of documentary in particular, in the Poland of the 1960s and 1970s, stood in a class of its own. These documentaries played a dual role in that they were both artistic and political – political in the sense that, with the help of various ruses at the expense of the censors, they strove to depict reality as it was and not as the Communists claimed it to be. In this way, they were precursors of the 'cinema of moral anxiety', a movement in feature films which strove to awaken social consciousness. As naturally as the 'cinema of moral anxiety' developed from the documentaries of the 1970s, so Kieślowski's features developed from his documentaries; so much so that in *Personnel* (*Personel*), for example, documentary devices were used to enhance and add authenticity to a fictitious plot. To this day, Kieślowski claims to make features according to documentary principles as his films evolve through ideas and not through action.

Kieślowski argues that all his films except one, perhaps – *Workers '71* (*Robotnicy '71*) – are about individuals and not politics, but it would be hard to deny that most of them, especially the earlier works, strongly reflect the political climate of their time. A general view of recent events in Poland will therefore help the reader of this book to understand why Kieślowski is considered not only a leading film-maker in his home country but also a controversial one. Many Poles love him but others view his work and person with considerable reservation, believing that he flirted with the Party in making such films as *Curriculum vitae* (*Życiorys*). He has been accused of being an opportunist, and of having betrayed himself and Poland.

In person, he is certainly a self-declared pessimist, his expression serious more frequently than not, his eyes intent behind the glasses. But when a smile does make an appearance, you immediately sense its sincerity. There's a wealth of unsuspected warmth and dry humour behind the daunting seriousness of his demeanour. When I spoke to him in Paris he was tired. Tired from an extremely heavy schedule, certainly, with three features to write and complete in two years, but also tired of politics, and tired of the Poles' expectations of him to be something he doesn't want to be – a political animal. As he frees himself from the oppressive confines of politics, so his films more evidently touch upon themes common to humanity, and the question of what it means to be human.

Kieślowski was born in June 1941 in Warsaw. His childhood was nomadic, as Krzysztof, together with his mother and sister, followed his father, who was suffering from tuberculosis, from one sanatorium town to another. (It is surprising to hear him speak of tuberculosis between one puff of a cigarette and another, between one cough and another.) No doubt the majority of children brought up in Poland at this time suffered numerous hardships but that in no way lessens individual suffering and it is hard to imagine that the constant uprooting which young Krzysztof experienced did not leave any trace on him. He didn't speak much about his childhood when I questioned him. Certainly, he told me the odd anecdote or reminiscence, but it all seemed fragmented. The phrase 'I can't remember' kept recurring – possibly as a subconscious way of obliterating pain. But that's conjecture – Kieślowski is reticent and wary by nature. Yet he does seem to have mastered the art of manoeuvring his answers to suit his purpose or to cut them short. Be that as it may, I did find him very responsive and co-operative in many talks with him in his Paris flat.

Kieślowski's first professional training, at the age of sixteen, was at Firemen's Training College and was short-lived, inspiring a hatred for uniforms and discipline. Anything was better than regimented life, so in order to avoid compulsory military service he went back to school, then on to the College for Theatre Technicians in Warsaw (Państwowe Liceum Techniki Teatralnej). At his third attempt, he was accepted into Łódź Film School where he completed the four-year course of film director.

During these years, the First Secretary of the Communist PZPR (the Polish United Workers' Party) was Władysław Gomułka, brought to power during the Polish October of 1956 (three years after Stalin's death) on a wave of popular unrest. He was welcomed both by Nikita Khrushchev, who then recalled his troops from their march on Warsaw, and by the Polish people. Gomułka wanted to 'lead Poland on a new road to Socialism' and the extreme restrictions on personal and public freedom enforced during the Stalinist era were slightly relaxed. A brief period of relative freedom followed, but by 1968, some thought Gomułka was becoming incompetent. A number of Party members, among them General Mieczysław Moczar, the head of security services, were simply waiting for the right moment to discredit Gomułka and to take power. The opportunity Moczar had been looking for came in January 1968. Adam Mickiewicz's *Forefathers' Eve* (*Dziady*), first published in 1823, was playing at Warsaw's National Theatre to students who cheered the anti-Russian references. The government took the drastic measure of banning the play. The resulting student demonstrations were violently repressed and many students were arrested or expelled from the University. Demonstrations spread to other student communities including the Łódź Film School. General Moczar accused Zionist agents of subversion. In the spring of 1968 there followed a purge of thousands of Polish Jews from the Party and from Poland. Gomułka was lenient in issuing exit visas for Jews and many, including a large percentage of the intelligentsia, emigrated. Łódź Film School lost many of its finest professors. The Party, blaming the demonstrations on Zionist conspiracies, managed quite successfully to set the media and, most importantly, the workers of large factories against the rebellious students. Many students, if not themselves arrested, suffered great disillusionment. They had been duped but their social and political awareness had been sharpened. Kieślowski graduated from Łódź Film School in 1969.

The turn of the decade, 1970, was a time of unrest in Poland generally. A combination of Gomułka's resistance to imports and the bad harvests of 1969 and 1970 led to severe food shortages, while throughout the 1960s the cost of living had risen and wages had remained low. Gomułka's announcement on 13 December 1970 of a 30 per cent price-rise in basic foodstuffs burst the dam. Workers at the Lenin Shipyard in Gdańsk went out on strike and marched on the Party headquarters where police opened fire on the crowd. The workers burnt down the building. Other shipyards followed, the army was called in to restore order, but fighting broke out, and hundreds died. An emergency session of the Politburo was held without Gomułka, who had allegedly suffered a stroke, and, after infighting between Edward Gierek's and Moczar's factions, Gierek, First Secretary in Katowice, Silesia, the most industrial area of Poland at the time, succeeded Gomułka.

Gierek brought in his own men from Silesia, true Soviet-style apparatchiks who, rather than bear a commitment to socialism were eager to promote their own personal well-being. In contrast to his predecessor, Gierek put into motion a large programme of economic and social expansion. He incurred great debts in the West in order to build new factories which were to produce export goods. Food prices were frozen. The standard of living shot up for a short time while its cost went down. But it was not long before the inherent flaws in the economy were to have effect. The new factories weren't completed on time and home-produced goods proved inferior in quality and difficult to sell in the West. In an attempt to meet rocketing debts, coal and goods intended for the home market went for export. Shortages became more frequent and on 24 June 1976 Gierek repeated Gomułka's mistake. He raised food prices by an average of 60 per cent. Strikes and riots broke out again throughout the country, forcing Gierek to withdraw the price increases. Hundreds of workers were beaten up by the militia, dismissed from work, or arrested and imprisoned.

Since the late 1960s, despite continuing censorship, culture and thought had been awakening the public's social consciousness. There was a general sense of sharing. Because food, household and other basic goods were in short supply, people turned towards immaterial goods – art, culture, religion, and each other's company. By the mid-1970s a sense of solidarity was already growing. This was reinforced by the fact that the East–West divide in respect of travel and cultural exchanges was becoming a little less pronounced. Films from the West began to be shown in Poland with increasing frequency and the works of Western playwrights were performed. Polish theatre itself experienced a rebirth with such innovative movements as that of Jerzy Grotowski in Wrocław and Tadeusz Kantor in Kraków. An active underground press provided people with uncensored literature and a Flying University was unofficially founded. Lectures and seminars were held in private homes. The venues were constantly changed to avoid police raids though many people were, indeed, arrested and harassed while much equipment was seized.

Throughout the 1960s and 1970s, film played an exceptionally important role in Poland. Its impact was visual, direct, whilst underlying unspoken messages still managed to elude the censors. A cinematic code evolved which the audience understood only too well but which the censors could not pin down. Cinema – both documentaries and features – became, as it were, the social conscience of the people as film depicted a way of life denied by the Communists. Documentaries, at this time, were considered to be just as important as features – they weren't television schedule fillers or mere supporting programmes. Many were shot with the intention of cinema release, and people would frequently flock to see a documentary, rather than the fictional feature which the documentary was supposed to support, for they knew it would show them the world of their everyday experience.

In a certain respect it was easier, at that time – and especially in the latter half of the 1970s – to make films in Poland than it was in the West. The commercial pressure was not so great. There wasn't such an urgency to please the producer or the audience in order to get the necessary finances. The film industry was run on State money so the money didn't belong to anybody in particular.

Although it still remained under the censorial eye of the Ministry of Arts and Culture, the Polish film industry was decentralized in 1955. Eight self-governing but State financed *Zespóly*, or Production Houses for feature films (a *zespól* literally means a team), were set up, each with its own artistic head – usually a film director – a literary manager, and a production executive. Each Production House was responsible for commissioning scripts, and arranging all stages of production. Thus, film-makers of similar tastes and beliefs were drawn to the same Production House.

Completed films were submitted for the approval of the Vice-Minister of Arts and Culture as well as the State Board of Censorship. Some scripts were written in a way to outwit the censor, but were made according to the film-maker's original, covert intentions. Documentaries, although also State-financed, were produced in separate production houses usually called Studios. Certainly, numerous films were shelved for many years – such as *The Calm* (*Spokój*) made by Kieślowski for television in 1976 – or were shown only to selected audiences – *Curriculum vitae* (*Życiorys*) and *From a Night Porter's Point of View* (*Z Punktu Widzenia Nocnego Portiera*) made by Kieślowski in 1975 and 1978 respectively – but still they were made and were seen at semi-clandestine screenings by a hard core of Warsaw's intellectuals.

I remember sliding past the porters at the State Documentary Film Studios (Wytwórnia Filmów Dokumentalnych) in Warsaw, to attend a number of such screenings. It was ironic that my husband, who had been working at the Studios as a lighting cameraman for a good many years, was always – and not too politely – asked to show his identity card while I somehow managed to glide past unharassed. Fortunately so, because I had no permit and a strict list of guests would always be drawn up prior to any such screening. The screenings were called 'kolaudacje' and were intended to allow a closed circle of film-makers to view a film and critically evaluate it. The films were shown in small viewing theatres on studio premises but instead of the ten or fifteen guests that the theatres were designed to hold, the rooms would be crammed tight with directors, cameramen, writers, poets, all peering intently at the screen through a thick fog of foul-smelling (Polish cigarettes!) smoke. If, by any chance, an executive or official of the studio should turn up, I – an illicit guest – would have to hide away or try to merge in with the surroundings as inconspicuously as possible.

By the mid-1970s society had become far more united and protective of dissidents than it had been half a decade previously. Workers and intelligentsia had joined forces. In September 1976, a group of intellectuals and dissidents, including Jacek Kuroń (who, after the Round Table talks of 1989, was to become Minister for Labour) and Adam Michnik formed the oppositionist Workers' Defence Committee (KOR). This organisation gave legal advice to arrested workers and informed the public of how workers were treated during their trials. It collected money to pay their fines and to provide aid for their families. The election of Cardinal Wojtyła as Pope in October 1978 and his subsequent triumphant tour of the country further consolidated the Poles in the belief of their own strength and unity, and of their right to freedom.

In July 1980, Gierek once more tried to set his debts to rights by increasing food prices. Again strikes broke out, but this time there was far more order and prescience to them. On 14 August 1980, Lech Wałęsa, an electrician, declared a strike at the Lenin Shipyard in Gdańsk over the illegal dismissal of a colleague, Anna Walentynowicz. Unlike the demonstrators against the strikes of 1976, these workers didn't march to torch Party headquarters. Instead they staged a peaceful sit-in, demanding to see representatives of the government. An Interfactory Strike Committee was created to co-ordinate the large number of other industrial centres which now followed suit. On 31 August 1980, the government signed an agreement with the workers allowing free trade unions, civil rights, freedom of information. Access to the media was also given to the free trade unions and the Catholic Church. Solidarity, the free trade union, was born. There was a genuine feeling of shared excitement. People really did believe that something might change, that their voice would be heard and, more importantly, respected. They became more open, less afraid of expressing their rights and their hatred of the repressive Party. Millions of people returned their Party membership cards and openly criticized the Party.

While society was enjoying its new freedoms, the Party's policy had brought about an economic crisis with even greater shortages, including those of much needed medical supplies, and it soon became evident that the Party itself was falling apart. One million of its members joined Solidarity. But while the Party's hold weakened, so various factions broke out within Solidarity, and conflict grew between moderates who considered Solidarity as primarily a trade union and not a political party, and militants who believed that Solidarity should share in power.

One thing Moscow could not allow, however, was the Party's total disintegration in Poland. In February 1981, in fear of losing control of Poland, Moscow introduced one of several measures designed to begin a clamp-down. General Wojciech Jaruzelski, faithful to Moscow, head of the Polish army and, since October of the previous year, First Party secretary, was declared prime minister.

On the night of 12 December 1981, I was at a friend's party. There were a lot of people there, many of them from the film world and other artistic circles. Someone tried to phone for a taxi but the phone was dead. One of the guests, a writer, disappeared to fetch a script he had just written from his flat upstairs. Time passed, he didn't reappear. His wife, anxious, went to look for him and came running back in tears: 'Michał's been arrested!' We looked out of the windows at the snow-covered street. It was uncannily still. On the way home, we stopped at a couple of telephone boxes, just to check the phones. They were all dead. We managed to catch a taxi and asked the taxi-driver to drive past Mokotowska Street where the local Solidarity headquarters were based. It was cordoned off by a row of police cars. We could only conjecture as to what was happening and fell asleep in ignorance. The following morning, I switched on the radio to hear solemn classical music and General Jaruzelski's voice: 'Last night a state of martial law was declared...' Communications remained cut and tanks appeared in the streets. Numerous people were arrested and interned, while several members of the Solidarity leadership went into hiding to continue their campaign underground. In the days that followed, hundreds if not thousands of people, including film-makers, were summoned by the police to sign statements of loyalty to the new government. Many of those summoned were forewarned and managed to evade signing by not being at home when the summons was delivered. Ironically, the sense of euphoria continued. In all appearances, the people were prepared to fight and to remain loyal to each other in the war against the Soviet hold. The sense of human solidarity was reinforced. But as the weeks, then months, wore on, the principles turned to disillusionment. It was proving hard enough to survive let alone rebel. People wanted bread, they wanted peace. They were tired. Petty jealousies and bitterness started to poison friendships. Many Poles emigrated to the West. In October 1982, the banned Solidarity was finally dissolved by order of the courts.

With the introduction of martial law, the film industry became practically non-existent. There was a drastic shortage of film stock, and equipment, hitherto owned by the State-financed Production Houses, became unavailable. Many film-makers sought alternative, hopefully temporary, employment. There was a sudden increase in the number of talented and educated taxi-drivers! Television, on the other hand, continued to function but purely as the voice of the military state. Writers, actors and directors boycotted television, and working for the television industry became synonymous with working for the Party and, consequently, for the Soviets.

Gradually, as 'stabilization' was achieved, with General Jaruzelski no longer appearing on television in full military uniform but in civilian clothes, some films started to be made. In December 1982, martial law was 'suspended', but economically the country was in a worse state than it had been in 1980. Following the death of Brezhnev, and the rapid successions and deaths of Andropov and Chernienko, the reformist Gorbachev instigated a tide of change in the Soviet Union. This, inevitably, had repercussions in Poland. In February 1989, the Round Table talks between the opposition and government began, and in April 1989, an agreement was signed on a new democratic system of election to the Seym (the Parliament of Poland). Solidarity was reinstated and given a share in power as a kind of bloodless *coup d'état*. Poland was free for the first time since the Second World War. There was no longer any political censorship. But there was an even deeper economic crisis.

In the light of recent history, it is difficult to envisage how any film made in Poland during the 1960s, 1970s or the 1980s could be entirely free of politics. And anything tainted by politics – especially the changing tides of post-war politics in Poland – lends itself to controversy. But the tide has shifted dramatically and Kieślowski, like all other film-makers, can now focus his concentration on the individual and his plight. Ironically, though, Kieślowski's production base has also shifted – to France. Lack of funds in Poland has driven him towards co-productions with the West. But perhaps it is also the remaining drabness of his home country and its claustrophobic attitudes which have equally prompted his 'escape' or, should one say, an 'opening'.

DANUSIA STOK
January 1993

Epigraph

Film-making doesn't mean audiences, festivals, reviews, interviews. It means getting up every day at six o'clock in the morning. It means the cold, the rain, the mud and having to carry heavy lights. It's a nerve-racking business and, at a certain point, everything else has to come second, including your family, emotions, and private life. Of course, engine drivers, business men or bankers would say the same thing about their jobs. No doubt they'd be right, but I do my job and I'm writing about mine. Perhaps I shouldn't be doing this job any more. I'm coming to the end of something essential to a film-maker – namely patience. I've got no patience for actors, lighting cameramen, the weather, for waiting around, for the fact that nothing turns out how I'd like it to. At the same time, I mustn't let this show. It takes a lot out of me, hiding my lack of patience from the crew. I think that the more sensitive ones know I'm not happy with this aspect of my personality.

Film-making is the same all over the world: I'm given a corner on a small studio stage; there's a stray sofa there, a table, a chair. In this make-believe interior, my stern instructions sound grotesque: Silence! Camera! Action! Once again I'm tortured by the thought that I'm doing an insignificant job. A few years ago, the French newspaper *Libération* asked various directors why they made films. I answered at the time: 'Because I don't know how to do anything else.' It was the shortest reply and maybe that's why it got noticed. Or maybe because all of us film-makers with the faces we pull, with the money we spend on films and the amounts we earn, with our pretentions to high society, so often have the feeling of how absurd our work is. I can understand Fellini and most of the others who build streets, houses and even artificial seas in the studio: in this way not so many people get to see the shameful and insignificant job of directing.

As so often happens when filming, something occurs which – for a while at least – causes this feeling of idiocy to disappear. This time it's four young French actresses. In a chance place, in inappropriate clothes, pretending that they've got props and partners they act so beautifully that everything becomes real. They speak some fragments of dialogue, they smile or worry, and at that moment I can understand what it's all for.

KRZYSZTOF KIEŚLOWSKI

CHAPTER I

Background

Returning Home

Half an hour's wait for luggage at the airport in Warsaw, as usual. The belt keeps going round and round – a cigarette butt, an umbrella, a Hotel Marriot sticker, the buckle from a suitcase belt and a clean, white handkerchief. Despite the 'No Smoking' signs, I light up a cigarette. Four men from the luggage service have been sitting near by on the only four available chairs. 'Smoking's not allowed here, boss,' one of them says. 'But sitting doing nothing is?' I ask. 'Doing nothing in Poland is always allowed,' another one says. They roar with laughter. One of them is missing two top teeth, another is missing his canine teeth and another tooth on the right side. The third hasn't got any teeth at all, but he's older, about fifty. The fourth, about thirty, has all his teeth. I wait another twenty minutes for the luggage, nearly an hour all in all. Since we already feel we know each other, the luggage guys don't say anything when I light up another fag.

There are thousands of traders in the centre of Warsaw. They sell meat, towels, shoes, bread or sugar from their cars parked along the roads. That's good – it's easy to buy things although it's harder to drive through. On the pavements are spread goods from the cheapest supermarkets in West Berlin, 'Bilka' and 'Quelle', and from Kreuzberg: chocolates, televisions, fruit, everything. I come across an elderly man holding a beer can. 'Empty?' I ask. He nods. 'How much?' '500 złotys.' I think this over. He no doubt thinks I want to buy the can. He encourages me: 'I'll give it to you for 400.' I ask him: 'What do I need an empty beer can for?' 'That's your business. If you buy it, you can do what you like with it.'

My love for Poland is a bit like love in an old marriage where the couple know everything about each other and are a bit bored with each other, but when one of them dies, the other follows immediately. I can't imagine life without Poland. I find it very hard to find a place for myself in the West, where I am now, even though the conditions are wonderful; drivers are generally considerate and people say 'good morning' in the shops. Yet when I think of myself in the future, I can only see myself in Poland.

I don't feel myself to be a citizen of the world. I still feel a Pole. In fact, everything that affects Poland, affects me directly: I don't feel so distanced from the country as to feel no concern. I'm no longer interested in all the political games, but I am interested in Poland itself. It's my world. It's the world I've come from and, no doubt, the world where I'll die.

When I'm away from Poland, it feels as if it's only for a while, as if I'm in transit. Even if I'm away for a year or two, I feel as if I'm only there temporarily. In other words, on going to Poland there's a sense of returning, a sense of coming back. Everyone ought to have a place to which they return. I have a place; it's in Poland, either in Warsaw or in Koczek[1] in the Mazurian lakes. Things don't change to such an extent as to change my basic feelings. When I return to Paris, I don't have this sense of coming back. I come to Paris. But I come back to Poland.

My father was more important to me than my mother because he died so young. But my mother was important too and she was one of the reasons, in fact, why I decided to go to film school.

One of the things that spurred my ambition happened just after I had taken the entrance exam for the second time. I got back home and, over the phone, arranged to meet my mother in Warsaw by the escalators in Castle Square (Plac Zamkowy). She was probably counting on my getting into film school, but I already knew I had failed. She arrived at the top of the escalators and I arrived at the bottom. I rode up and went out. It was raining like hell. And Mum just stood there completely drenched. She was so sorry that I hadn't got in the second time around. 'Look,' she said, 'maybe you're just not cut out for it.' And I don't know whether she was crying or whether it was the rain but I felt very sorry that she was so sad. And that's when I decided that I'd get into that film school no matter what. I'd prove to them that I was cut out for it, simply because she was so sad. That's when I really made the decision.

We were quite a poor family. My father was a civil engineer, my mother an office clerk. My father had tuberculosis and for twelve years after the Second World War he was dying of it. He'd go to

1 'My father was a very wise man but I couldn't make much use of his wisdom. It's only now that I can understand some of the things he did or said.'

2 'My father was more important to me than my mother because he died so young. But my mother was important too and one of the reasons I decided to go to film school.'

3 'My father had tuberculosis. He'd go to sanatoria and my mum, me and my sister, we'd follow him.'

sanatoria and since we wanted to be near him – my mum, that is, and the two of us, me and my sister – we'd follow him. He'd be in a sanatorium and my mum would work in an office in the same town. He'd go to another sanatorium and we'd move to another town and Mum would work in an office there.

A great deal in life depends on who smacked your hand at breakfast when you were a child. That is, on who your father was, who your grandmother was, who your great-grandfather was, and your background in general. It's very important. And the person who slapped you at breakfast for being naughty when you were four, later put that first book on your bedside table or gave it to you for Christmas. And those books formed us – at least, they did me. They taught me something, made me sensitive to something. The books I read, particularly as a child or a boy, made me what I am.

Throughout my childhood I had bad lungs and was in danger of getting TB. Of course, I'd often play football or ride a bike as all boys do, but because I was sick I spent a lot of time sitting covered in a blanket on some balcony or veranda, breathing in the fresh air. So I had an enormous amount of time for reading. At first, when I didn't know how, my mum would read to me. Then I learnt to read pretty quickly. I'd even read at night, by the light of a small torch or candle, under the bedclothes. Right into the morning sometimes.

Of course, the world which I inhabited, the world of friends, bicycles, running around, and in the winter skiing on skis made out of planks from pickled-cabbage barrels, this was the real world. But equally real to me was the world of books, the world of all sorts of adventures. It's not true that it was only a world of Camus and Dostoevsky. They were a part of it, but it was also a world of cowboys and Indians, Tom Sawyer and all those heroes. It was bad literature as well as good, and I read both with equal interest. I can't say whether I learnt more from Dostoevsky or from some third-rate American writer who wrote cowboy adventures. I don't know. And I wouldn't like to make any such classifications. I'd known for a long time that there was something more to life than material things which you can touch or buy in shops. Precisely through reading books.

I'm not someone who remembers dreams for long. I forget them as soon as I wake up – if I've had any, that is. But as a child I had them like everyone else: horrible dreams where I couldn't escape or somebody was chasing me. We've all had dreams like that. I also dreamt that I was flying above the earth. I had dreams in colour. I had dreams in black and white. These childhood dreams I remember well but in a strange way. I can't describe them, but when I have a similar dream now – and I do sometimes have those dreams now, both the good and the bad ones – I know immediately that it's from my childhood.

There's something else which I think is more important to me. There are many events in my life which I believe to be a part of my life and yet I don't really know whether or not they happened to me. I think I remember these events very accurately but perhaps this is because somebody else has talked about them. In other words, I appropriate incidents from other people's lives. I often don't even remember who I've appropriated or stolen them from. I steal them and then start to believe that they happened to me.

I remember several incidents like that from childhood which I know couldn't have happened to me, yet at the same time I'm absolutely sure that they did. Nobody in my family could explain where they came from, whether they were dreams of such power that they materialized into what I thought were actual incidents, or whether somebody described similar events to me and subconsciously I stole them and made them mine.

For example, I remember one scene perfectly well. Not so long ago, I went skiing with my daughter and sister. We passed through Gorczyce, a very small town in the Regained Territories,[2] where the incident I remember took place in 1946 or '47 when I was five or six. I was going to infant school and clearly remember walking with my mum. An elephant appeared. It passed us by and walked on. Mum claimed she'd never been with me when an elephant walked by. There's no reason why, in 1946, after the war, an elephant should appear in Poland, where it was hard even to get potatoes. Nevertheless, I can remember the scene perfectly well and I clearly remember the expression on the elephant's face. I'm absolutely convinced that I was going to school, holding my mum's hand when an elephant walked towards us. He turned left and walked on while we went straight ahead. Nobody even paid any special attention to it. I'm convinced that this happened although my mum claimed it never did.

After a while, I lose control of these incidents which I steal and which I start to describe as having happened to me. That is, I forget that they happened to somebody else and start to believe that they really happened to me. And it's more than likely that that was the case with this elephant. No doubt somebody had told me about it.

I realized this very clearly quite recently when I went to America. *The Double Life of Véronique* was about to be released through a regular, decent distributor called Miramax. At a certain moment during its screening at the New York Film Festival, I realized that the people in America were absolutely baffled by the ending of the film. There's a scene in which Véronique returns to her family home where her father is still living. The scene is very enigmatically done and it's not made obvious that it's the family home she's returning to, but I don't think that anybody in Europe has any doubt. But in America I noticed that people were confused. They weren't sure that she returns to the family home, to where her father lives. They weren't sure that the man who is there is her father. And, even if they were sure, they couldn't understand why she goes back.

For us, Europeans, going back to the family home represents a certain value which exists in our traditions, in our history and also in our culture. You can find it in the *Odyssey*, and literature, theatre and art through the ages have very often taken up the subject of the family home as a place which constitutes a set of values. Particularly for us Poles, who are very romantic, the family home is an essential point in our lives. And that's why I ended the film the way I did. But I realized that nobody understood it in America. So I suggested to the Americans that I should make another ending for them, to make it clear that it's the family home. So that's what I did. Later, I thought about why Americans can't understand this notion. I don't understand America, but I tried to figure out what lay at the bottom of this, and I remembered a certain story.

I started telling this story to all sorts of people – journalists, distributors, friends – and suddenly, when I'd told it a number of times, I realized that it hadn't happened to me at all. It was a friend's story, and I'd begun telling it exactly as if it had happened to me. Not only had I stolen it, and then sold it as my own, but in between I was absolutely convinced that it had really happened to me. Only later did it occur to me that it hadn't happened to me at all and that I'd simply stolen it.

Here's the story. I always say that it's me who's flying to America. Sitting next to me is this guy. Well, I wanted to take a nap or read a book and not talk to this guy, but unfortunately he was talkative and started up a conversation. 'What do you do?' he says. 'I make films,' I say. He says, 'That's very interesting.' I say, 'Yes, it is.' He says, 'And I make windows, you know.' 'That's very interesting,' I say. 'Yes, yes,' he says, 'incredibly interesting.' I was being sarcastic, of course, but he took me literally and started telling me this story. It turned out that he manufactured windows in Germany. He's a German. We didn't have any problems understanding each other because his English was just like mine. It was much easier to talk to him than to an American or Englishman.

And what happens in his story? He was going to America just like me. Well, this guy has the biggest and the best window factories in Germany. They make the best windows. He sells these windows in Germany for quite a high price with a fifty-year guarantee. Of course the Germans happily buy them because, being practical, they think that if something's got a fifty-year guarantee on it then it won't break for fifty years. Because this guy's the best manufacturer of windows in Germany, like every European who has excelled in something, he immediately wanted to do the same in America. So he opened a factory in America. And he says to me, 'Look, I opened this factory. I really make fantastic windows, I tell you. I made out a fifty-year guarantee. I set a price. Nobody wanted to buy the windows. Nobody. Simply nobody. I put a lot of money into advertising – newspapers, television, whatever. I sent out leaflets. I sent out catalogues, whatever you can think of. But nobody wanted to buy these windows. So I lowered the guarantee to twenty years, but left the price the same. And listen, they started to buy the windows. I lowered the guarantee to ten years. Left the price the same. They started to buy four times the number of windows. Right now, I'm going to America to buy a second factory and lower the guarantee to five years. The price is going to stay the same. They're buying the windows. Why are they buying windows with a five-year guarantee and not a fifty-year guarantee? Because they just can't imagine sitting in one place for fifty years. It's inconceivable to them.'

And so the idea of a family home as a place through which successive generations pass is inconceivable to them because they're constantly changing where they live. I started telling this story as my own to explain the position of the family home in

America and, after a while, I realized it wasn't mine. But I needed this story so much in order to understand the American inability to grasp the importance of the family home, that I simply usurped it. Nevertheless, if you were to ask me what this German sitting next to me had looked like, I could describe him to you in detail. Even though there wasn't any German sitting next to me, I know what he looked like, because he's my German now. It had happened to me. So those are the kinds of stories I have – ones which somebody else has told me, probably my mum or dad, and which I then think I remember.

I remember certain images too, but they're probably not authentic. However, some must have happened to me because nobody, for example, could have told me about a German soldier standing and drawing water from a well. He moves his arms or lips as he drinks, the helmet slips back as he tilts his head. He catches hold of the helmet but it isn't any dramatic event worth talking about. Nothing comes before it, nothing comes after. I must have been three at the time.

I think we do remember a lot, only we just don't know it. Digging hard and decisively, digging sensitively around in our memories makes the lost images and events come back. But you must really want to remember and you have to work hard.

Soon after the Occupation of Poland in 1939, the Germans started to throw everybody out. So we left. Then, after the war, we lived in various places in the Regained Territories including Gorczyce. They were good times for our family – when we lived in Gorczyce – because my father was still fairly healthy and working. We had a house; a real, normal, big house. My sister and I went to school and life was pretty good. This house had belonged to the Germans before the war and was full of German bits and pieces. I've still got some of them: a knife, and a set of compasses. Something is missing from the set but it used to be complete. My father, who was an engineer, used these compasses for his drawings, and I inherited them. There were also a lot of German books. I've kept a German book from that house to this day. It's called *Mountains in the Sun*. There are photographs of skiers in it. In the sun.

But I don't know where we were during the war. And I'll never find out. Some letters and documents do survive, but none of them show where we were. My sister doesn't know either. She was born three years after me, towards the end of the war, in 1944. I do know where she was born, in Strzemieszyce, a tiny part of Silesia which was the last part of that region to belong to Poland before the war. But during the war that didn't mean anything because the Germans were everywhere anyway. That was where my father's mother lived, and we lived with her, in a little room. She knew German well but after the war she taught Russian. It was difficult to be a German teacher in Poland then, so, since she knew both German and Russian well, she became a Russian teacher. I even went to her class.

We lived in Strzemieszyce several times after that. We'd move here and there, then return to Strzemieszyce because that was a place where we knew we could stay for a while. It is a terrible place. I went there recently and found the house and yard. As always happens on such occasions, everything seemed smaller, greyer and dirtier than before.

I went to so many schools that I often get them mixed up, and don't remember even where I went. I would change schools twice or even three times a year. But I think I went to the second or third form, when I was eight or nine years old,[3] in Strzemieszyce. Then, later on, I went to the fourth or fifth form for a while when I was about eleven. I did well at school but I was never a goody-goody or a swot. I got good marks but didn't make any special effort. I think my schoolfriends quite liked me because I let them copy from me. The level at school was simply very low at the time, and things came very easily to me. But I didn't waste much time on learning and I can't remember anything I was taught then. I can't even remember multiplication tables or spelling. I'm always making spelling mistakes. Nothing has stayed with me, except maybe a few dates from history. Looking back, I don't think I gained much from school.

I don't remember anybody being so unpleasant that it upsets me to think about it now. The children would beat me up, that's true. Or rather, they wanted to beat me up, but somehow or other I usually managed to escape. I remember there were times, especially in winter when I'd be going home from somewhere in the evening, sledging or school, and I'd have this feeling that there was a group of boys who wanted to beat me up. I reckon it was mainly because I was their teacher's grandson. My grandmother probably used to give them bad marks and they wanted to beat me

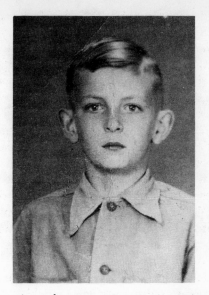

4 'I was never a goody-goody or a swot. I got good marks but didn't make any special effort.'

5 'I used to go to sanatoria for children. The whole idea was to spend
time in a good climate and to have healthy food.'

up in revenge. But I never talked to her about it so I don't know whether that's true or not. Maybe they beat me up because this was Upper Silesia. Upper Silesia was quite particular in that it was very hard to fit in there. Silesians spoke a different dialect from the one used in Warsaw. And if you talked differently in Upper Silesia, you were an outsider. Maybe that's why they wanted to beat me up.

I remember I used to go to sanatoria for children which were called 'preventoria' in Poland. They were for children threatened with TB or who were weak. The whole idea was to spend time in a good climate and to have healthy food. The food there was probably pretty good for those times. And there would always be a couple of hours' school in the mornings.

The main reason why I went there was because my parents weren't really in a position to keep us. Father was constantly ill. Mother earned far too little. And I think the preventoria were free. My sister often went too, sometimes to the same one, sometimes to a different one. My parents were terribly sad that they had to send us there but they probably didn't have any choice. They came to visit us whenever they could and we always looked forward to their visits. Especially me. Usually it was our mother who came, of course, because my father was often ill in bed. I loved them and I think they loved me and my sister very much, too. We were extremely sad that we had to part, but that's the way things were.

We lived in such small communities that the Communist authorities didn't really get to us. That is, they didn't manifest themselves as they did in the towns. The places we lived in were so small that there wasn't even a policeman there. There were only about 600 to 1,000 inhabitants in these places, with a teacher, and a bus-driver who would go to the larger town once or twice a day. That's all. Of course, there was the manager of the sanatorium, who was probably a Party member, but I can't remember whether I ever saw him. I haven't even any idea where I was when Stalin died.[4] It had nothing to do with me: I don't even know whether I was aware that he'd died – most probably not.

The first film I remember seeing – but maybe I've imagined it again – was in Strzemieszyce where they showed a French film with Gérard Philipe. It must have been *Fanfan la Tulipe*. It was an absolute sensation that a French film was being shown because all films were normally Czech, Russian or Polish. I must have been

6 'My father eventually died of TB. He was forty-seven, younger than I am now.'

seven or eight at the time and under-sixteens were not allowed to see the film. So there was this problem – my parents wanted me to see the film and, of course, I wanted to see it too. They thought it was a beautiful film and that I'd enjoy myself. So my great-uncle, who was an eminent doctor there, went to the four or six o'clock screening, realized that the film was suitable for me and, taking advantage of his authority as a doctor, sorted things out with the director of the cinema and they let me in. I don't remember anything whatsoever from the film. My parents had kept talking about it for a few days beforehand, that they'd probably manage to get me in to see it and so on. I was terribly excited, of course, and was quite anxious about whether they'd let me in or not. And I remember absolutely nothing of the film.

Then we lived in a place called Sokołowsko, near Jelenia Góra in Lower Silesia, in the Regained Territories. We lived there about three times and that's the place I remember best from my childhood. There was a sanatorium there where my father stayed. It was only a health resort really. Well, it's actually hard to call it a health resort because then one always imagines a place like Cannes, for example. This was nothing like that. It was a tiny place with two or three sanatoria. There weren't any Silesians there because they'd either fled or been driven out after the war. It was a place of about 1,000 people, most of whom were patients, and there were another 200 or so people to help with the patients. And their children.

There was a hall there in the House of Culture where the travelling theatre or cinema would come. The cinema came more or less once a week. It was a good hall, decently fitted out with good projectors and so on, and not some old fire station. But there was a different problem there; this time I was not too young to see the films, as they also showed films for children. The problem here was that I didn't have any money to buy a ticket. Neither did many of my friends. Our parents simply couldn't afford to give us any money for tickets – or if they could then it was only very rarely. So I'd climb up on to the roof of the hall with my friends. There was a sort of large ventilator there, a chimney with vents in the sides. These vents were great to spit through, down at the audience. We were jealous that they could go to the cinema and we couldn't. We spat not through our love of the cinema but our anger at the people inside.

We would watch a tiny bit of the screen. From my usual position I'd see the bottom left-hand corner, maybe one and a half square metres. Sometimes I could see the actor's leg if he was standing, or his hand or head if he was lying down. We could hear more or less, too, so we cottoned on to the action. And that's how we watched. We'd spit and watch the films. They'd chase us away from there, of course, from that roof. It was very easy to climb up there because Sokołowsko was a hilly place and the House of Culture stood right up against a hill. Its roof touched the hillside, so it was easy to climb up the hill, then up a tree and from the tree down to the roof. And that's where we played our childhood games, up there on the roof.

I always climbed roofs a lot. One of my friends, for example, a boy from Warsaw, did nothing but climb roofs. If there was any wine or vodka to drink, he'd have to do it up on a roof. He'd climb the highest roofs with his friends. I'd climb with him, too, and we'd always drink the wine somewhere high above the town.

Later on, I travelled around a lot, looking for these places. I thought of meeting up with these people but when I'd get there the desire would pass. I'd look at the places and leave. I used to think it would be nice to arrive, see someone I hadn't seen for thirty or forty years; see how he looks, who he is today. It's an entirely different world but that's precisely why it's interesting. You talk about how things are, what has happened. But then later, after I'd met a couple of friends like that, I didn't want to meet any others. To be honest, I was ashamed. I'm quite well off, drive a good car. And I'd arrive at places where there were slums, and see poor children, poor people. No doubt I've been lucky once or twice in my life and that's all. But they haven't, and it makes me ashamed. I suspect it would make them ashamed, too, if it came to a meeting. But since I'd initiated these reunions, I was the one who felt the shame and it became a great problem.

My parents couldn't afford to send me away to school, because they couldn't afford to pay for lodgings and so on. Besides, I didn't want to study. I thought I knew everything I needed to know, like most teenagers. That was after first school. I must have been fourteen or fifteen, and I did nothing for a year. My father was a wise man. He said, 'All right, go to the fireman's training college. At least you'll learn a profession and be able to work as you want to.' I wanted to work. Board was free there. So was the food. And

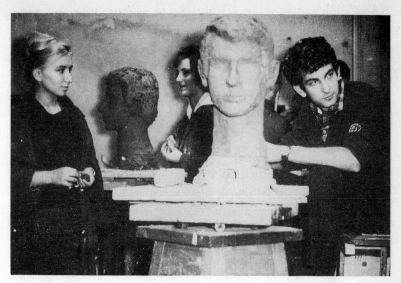

7   'Then, by chance, I got into a school in Warsaw which was an arts
school. It was a fantastic school.'

it was easy to get in. My father knew perfectly well that when I got back from that fireman's training college I'd want to study. He was right, of course. In three months I came back, wanted to study – at any cost – and went to all sorts of different schools.

Then, by chance, I got into a school in Warsaw which was an arts school. That really was pure chance. It turned out that my parents had approached some distant uncle whom I hadn't known before and who was the director of the College for Theatre Technicians in Warsaw (*Państwowe Liceum Techniki Teatralnej*). It was a fantastic school. The best school I've ever been to. Schools like that don't exist any more, unfortunately. Like everything that's good, they soon closed it down. It had excellent teachers. Teachers in Poland – and in the rest of Europe, I dare say – didn't treat pupils like younger colleagues. But here they did. They were good, too, and they were wise. They showed us that culture exists. They advised us to read books, go to the theatre or the cinema, even though it wasn't such a fashionable thing to do then, at least not in my world, my environment. Besides, I couldn't have done so because I'd always lived in those tiny places. Then once I saw that such a world existed, I realized that I could live like that, too. I hadn't known this before. Well, that was pure chance. If my uncle hadn't been the director of that particular school but of another, then I'd have attended a different school and no doubt be somewhere else today.

My father eventually died of TB. He was forty-seven, younger than I am now. He had been ill for twenty years and I suspect he didn't want to live any longer. He couldn't work, couldn't do what he believed he ought to do for his family and, no doubt, felt he hadn't entirely fulfilled himself in professional matters – since, being ill, he wasn't in any condition to do so. He didn't fulfil himself in emotional matters, family matters. I didn't talk to him about it but I'm sure that's how it was. One can feel these things. I can understand it.

Later on, my mother lived in Warsaw. Life was very hard because we didn't have any money then – I didn't have any either, of course. It was terribly difficult to find a means of staying in Warsaw, because you weren't allowed to register there.[5] This was at the end of the 1960s and the beginning of the 1970s. Then step by step, she moved to Warsaw. Somehow she managed to get herself registered there. I had already started to work in films and

8 'Later on, my mother lived in Warsaw. Life was very hard.'

was living in Warsaw, so could help her a bit. Which, of course, I did.

My mother was sixty-seven when she died in a car accident when a friend of mine was driving. That was in 1981. So I haven't had any parents for quite some time now. Besides, I'm over fifty. Hardly anybody has parents when they're over fifty. There are thousands of things we didn't talk about. Now I'll never find them out. I've only got my sister and I can't be very close to her because I simply haven't got the time. I haven't been close to anybody recently. For the last few years I've been quite alone in day-to-day life.

I've certainly got something in common with my sister; we were always together as children. In the sort of life we led – with those constant moves and so on, and a sick father – any permanent ties we had were extremely important. Now, we often think about various things which happened in the past, but we can't recreate the chain of events. Those who played the main roles in those events simply aren't there any more and can't tell us what happened. One always thinks there's plenty of time: that one day, when the opportunity arises . . .

Relationships with parents are never fair. When our parents are on top form, at their best, their most energetic, their most lively and their most loving, we don't know them because we don't exist yet. Or we're so tiny that we can't appreciate it. Then, when we grow older and start to understand certain things, they're already old. They no longer have the energy which they used to have. They no longer have the same will to live as they had when they were young. They've been disillusioned in all sorts of ways, or they've experienced failure. They're already bitter. I had wonderful parents. Wonderful. Except I wasn't able to appreciate them when I should have. I was too foolish.

People don't have time for love any more because they all have their separate lives; we all have our own families and our own children. Of course we try to phone home and say 'I love you, mum'. But that's not the point. We don't live at home any more. We are somewhere else. Whereas, in actual fact, our parents need us around: they still think we're little and need to be looked after. But we try to break away from this care and we have the right to do so. That's why I think the relationship between children and parents – and particularly between parents and children – is

9, 10   'I don't really talk to my daughter about important matters. I write her letters.'

terribly unfair. But that's the way it has to be. Every generation has to go through this injustice. Maybe what counts is simply to be able to understand this at a certain moment.

My daughter, Marta's, attitude is just as unfair. It's the natural order of things. She's repaying me for the unfair attitude I once had towards my parents. That sounds as if it were premeditated, but it's not calculated at all; it's natural, biological. She's nineteen and it's only natural that she should want to leave home. Of course, she wants something I don't want her to want. But that's the way it must be. It's natural.

My parents were too fair with me. My father was a very wise man but I couldn't make much use of his wisdom. It's only now that I can understand some of the things he did or said. I couldn't understand at the time; I was too foolish, too inconsiderate or too naïve. So I don't really talk to my daughter about important matters, or if I do, then very rarely. I do talk about practical things, of course, but I don't talk to her about the really important things in life. I write her letters, because she can keep them, look back over them. When you get a letter like that it doesn't mean much, but later on, in the future . . .

It's essential that your father is an authority to you, and that he's somebody you can trust. Maybe one of the real criteria of our behaviour in life is to enable our children to trust us – at least a little. That's why we don't disgrace ourselves completely, behave badly or shamefully. At least that's why I behave the way I do, in most cases.

Film School

At the College for Theatre Technicians, they showed us that there's a world of values which doesn't necessarily have to do with such everyday and socially accepted values as how to settle down, how to make comfortable lives for ourselves, own material goods, make money, have good positions. And they showed us that you can fulfil yourself in that other world, the so-called higher world. I don't know whether it's higher, but it certainly is different.

Consequently, I fell totally in love with the theatre. From about 1958 to 1962 was a great period in Polish theatre. It was a period of great directors, writers, actors and designers. In 1956 plays by authors from the West began to be shown in Poland, too. This was theatre of an internationally high standard. Of course, there was the Iron Curtain. There was no question of cultural exchange as there is now. Maybe this happened sometimes in the cinema, but rarely. In the theatre, it was impossible. Nowadays, Polish theatre companies travel all over the world. At that time, they didn't travel anywhere. They performed in their own buildings and that was it.

I don't see theatre of this quality anywhere nowadays. I go to the theatre in New York or I go to the theatre in Paris, in Berlin, and even there I don't see performances of such class. No doubt these are memories from a time when I was young and had the feeling that I was discovering something completely new and wonderful. Now, I don't see the same standard of directors, actors, designers, the same inventiveness in putting on a play, as I saw then, when I was dazzled by the discovery that something like that could be possible.

So obviously I decided to become a theatre director. But since you couldn't become a theatre director in Poland without first finishing some other form of higher studies – and it's still like that now – I wanted to get some sort of higher education. There were a lot of possibilities but I thought: 'Why not study at film school to become a film director, as a way to becoming a theatre director?' They're both directors.

It's not easy to get into Łódź Film School. As I've explained, I didn't get in either the first time, or the second. If you fail you have to wait a year before you can try again. In fact, it was only through sheer ambition that I took the exams a third time, to show them that I could get in. By then, I was no longer motivated because in the meantime I had stopped liking the theatre. The beautiful period had come to an end somewhere in 1962, and the plays were no longer as good. Something had happened – I don't know what. After 1956, there'd been an explosion, no doubt, of a certain degree of political freedom and this was expressed in the theatre. This had lasted for a few years, then in 1961 or 1962 it simply started to peter out. I decided that I didn't want to be a theatre director at all any more, or any sort of director for that matter. Even less a film director.

In the meantime, of course, I worked because I had to have something to live on. I was grown up and couldn't expect my mother, who didn't have any money anyway, to help me. I worked for a year or so as a clerk in the Department of Culture at the Council in Żolibórz.[6] I worked there for a year and wrote poetry. I also worked in the theatre for a year as a dresser. That was more interesting and was connected with my profession. But I had to spend most of my time studying something to get out of the army,[7] so I went to teachers' training college and studied drawing for a year. I had to pretend that I wanted to be an art teacher.

I drew very badly. The others drew just as badly as they learnt history, Polish, biology or geography at that teachers' training college. Everybody was bad at their subject. All the boys there were running away from the army and most of the girls were from outside Warsaw and were counting on catching a husband or maybe finding a job in a school in Warsaw and so acquiring a residence permit. People schemed like that and nobody there really wanted to be a teacher, which was a shame because it's a fine profession. Anyway, I don't think I met one single enthusiast of teaching.

So all this time I was trying to wangle my way out of the army. And I succeeded in the end. I was finally placed in a category which states that I'm unfit for military service even in the event of war. They're very rare, cases like that. I've got papers which certify me as having schizophrenia duplex which is a very dangerous form of schizophrenia and could mean that, given a rifle, I might, first and foremost, shoot my officer. The whole thing made me aware yet again of how complicated we all are because I didn't lie to the Conscription Board. I spoke the truth. I simply exaggerated a little and didn't tell the whole truth, and this proved credible.

First of all, I decided to lose weight. When I went before my first Conscription Board, it just happened that I was 16 kilos underweight. You calculate how much you're underweight by subtracting your weight in kilos from your height in centimetres and then subtracting 100. That is, if you're 181 cm tall – and I am 181 cm – then you should weigh 81 kilos. That's the way they calculate it in the army. So when I weighed 65 kilos, I was 16 kilos underweight. Consequently, they gave me Category B. That means I was relieved from military service for a year due to my poor physical condition.

I was simply slim and 16 kilos underweight. I didn't know the rules, but I took it that if I was 16 kilos underweight and was relieved for a year, then if I were, for example, 25 kilos underweight, they might let me off altogether. So I started to lose weight intensively. For a couple of months I began to eat less and less, until eventually I ate only a little. I ran and exercised. Then for the last ten days before I was due to see the Conscription Board again, I didn't eat or drink anything. Literally. It turns out it's possible. It's not at all true that people need liquids. I didn't drink a drop of water, not a drop of anything, and I didn't eat a single thing for a whole ten days. And at the beginning of those ten days, I went to the public baths because I didn't have a bathroom at the time. I was living in some awful rented room just outside Warsaw. So I visited the steam baths. I was nineteen and the thought of having a heart attack or anything like that didn't occur to me. Besides, I didn't care. I preferred to have a heart attack than go into the army. I preferred to have anything rather than go into the army. I had been to the firemen's training college and ever since then I knew that I preferred anything rather than wear another uniform.

They didn't beat me at firemen's training college; I just realized that I can't do things which are subject to rules, a trumpet, whistles, a set time for breakfast and so on. I want to eat breakfast when I feel like breakfast or when I'm hungry. It comes from a certain individualism which Poles have, or maybe from my own individualism. I simply don't agree to anyone organizing everything for me even though it may be convenient. That's why I'd find it hard in prison although there's much more freedom in prison than there is in the army.

So for ten days I didn't eat or drink anything whatsoever. Then I went to these baths. There was both a sauna and a steam bath there. All the men walked around naked, of course. This small guy attached himself to me. Since I went there every day or every other day, I noticed that this guy was getting closer and closer to me. I thought he must be gay and that this was some sort of meeting place for homosexuals. He came closer, closer and closer and finally, one day, he approached me, stood next to me, nudged me, looked at me and said, 'A skinny cockerel's a fine cockerel.' It turned out that he wasn't gay, just that he was as thin as I was and because of that he thought we were both great – and friends, of course. He must have been about fifty, and he really was as thin as a lath – like something straight out of Auschwitz, as they say in Poland. It's awful but that's what they say. And I looked as if I'd just got out of Auschwitz, too.

The last day really was hard for me. My mother came, made me a steak and I ate it. I got up, went to the Conscription Board. As usual, I got undressed and walked up to the table. I was 23 or 24 kilos underweight by then and that was a lot. I stood in front of that Board. Of course, there had to be all that military yelling as usual. 'You there! Get yourself over here! Stand over there! There, I said! . . . ' Because it was the same Board and the same time and place as before, I automatically made my way to the scales. I was going up to the scales when: 'Where do you think you're going?! The scales are broken! Come back here!' And that was the end of my losing weight. It got me nowhere.

And it all ended with schizophrenia. I didn't read a single word of any book. I realized that if I pretended, if I cheated, then they'd catch me out. It cost me a good bit of time, particularly as those Boards are no joke. I was locked up in a military hospital for ten days and every day I had a couple of hours of – I don't know what to call them – interrogations. In fact, they weren't really interrogations but sort of medical examinations with some eight or ten army doctors present.

Of course, a long time before that I'd already started attending a psychiatric clinic. I'd started going there about half a year earlier. I signed myself in saying that I felt unwell, that I'd simply lost all interest in anything whatsoever. That was my main argument; that I didn't care about anything, that I didn't want anything.

It was true that I felt a little that way throughout my whole life, but I felt it more deeply then, when I hadn't managed to get into film school for the second time. I really was, shall we say, resigned. It seemed more important for me to get out of military service than to get into film school.

I started going to the clinic during the winter and went there once a month. Then I was called up before the Board. They asked me whether there were any obstacles to my doing military service. I said there weren't. They weighed me. I'd regained weight. I was 15 kilos underweight again but not 25. Finally, they asked me what sort of military service I'd like to do. So I said I'd prefer some sort of peaceful service. 'Peaceful?' they said. 'There's no peaceful service in the army. What are you thinking of? What d'you mean peaceful? Why peaceful?' 'Well, peaceful because I'm being treated at the psychiatric clinic.' 'What d'you mean treated? Treated where? How long have you been treated?' 'Well, I've been going

there for half a year,' I said. 'What're you being treated for?' 'Well,
I don't know,' I said. 'I don't feel very well mentally, so I'm being
treated. That's why I wanted to join a peaceful military unit.' They
started to mumble something among themselves and said, 'Listen,
take this note. Go to Dolna Street, in Warsaw.' This was a military
hospital just next to the State Documentary Film Studios (Wytwórnia Filmów Dokumentalnych). It used to be a psychiatric
military hospital.

I spent ten days there in my pyjamas, not really knowing who
my room-mates were. And I just kept repeating the same thing
over and over again – that I wasn't interested in anything –
throughout the few daily hours of interrogations. They were very
searching, of course. For example, they asked, 'What have you
been doing if nothing interests you?' 'I did do something interesting recently,' I said. 'So what did you do?' 'I made my mum a
plug.' 'What d'you mean a plug?' 'You know, an electric plug.'
'Yes, but what did you do with the plug? The plug was there,
wasn't it? In the house?' I said, 'Yes, but there was only one plug in
the house and my mum has two machines. How could she plug
them in if she wanted to make soup and tea at the same time? I had
to make another plug.' 'All right,' they said, 'so what did you do
with this plug?' I took four hours to explain how to connect the
wires. 'How do you cut a wire? Well, first of all, you've got to cut
the cable, right? And how do you cut that? You have to peel the
first skin off the cable,' I explained to them, 'because there are two
cables there. One is positive and the other is negative, right? There
are two of them. They're in a sort of rubber protective casing. So
you have to cut through that. So I have to sharpen my knife, right,
and cut. But when I cut it I cut through the protective casings
which surround the little cables. So there could be a short-circuit.
You have to cut so as not to cut through the little protective
casings, too. Then when you take off the main protective casing,
there are two little cables, each in its own protective casing. Now
you have to cut each one so as to get to the wire because the
current doesn't run through the plastic. No, it has to go through
the wire. But there are seventy-two of these wires at each point.'
'Seventy-two?' he said. 'How do you know?' 'Because I counted
and there are seventy-two little wires.' They noted down scrupul-
ously that I'd counted the wires. 'You have to cut so as not to cut
through the wires. So the knife can't be too sharp. Because if you

press too hard you'll cut through the wire. Well, and you have to twist the wires together because, when you take the protective casing off, they spread out all over the place. So you have to twist them together again. There used to be one cable but this cable was made up of seventy-two wires. You have to be careful to twist them together accurately. And then you have to unscrew the screw and connect it in the right place. Get everything inside, case it again, tie it up and so on.'

It took me three or four hours to tell them about this little wire, because I explained it all in great detail. I'd simply realized that this interested them. When I started to describe something in detail, they started noting something down. I didn't know why but I did know it was important because I saw that they obviously concentrated at this point.

Then I told them about how I'd gone down into the basement to tidy things up. That took me about two days. I explained what was on the shelf, how dusty it was, that I had to move it, that it was damp down there, that I had to wipe the floor, that I had to go outside to wring the rag. Because if I were to wring the rag on the floor, then it would be wet again. So every time I had to go outside. So they said, 'Didn't it occur to you to take a bucket?' 'Yes,' I said. 'I realized later on that I had to get a bucket. It was a very good idea because I didn't have to go outside any more and could wring the rag into the bucket.'

So that's how we spent the next two days. Then there were about two days during which they made all sorts of ink blots and told me to guess what they reminded me of. Typical psychiatric tests.

Anyway, after ten days there, I got a sealed envelope. I unsealed it at home and read: Diagnosis: schizophrenia duplex. I resealed the envelope, went to my Conscription Board and gave it to them. They asked me for my Military Service Book and stamped it Category D: unfit for military service even in the event of war.

That's how my adventure with the army came to an end. I kept telling them that I didn't feel like doing anything. That I didn't want anything from life be it good or bad, that I didn't expect anything. Nothing at all. I told them that sometimes I read books. So they asked me to describe the books. And I recounted W Pustyni i w Puszczy,[8] sentence by sentence, for example. It took hours. It interested them that I found all sorts of connections, such as, if the author described the end as he did, it means the hero must have met the heroine and so on and so on.

Exactly four days later the film school entrance exams started and I passed. It was quite risky because, on the one hand, for the ten days that I was with the Conscription Board, I behaved as if I didn't feel like doing anything, while, on the other hand, I had to feel like doing everything the moment I went to take the film school exams.

I was happy when I got in to film school. I'd simply satisfied my ambition to show them that I could get in – nothing else – although I do believe they shouldn't have accepted me. I was a complete idiot. I can't understand why they took me. Probably because I'd tried three times.

To begin with, you had to show the examiners some work and then they graded you. You could show them films, or a script, or photographs. You could show them a novel, or paintings if you were a painter, whatever. I showed them some absurd short stories – absurd in the sense that they weren't any good. Once, during an earlier exam, I showed them a short film which I'd shot on 8 mm. Terrible. Absolutely terrible. Pretentious rubbish. If anybody had brought me anything like that I'd never have accepted them. They didn't take me then, of course. So I wrote a short story. Maybe it's when I wrote the story that they accepted me. I can't remember.

They're very long, the film school entrance exams. It's still like that now. They last two weeks. I always managed to get through to the last stage. This was quite difficult because there were something like five or six places and always about 1,000 candidates, which was a hell of a lot. You had to get through to the last stage where there were about thirty to forty candidates. Then from these, they chose five or six. I always got through to this stage without any problems. But I'd never get past that last stage.

I was quite well read and I was good at history of art because that had been very well taught at the PLTT, the College for Theatre Technicians. I wasn't bad at history of the cinema and so on. But, to be honest, I was a pretty naïve boy – or man, really, because I was over twenty – pretty naïve and not very bright. Anyway, I clearly remember what they asked me, in one of those last exams – an oral which was to decide whether or not I'd be accepted. There were always a couple of candidates whom they

11 'I was a complete idiot . . . pretty naïve and not very bright.'

thought they ought to accept and, no doubt, I was in that group because that's the way they treated me, and I remember them asking me, 'What are the means of mass communication?' So I said, 'Tram, bus, trolley-bus, aeroplane.' I added aeroplane as an afterthought. I was absolutely convinced that was the correct answer, but they probably thought that the question was so silly that I'd answered sarcastically, not outright, because that would have been below me. To answer outright and to say, the radio or television would have been well below me, so I answered derisively. And that's probably why I got in. But I really did think that the means of mass communication was a trolley-bus.

They asked various things during the exams. For example, How does a toilet-flush work? How does electricity work? Do you remember the first take of a film by Orson Welles? Or, Do you remember the final sentence of *Crime and Punishment*? Why do you have to water flowers? They asked all sorts of things. They tried to work out your intelligence, your association of ideas, because they were trying to see if you could describe things. It's very easy in a film to show a toilet flushing, but, in actual fact, it's quite difficult to explain it. Try to describe how a toilet-flush works in whatever language – it's not that easy. You can gesticulate but the point is to explain why water collects, why, when you press a button, something happens which makes all the water flush and then just the right amount of water collects for you to be able to flush again next time. Well, you simply had to be able to describe it all. With the help of questions like that, they examined your narrative skills, your skills of concentration, and your intelligence, too.

Classes at the Łódź Film School are much like those at any other film school. You learn the history of films, the history of aesthetics, photography, how to work with actors. You learn everything, one step at a time. Of course, you can't learn any of these things from theory alone, apart from the history. You simply have to experience them for yourself. There's no other way.

The whole idea of the school is to enable you to watch films and to talk about them, nothing else. You have to watch films, and because you're watching them and making them, you're always talking about them. It doesn't matter whether you talk about them during history lectures, or lectures on aesthetics or even if you talk about them during English classes. It's all the same. What is important is that the subject is always present. That you're always talking about it, analysing, discussing, comparing.

Fortunately, that school was well thought out. It enabled us to make films. We made at least one film each year. But if we were clever or a bit lucky, we could make two. I always managed to make one or two films a year. That was one of the school's objectives; to enable us to enter that world, as it were, and stay there for a bit. Another objective was to give us the opportunity to make films which was the practical realisation of all these discussions.

We had to make feature films and documentaries. I made both. I think I made twenty-minute features in my third year. We'd sometimes base our work on short stories. The films had to be short so there was no question of adapting a novel. But on the whole, most of us wrote our own scripts.

There wasn't any particular censorship at the School. They showed us various films which people usually didn't see. They imported films so that students would be educated by them and not merely watch them as scraps of interesting information or forbidden news, albeit political. Of course, we weren't shown any James Bonds fighting the KGB, but we did see films which weren't generally shown in Poland or we saw them long before they were shown. I don't think there was any political censorship in their choice of films. Maybe there was and I just didn't know about it. They would show us Eisenstein's *Battleship Potemkin* and other good Russian films which had a reason for being interesting. The school wasn't tinged with Communist propaganda. It was really open-minded, and that's why it was so good, up until 1968.

A number of films have stayed in my memory simply because they're beautiful. I remember them because I always thought that I'd never be able to do anything like that in my life (no doubt those are the films which always make the greatest impression), not due to lack of money or because I didn't have the means or technicians, but because I didn't have sufficient imagination, intelligence or enough talent. I always said that I never wanted to be anybody's assistant but that if, for example, Ken Loach were to ask me, then I'd willingly make him coffee. I saw *Kes* at film school and I knew then that I'd willingly make coffee for him. I didn't want to be an assistant or anything like that – I'd just make coffee so I could see how he does it all. The same applied to Orson Welles, or Fellini, and sometimes Bergman.

There were wonderful directors once but now they're dead or retired. It's all in the past – the period of great film personalities. Watching the great films, it wasn't even jealousy I felt because you can only be jealous of something which, theoretically, is within your reach. You can envy that, but you can't envy something which is completely beyond you. There was nothing wrong with my feelings. On the contrary, they were very positive; a certain admiration and bedazzlement that something like that is possible – and that it would always be beyond my reach.

Once, somewhere in Holland I think it was, they asked me to choose some films which I had liked a lot. I made a selection. I can't even remember them all, but I made my selection and I even went to two screenings. Then I stopped going. I'd simply understood that somewhere along the way, these expectations and notions which I had had of the films, which I can clearly remember, completely lost their myth.

I remember watching Fellini's *La Strada* and not being disillusioned at all. I liked it just as much as before, if not more. And then I watched a film by Bergman called *Sawdust and Tinsel* and I remember I'd had beautiful recollections of that film. But I found myself watching something on the screen which left me completely indifferent, which was completely alien to me. I couldn't understand what I'd seen in it before, apart from perhaps three or four scenes. I didn't experience any of the tension which I'd felt when I'd watched it before. But then Bergman went on to make some more beautiful films which still create this tension. This, among other things, is where the magic of the screen lies: that suddenly, as an audience, you find yourself in a state of tension because you're in a world shown to you by the director. That world is so coherent, so comprehensive, so succinct that you're transported into it and experience tension because you sense the tension between the characters.

I don't know why this happened, because these two films were made at more or less the same time. Fellini and Bergman are, more or less, of the same period. They're both great directors. But *La Strada* hasn't aged while *Sawdust and Tinsel* has. I don't quite know why. Of course, you could analyse it and, no doubt, might even understand the phenomenon but I don't know whether it's worth it. That's philosophizing, the work of critics.

Andrei Tarkovsky was one of the greatest directors of recent

years. He's dead, like most of them. That is, most of them are dead
or have stopped making films. Or else, somewhere along the line,
they've irretrievably lost something, some individual sort of imagination, intelligence or way of narrating a story. Tarkovsky was
certainly one of those who hadn't lost this. Unfortunately, he died.
Probably because he couldn't live any more. That's usually why
people die. One can say it's cancer or a heart attack or that the
person falls under a car, but really people usually die because they
can't go on living.

They always ask me, in interviews, which directors have
influenced me the most. I don't know the answer to that. Probably
so many, for all sorts of reasons, that there's no logical pattern.
When the newspapers ask, I always say, Shakespeare, Dostoevsky,
Kafka. They're surprised and ask me whether these are directors.
'No,' I say. 'They're writers.' And that's as if more important to
me than film.

The truth is that I watched masses of films – especially at film
school – and I loved a lot of them. But can you call that influence?
I think that to this day, apart from a few exceptions, I watch films
like a member of the public rather than a director. It's a completely
different way of looking at things. Of course, I watch with a
professional eye if somebody asks me for advice or something.
Then I try to analyse the film, watch it professionally. But if I go to
the cinema – which happens very rarely – I try to watch films like
the audience does. That is, I try to allow myself to be moved,
surrender to the magic, if it's there, on the screen, and to believe
the story somebody's telling. And then it's hard to talk of
influence.

Basically, if a film is good, and if I like it, then I watch it far less
analytically than if I don't like it. It's hard to say that bad films
have an influence; it's the good ones that influence us. And I try to
watch – or rather, do watch – good films in the spirit in which they
were made. I don't try to analyse them. It was the same thing at
school, too. I watched *Citizen Kane* a hundred times. If you
insisted, I could sit down and probably draw or describe individual takes, but that's not what was important to me. What was
important, was the fact that I took part in the film. I experienced
it.

Nor do I think that there's anything wrong in stealing. If
somebody's gone that way before and it's proved to be good, then

you have to steal it immediately. If I steal from good films, and if this later becomes part of my own world, then I steal without qualms. This often happens completely without my being aware of it, but that doesn't mean that I don't do it – it did happen but it wasn't calculated, or premeditated. It's not straight plagiarism. To put it another way, films are simply part of our lives. We get up in the morning, we go to work or we don't got to work. We go to sleep. We make love. We hate. We watch films. We talk to our friends, to our families. We experience our children's problems or the problems of our children's friends. And the films are there somewhere, too. They also stay somewhere within us. They become part of our own lives, of our own inner selves. They stay with us just as much as all those things which really happened. I don't think they're any different from real events, apart from the fact that they're invented. But that doesn't matter. They stay with us. I steal takes from films, scenes, or solutions, just as I steal stories and afterwards I can't even remember where I stole them from.

I keep persuading younger colleagues to whom I teach script-writing or directing, to examine their own lives. Not for the purposes of any book or script but for themselves. I always say to them, Try to think of what happened to you which was important and led to your sitting here in this chair, on this very day, among these people. What happened? What really brought you here? You've got to know this. That's the starting point.

The years in which you don't work on yourself like this are, in fact, wasted. You might feel or understand something intuitively and, consequently, the results are arbitrary. It's only when you've done this work that you can see a certain order in events and their effects.

I tried to fathom out what brought me to this point in my life, too, because without such an authentic, thorough and merciless analysis, you can't tell a story. If you don't understand your own life, then I don't think you can understand the lives of the characters in your stories, you can't understand the lives of other people. Philosophers know this. Social workers know this. But artists ought to know this too – at least those who tell stories. Maybe musicians don't need such an analysis, although I believe that composers do. Painters maybe less so. But it's absolutely necessary to those who tell stories about life: an authentic understanding of

one's own life. By authentic I mean that it's not a public understanding, which I'll share with anybody. It's not for sale, and, in
fact, you'll never detect it in my films. Some things you can find
out very easily but you'll never understand how much the films I
make or the stories I tell mean to me and why. You'll never find
that out. I know it, but that knowledge is only for me.

I'm frightened of anybody who wants to teach me something or
who wants to show me a goal, me or anybody else, because I don't
believe you can be shown a goal if you don't find it yourself. I'm
fanatically afraid of all those people. That's why I'm afraid of
psychoanalysts and psychotherapists. Of course they always say,
We don't show you, we help you find it. I know all those argu-
ments. Unfortunately, that's only theory while in practice they do
show you. I know masses of people who feel wonderful afterwards. But I also know a great many people who feel terrible and I
think that even those who feel good today won't feel so good
tomorrow.

I'm very unfashionable about such things. I know it's in vogue
to run to all sorts of places like that, to various group or individual
therapies with psychotherapists, or to seek the help of psychiat-
rists. I know masses of people do it. I'm afraid of it, that's all. I'm
just as fanatically afraid of those therapists as I am of politicians,
of priests, and of teachers. I'm frightened of all those people who
show you the way, who know. Because really – and I'm deeply
convinced of this, I firmly believe it – nobody really knows, with a
few exceptions. Unfortunately, the actions of these people usually
end in tragedy – like the Second World War or Stalinism or
something. I'm convinced that Stalin and Hitler knew exactly
what they were to do. They knew very well. But that's how it is.
That's fanaticism. That's knowing. That's the feeling of absolutely
knowing. And the next minute, it's army boots. It always ends up
like that.

I went to a good film school. I finished there in 1968. The School
used to have a certain amount of freedom and wise teachers but
then the Communists destroyed it. They started by throwing out
some of the teachers because they were Jewish, and they ended by
taking away such freedom as the School enjoyed. That's how they
destroyed it.

They tried to disguise the censorship they introduced with grand
words. For example, at one stage there was a group of young

people who wanted to hold positions of power in the School, but they were advocates of experimental cinema. That is, they cut holes in film or set up the camera in one corner for hours on end, filming the result, or scratched pictures on to film, and so on. Totalitarian authorities always support movements like these if the movement can destroy another movement. And that movement was in a position to destroy a movement at School which was based on our trying to see what was happening in the world, how people were living and why they weren't living as well as they could, why their lives weren't as easy as the paper described them. We were all making films about that.

The authorities could have closed the School down but it would have looked bad because then people would have said that the authorities were destroying artistic freedom, so they acted far more subtly. The authorities vested their interest in people who claimed to make artistic films. 'There's no point in filming people and their living conditions. We're artists, we have to make artistic films. Experimental films preferably.'

I remember going back to the School in 1981 with Agnieszka Holland,[9] when those young people were there. They were being led by a former colleague of mine who desperately wanted to be Principal and who spent most of his time cutting holes in magnetic tape. White holes. There was a black screen and every now and again a white hole, sometimes small, sometimes large, would flash on one side or other of the screen. This was accompanied by some sort of music. I'm not an advocate of films like that and I don't hide the fact that they irritate me. But that's not the point, because there are people who do like films like that and holes have to be made to cater for them. I've got absolutely nothing against that provided that with the help of those holes you're not going to destroy something else.

I was Vice-President of the Polish Film-makers' Association[10] at the time and this was one of the many actions which we took and in which we failed; Agnieszka and I went to the School to try and explain to the students that the film school was there to enable them to make films, to teach them where to set the camera up, how to work with actors, what films had been made to date, the basics of dramaturgy, script structuring, how a scene differs from a sequence, and how a wide-angle lens differs from a telephoto lens. At that, the students threw us out, shouting that they didn't want a

professional school. They wanted to study yoga, the philosophy of
the Far East and various schools of meditation, claiming that this
was very important. And that they wanted to cut holes in film and
believed that yoga and the art of meditation was a great help to
them in this.

They simply threw us out of the school. This was only one of the
numerous undertakings of our Film-makers' Association during
which I realized how ineffective we were. Perhaps I was wrong but
I personally believe that the school is there to teach these things.
But they thought otherwise. I don't know, maybe that's why
Polish cinema is in the state it's in today – because they thought
the way they did.

Back in 1968 there was a small revolution in Poland led by
intellectuals whom nobody supported. We, at the film school,
believed that the papers were lying, that Jews mustn't be thrown
out of Poland, and that perhaps it would be a good thing if people
who were more open and democratic than Gomułka's[11] party,
were to come to power. We thought that if we spoke out for
something which appeared to be good or better than what had
been before – an expansion of freedom, what appeared to be more
democratic or effectively more common to all (because, after all,
that's what democracy boils down to, to that which is most
common to most people) – then, even if we didn't achieve it, at
least we'd have expressed ourselves decently. Later on, it turned
out that we'd been manipulated by people who wanted to gain
power but who were far crueller and more cynical than Gomułka.
We'd been used by Moczar[12] and his followers.

Twice in my life I tried my hand at politics and twice I came out
very badly. The first time was then, in 1968, when I took part in a
students' strike in Łódź. That was not very important; I threw
stones and ran away from the militia. That's all. And then they
interrogated me five times, maybe ten. They wanted me to say
something, sign something, which I didn't do. Nobody beat me up,
nobody threatened me. I never even got the impression that they
wanted to arrest me. What was worse was the fact that they threw
people out of Poland. Anti-Semitism and Polish nationalism are a
stain on my country which has remained to this day and I don't
think we'll ever be able to get rid of it.

It's only now that I realize how good it is for a country not to be
ethnically pure. Now I know. Then I didn't. Still, I did know that

some terrible injustice was being perpetrated, and I knew that I couldn't do anything about it, that nobody could do anything about it, and that, paradoxically, the more I shouted against the authorities, the more I threw those stones, the more people would get thrown out of the country.

For some time afterwards, I managed to avoid politics. And then I got involved in politics on a small scale as Wajda's[13] Vice-President, although effectively I was doing the work of an acting president of the Polish Film-makers' Association, which was quite important at the time. That must have been from about 1976 or 1977 to 1980. I very quickly realized what an unpleasant and painful trap it was to be in such a position. And this, as I said, was only politics on a small scale. But it was politics. We were trying, as an Association, to fight for some sort of artistic freedom, some sort of freedom of expression in films to stop them from clashing so painfully with the censors. Nothing came out of it. We thought we were very important and then it turned out that we were completely insignificant.

I had a painful feeling of having walked into a room where I absolutely shouldn't have gone, that the compromises which I had to make – and I was constantly having to make compromises, of course – that those compromises embarrassed me because they weren't my own private ones: they were compromises made in the name of a number of people. This is deeply immoral because, even if you can do some good for somebody, achieve something which people need, there's always a price to be paid. Of course, you pay with stress but it's the others who really pay. There's no other way. I realized it wasn't my world.

I keep making compromises in my own private and professional life, as well as artistic compromises, but I make them on my own account. They concern my own films, something which I, myself, have imagined, and I'm the only one who bears the consequences. In other words, I don't want to be responsible for anybody else. And that's what I realized, despite the fact that I'd got myself mixed up in this Association affair. When Solidarity came along, I simply asked the Association to dismiss me – I wasn't cut out for such revolutionary times.

But going back to the subject of film school, I was there along with Jerzy Skolimowski,[14] who was just leaving when I joined. Then when I was in my second year, Krzysztof Zanussi,[15] Edek

Żebrowski,[16] and Antek Krauze[17] left. We were a good team, my year, and got on very well together. I was very good friends with Andrzej Titkow[18]. Then I was great friends with Tomek Zygad-ło.[19] Also with us were Krzyś Wojciechowski[20] and Piotr Wojcie-chowski[21] who was already a good writer then, and still is. There were some foreign students, too. That was my year. A very, very good year and we all liked each other very much.

Andrzej Titkow wrote a play for television called *Atarax* (Ata-rax is a tranquillizer). I directed the play as part of my work in my second or third year. That was one of the advantages of the School – the possibility of practical work. It wasn't obligatory but you could direct something if you wanted to. We were given relatively good professional conditions for those times. The machines we used are terribly old-fashioned by today's standards, but at the time they were decent. We were given professional camera opera-tors, electricians and sound technicians.

After film school, it turned out that we had different tastes or interests. I went into documentaries as quickly as I possibly could because I very much wanted to make documentary films, and did make them for a good many years. My friends went all sorts of different ways, although some of them went into documentaries, too, later on. This was the end of the 1960s and it wasn't easy, at the time, to get into documentaries. I don't really know how I succeeded so quickly. Kazimierz Karabasz,[22] one of my teachers, probably helped me. He was one of the better teachers and cer-tainly had a great influence on me at the beginning.

They used to call me 'engineer'. Maybe because my father was an engineer, but I suspect I've got the habit or obsession of always tidying up around myself. I keep drawing up various lists for everything and I try to put my papers into some sort of order. Or they'd call me 'orni' or 'ornithologist', probably because of the patience I used to have when making documentaries.

I used to be very patient when making documentaries, of course, because the profession demands it but now I'm absolutely impatient. It's a question of age. When you start off, you think there's plenty of time, and you're patient. Then you become more and more aware that there isn't any time after all, and you don't want to waste time on things which aren't worth it.

Then I started making feature films and found myself in a slightly different group, which later called itself the Cinema of

Moral Anxiety. That name was invented by Janusz Kijowski,[23] who was one of our colleagues. I think he meant that we were anxious about the moral situation of people in Poland. It's difficult for me to say what he had in mind. I always hated the name, but it works.

These friendships were completely different from those of my documentary film-making days, between entirely different people. They weren't so close, perhaps, not so human, and were more professional. I became friends with Krzysztof Zanussi, and then with Edek Żebrowski and Agnieszka Holland. And for some time, with Andrzej Wajda, too. We were all, as it were, in a group which shared the feeling that we could do something together, that we positively had to do something together, and that in such a group we'd have some sort of power. This was true considering the circumstances in Poland at the time. A group like that was necessary. There were about six years of this Cinema of Moral Anxiety, from 1974 to 1980.

However, all that came later. Soon after I finished film school, somewhere at the beginning of the 1970s, several of us thought it essential to create small pressure groups. We thought that we should create a studio which would bring together young people, which would serve as a bridge between school and the professional film world, and become a place from which one could really enter the professional world. This was because our main grievance against the organization of film production in Poland at that time was that it was immensely difficult to find a way into working in film from school. Later, in the mid-1970s, it became a bit easier but at the beginning of the 1970s or the end of the 1960s even, it seemed that there was no way in. So we tried to create one.

The idea came from a studio in Hungary called the Bela Balasz Studio. Bela Balasz was a Hungarian film theoretician, an intelligent man who was working before and after the Second World War. Our studio in Poland was to be called the Irzykowski Studio. Irzykowski was very close to Bela Balasz as a film theoretician before the war. He was a serious theoretician, and a good one. The main point of our studio was to make films cheaply. Our slogan was 'début for a million'. The average cost of a film, at the time, was six million złotys but we undertook to make first films for a million złotys.

We decided to concentrate on feature films but thought it might also be possible to make all sorts of films for various distributors. Short documentaries were still being distributed in cinemas as supporting programmes to feature films. We also thought that it might be possible to make documentaries for television. We were looking for all sorts of ways to finance this studio, although, at that time, money came from only one source, namely the State Treasury. It was only a matter of convincing those responsible for cultural politics that such a place was necessary. But, to be honest, we never managed to do that. We never managed to convince them, despite devoting several years to it.

I wasn't by any means the most important there. The group was made up of Grzés Królikiewicz[24] (who, I think, had the most energy), Andrzej Jurga,[25] Krzyś Wojciechowski and me. There was also a production manager. We wanted people from all disciplines. We needed a producer and a production manager to work out film budgets and the studio budget.

That's what we were trying to attain and we wrote various manifestos. We even managed to get the support of various important people from the film industry – Kuba Morgenstern,[26] Andrzej Wajda, Krzysztof Zanussi, and even Jerzy Kawalerowicz,[27] then President of the Film-makers' Association – even though this was very difficult at the time because we'd only just left school. We managed to get all those people to sign papers which stated that such a studio was necessary, that it would be a good thing for the film industry. But we always came up against a lack of goodwill on the part of – I don't really know who – the Ministry of Arts and Culture? Then again, the Ministry probably wasn't in a position to decide. It was probably the Department of Culture at the Central Committee which decided. I suspect we weren't trustworthy enough. We were too young for them to know us and none of us belonged to the Party.

In order to give ourselves credibility we even asked Bohdan Kosiński,[28] the documentary film-maker, to be artistic patron of the Studio. Later on, he became a known and very active member of the opposition. But at that time he was still Party Secretary at the WFD (State Documentary Film Studios). We thought that if we gained such support from the side of the Party, it would be easier. But it turned out that Kosiński, although Party Secretary, wasn't so trustworthy in the eyes of the Party. He had probably already sensed something because this was, firstly, after 1968 and the anti-Semitic purge in Poland, and secondly, after the invasion of Czechoslovakia by the Allied forces. I think the Party vetted everybody very carefully. In fact we had all been involved in the events of 1968. Bohdan, I suspect, was already expressing his attitude to the invasion of Czechoslovakia. Even if he wasn't doing so openly, he was probably doing it clearly enough at the Party forum to arouse their mistrust.

After a few years, this enterprise collapsed, and the studio only came into being later on, in 1980, during the period of Solidarity. Other young people created the studio under the leadership of Janusz Kijowski, and it's still functioning to this day. I've no idea how it's getting on because, to be honest, I'm not interested any more. I wanted to create this studio for people of my own generation but later it was the new generation who needed it. We didn't need it any more; we'd already made our way into the film industry.

I was interested in the new studio for a while because there were students there from the Katowice Film School, which had been founded in 1977, I think, and where I taught for three or four years, together with Krzysztof Zanussi, Edek Żebrowski and Andrzej Jurga. Those people who were finishing the School at the beginning of the 1980s were our students, our younger colleagues. So that's why I did have some interest in the way the studio was developing.

It's always like that – that people want something in the name of their ideals. They want to do something together, to define themselves in some way and then, when they get the money and a little bit of power, they start to forget those ideals and make their own films, not allowing anybody else in and, no doubt, that's how the Irzykowski Studio ended up. They're always wrangling. The studio management is forever changing. To be honest, I don't have much faith in that studio.

CHAPTER 2

The Unique Role of Documentaries

From the City of Łódź
Z MIASTA ŁODZI (1969)

My graduating film was also my first professional one, which I had made at the WFD (State Documentary Film Studios) in Warsaw, therefore my entry into the profession went very smoothly. The film had been jointly financed by the school and the Studios. I can't remember the financial terms any more – besides nobody cared then. I just know that I didn't have much money but it was enough.

It was called *From the City of Łódź*, and was a short documentary, ten or twelve minutes long. We were all making them at the time; short one-act documentaries which could be shown as supporting programmes in cinemas. It was about Łódź, a town I knew well since I'd lived there while at film school, and which I loved very much. Łódź was cruel and unusual. Singularly picturesque with its dilapidated buildings, dilapidated staircases, dilapidated people. It was much more dilapidated than Warsaw, but also more homogenous. Łódź had only been slightly damaged during the war so the town of my film-school days was, in fact, the pre-war town. And, because it stood just as it had before the war and there'd never been any money for repairs and renovations, the walls were all blistering, plaster was peeling away, crumbling everywhere. And all that was singularly picturesque. It's not an ordinary town.

When I was still at film school, my friends and I often played a game which was very simple but required integrity. On the way to school in the morning, we had to collect points. If you saw someone without an arm you got one point, without two arms two points, without a leg two points, without two legs three points, without arms or legs, a trunk that is, ten points, and so on. A blind person was five points. It was a great game. Then, at school we'd meet at about ten in the morning for breakfast and see who had won. We'd usually all get about ten or twelve points, on average. If anyone got fifteen, he was almost sure to have won that day. That shows you how many people there were in Łódź who didn't have arms or legs or who were mere trunks without both arms and legs. This was a result of the extremely backward, ancient textile industry there, where people were forever having limbs torn off. It was also the result of very narrow streets where trams went right up next to the buildings. You just had to take one inadvertant step and you'd find yourself under a tram. Anyway, that's the sort of town it was. Horrifying yet at the same time fascinating because of this.

We played this game for many years. There were other things, too, which we'd observe with a certain passion. I started taking photographs then, because there was an excellent photographic department at the School with a dark room in the basement. They'd give you a camera, and film; you could take endless photographs, and develop anything. We'd take hundreds of photographs. I loved taking photographs. And all the time the subjects were old people, contorted people, staring out into the distance, dreaming or thinking of how it could have been, yet reconciled to how things were.

I took lots of photographs. I've still got some which aren't all that bad. I showed them to my daughter recently because she's taken up photography, of her own accord. I don't know what suddenly made her want to take photographs.

That's basically the subject of *From the City of Łódź*. It's a portrait of a town where some people work, others roam around in search of Lord knows what. Nothing probably. Generally, it's the women who work hard and the men not so hard or not at all. A town which is full of eccentricities, full of all sorts of absurd statues, and various contrasts. There are trams and old horse-drawn coal carts still on the streets to this day. It's a town full of terrible restaurants and horrible milk bars. Full of stinking, shitty, pissed, foul toilets. Full of ruins, hovels, recesses.

It's a town where, for example, there were notices in the trams which said that if you wanted to transport a cabbage-slicer, you had to buy two tickets. I've never ever seen a notice like that since – that there's a special fare for transporting a cabbage-slicer. I don't know whether anybody knows what a cabbage-slicer is any

12–17 (Photographs by Krzysztof Kieślowski) 'Film School taught me how to look at the world. It showed me that life exists and that people talk, laugh, worry, suffer, steal in this life, that all this can be photographed and

that from all these photographs a story can be told. I didn't know that before.

　　To be honest, the one and only grudge I bear the school is that nobody told me – I still don't know why because the lecturers must have known – that the only thing I and nobody else can really call my own, is my own life and my own point of view. It took me many, many years to arrive at that conclusion.'

more. It's a long board, about four to five feet in length, with a slit in the middle. In that slit, there's a knife. You put the cabbage on it, press down with a board and move it up and down. In this way, the cabbage is shredded to make sauerkraut.

So in Łódź, there's a special tram fare which allows you to transport a cabbage-slicer if you've got two tickets. And various other things, too. I remember there was a notice saying that you have to buy two tickets if you wanted to transport skis. But skis means a pair, doesn't it? Two skis. So I'd take one ski and a friend would take one ski. The ticket inspector would come along. Well, the problem was that neither of us was carrying skis. Because each of us was carrying only one ski and the notice applied to a pair of skis. For the transportation of skis: two tram tickets. But nowhere was it written what you had to pay for the transportation of one ski. So there'd be endless discussions with the ticket inspector. 'But I've only got one ski.' 'Yes, but your friend has the other.' 'But my friend's got his ticket, I've got mine.' I remember that there was 'Skis. Cabbage-slicer. Wreath' on that notice, so that for two tickets you could transport three things. A funeral wreath, that also cost two tickets. Tram tickets were quite a problem for us then because, although they seemed very cheap, every penny counted. I didn't have any money. Mum gave me a little. I got a very small grant at film school. I had already married Marysia, my present wife, when I was in my fourth and final year, and we had very little money.

The town has changed now. A lot of modern buildings have gone up and the old ones have been demolished, but I don't think the modern ones are any better – they're worse, to be honest. Completely without character. The town's losing its character because they're demolishing those old buildings instead of repairing them. That strange, alluring power it once had is disappearing. And it used to be really strong. That's what the film *From the City of Łódź* is about. It's made with an enormous amount of sympathy for the town and for the people living in it. I don't remember it all that well to be able to say exactly what happens. There are women working. There was this guy in a park with a special machine which would give you an electric shock. You'd hold on to the negative charge, with one hand, and with the other a wire which was positively charged. And he'd turn on the power. The whole point was to see who could stand the highest voltage. How much will you stand? 120 volts? Proof of whether you were a man depended on whether you could bear 380 volts, for example. And not 120. A child could stand sixty or eighty then would let go immediately. But serious, fat men would hold on to 380 volts and say: 'Okay, give me more.' But the guy didn't have any more. He only had 380 volts. I think I stuck it to the end. I had to because the whole crew was watching and I didn't have any choice. Well, those were the sort of games we played in Łódź. But that guy made money out of it. He'd take a złoty for wiring you up.

We all lived in rented rooms. Later, when I got married, we lived in an attic. It was quite large; one of those places that had been used for hanging wet linen. The owner rented it out to us and Marysia and I turned this place into a room with a kitchen. And Andrzej Titkow lived with us for some time, too. There was this old-fashioned stove but we never had enough money to keep it burning. Also, there was a problem with buying coal; not only was it difficult to buy because we didn't quite know where to get it, but we didn't have enough money for it either. So every day, or every other day, we'd steal a bag of coal, a ten-kilo bag of coal, from the school. This would last us for two days and then two days later we'd be off stealing another ten kilos and so on. In this way we survived the winter. We simply stole coal.

There was another game we'd play. There was a woman who lived right next to the school. The road near the school was quite wide in one place because there was a park there. It was, say twenty-five metres wide. Every metre, we'd make a mark on the road. A chalk mark. The old woman's house was on one side of the road, opposite was the park. And where the park started, there was a public toilet where you had to go down some stairs if you wanted a pee. At more or less ten in the morning, when we'd be meeting for breakfast, that old woman would leave her house where she presumably didn't have a toilet, and make her way to that public loo. She was, well, very old. She moved with great difficulty. The way the betting worked was that every hour, at the end of a class, we'd go out and check which metre mark the old woman had reached. She moved so slowly that it took her eight hours to get to that toilet. Sometimes seven. Sometimes six. Then she had to climb down the stairs. Afterwards, she had to climb up again and, in the evening, she'd go back home. She'd go to bed.

18 'I had already married Marysia, my present wife, when I was in my fourth and final year.'

Sleep. Then get up in the morning and go to the loo again. And we took bets – not for stakes, of course, only honour and the fun of it – which mark the old woman would reach at twelve o'clock, for example. I'd say the fourth. Somebody else would say the third. Somebody else again the sixth. And then we'd go out and check where she'd got to.

Those were the kind of games we played. They may seem cruel today but we played them because of the interest we had in life, interest in the lives of other people, interest in worlds which were completely different to those in which we grew up. I had come to Łódź from Warsaw, after going to the college for Theatre Technicians. All of my friends were from Warsaw. Łódź was a completely different town, and a completely different world.

Marek Piwowski[1] photographed this world beautifully in his film *Fly-swat* (*Muchotluk*). This is a beautiful film about all those monsters in Łódź – the sort of people Fellini always uses in his films. But I think that the Communist monsters, living in Łódź at that time, were far more vivid than Fellini's, and Piwowski managed to use that in *Fly-swat*.

So those were the film school days. I never went back. Sometimes I went on a brief visit to shoot something at the Łódź studios, but I didn't ever really go back. In *From the City of Łódź* I wanted to film what I'd once liked so much in that town. Of course, I didn't manage to capture everything but I think that a little of the atmosphere is there in the film. I got my diploma for it.

Just after school – that must have been some time in 1969 – I made a couple of films for a co-op in Warsaw which produced some absolutely cretinous commercials. I don't even know what it was called – *Spółdzielnia Pracy* (Work Co-op) or *Spółdzielnia Usług Filmowych* (Film Services Co-op) or something. We called it *Spółdzielnia Woreczek* (Money-bag Co-op). I managed to live for about half a year thanks to that co-op. One film I made was about a watch-makers' co-op in Lublin and the other was about some craftsmen. Tanners or something like that.

Then I made two so-called commissioned films. One of these encouraged young people to come and work in the copper mines by saying that there were good working conditions there, good living conditions, that one could earn a lot and so on. The copper factories must have commissioned that. I made that at the WFD (State Documentary Film Studios) but the money came from rich

19, 20 'I made two so-called commissioned films.' *Between Wrocław and Zielona Góra (Między Wrocławiem a Zieloną Górą)* . . .

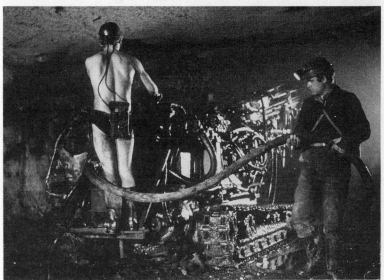

21, 22 ... and *The Principles of Safety and Hygiene in a Copper Mine* (*Podstawy BHP w Kopalni Miedzy*).

factories and sponsors. Masses of films like that were being made at the WFD at the time.

I think I made four things like that all in all. I didn't particularly want to but it wasn't a shameful thing to do. It's a profession – film director. Sometimes you just have to render some services. It was boring, far more boring than anything else I've done, but I could live because of it. Apart from those few films, I've never made a film which I didn't want to.

I Was a Soldier
BYŁEM ŻOŁNIERZEM (1970)

Initially I was employed as an assistant at the WFD but I never worked as one. Never in my life have I been an assistant. I strongly defended myself against it. They employed me as an assistant because those were the formal requirements. Then, later, I was employed as a director. I think I was the first of my generation to be officially employed as a director at the WFD.

There were three film studios in Warsaw; the WFD, Television[2], and Czołówka. Czołówka commissioned documentaries or films for the army, films about the army, about particular squadrons or life in a military unit. I don't really know what they made there.

I made one documentary at Czołówka in 1970 and it's quite a good film. It wasn't commissioned. It's called *I was a Soldier* and is about men who had been soldiers and lost their sight in the Second World War. Staś Niedbalski[3] was cameraman. The soldiers just sit there, in front of the camera, throughout the film, and talk. I asked them about their dreams. That's what the film's about really.

Workers '71
ROBOTNICY '71 (1971)

At that time, I was interested in everything that could be described by the documentary film camera. There was a necessity, a need – which was very exciting for us – to describe the world. The Communist world had described how it should be and not how it really was. We – there were a lot of us – tried to describe this world and it was fascinating to describe something which hadn't been described yet. It's a feeling of bringing something to life, because it is a bit like that. If something hasn't been described, then it doesn't officially exist. So that if we start describing it, we bring it to life.

Workers '71 is my most political film because it gives no humanistic point of view. It was intended to portray the workers' state of mind in 1971. At that time, this was still the ruling class. That's what it was officially called in Poland anyway. It seemed to us that it would be a good idea to show that this class did think and that it thought in what I then considered to be more or less the right way to think. That is, aiming for democratization everywhere: in places of work, in administrative districts, in towns throughout the whole country. We tried to give a broad picture showing that the class which, theoretically at least, was said to be the ruling class had somewhat different views than those which were printed on the front page of the *Trybuna Ludu*.[4]

This was after the strikes of 1970[5] and we made the film in 1971. We tried to show people who, in small towns, villages, and factories, had organized the strikes and had, through various government representatives, tried to convey to Gierek[6] in Warsaw, the idea that people in Poland awaited changes; more visible changes than those Gierek was making. This was during the year after Gierek had been made First Secretary. The people's desire for more radical changes, more evident in a film which I shot in 1981 called *Talking Heads (Gadające Głowy)*, eventually resulted in Solidarity which made it blatantly clear that people wanted to live differently.

Tomek Zygadło and I directed *Workers '71*. There was Tolo's[7] crew working with another crew. Then there was still another small sub-crew directed by 'Szajbus' (Madman) Wojtek Wiszniewski[8]. We travelled all over Poland and tried to film those heated times before they disappeared. Because we all knew they would end. We had to film them.

Somebody probably wanted to make a profit out of the film but they didn't succeed. If, for example, with the help of this film, a Party Secretary called Olszowski[9] – who at the time seemed a more liberal Secretary but who later turned out to be a far more stubborn and relentless enemy of liberalization than the previous Secretary – if, with the help of this film among other things, he'd have come to power, then I'd have held it against myself. But he

23, 24, 25
'Tomek
Zygadło and I
directed
Workers '71
(*Robotnicy
'71*).'

didn't. Maybe because the film wasn't one which could have helped a Party career. The upshot was that we were forced to make a version which we didn't like, neither in essence nor in form. The cuts were particularly nasty and galling. Fortunately, they don't matter since neither version – neither the one which the authorities brought about, nor the one which we proposed – was ever shown.

I had already started to realize it would be like this when we were nearing the end of the shoot. To be honest, I'd never have agreed to the cuts which they made if I had been the only director. That doesn't mean that Tomek Zygadło agreed and I didn't. God forbid. We simply realized that we had to agree to them and we made the decision jointly. If I'd made the film myself, I certainly wouldn't have agreed. But then I'd have been responsible only for myself. No doubt, if Tomek had made the film by himself, he wouldn't have agreed either. But then he'd have been responsible only for himself, too. But as it was, we were, in a way, responsible for each other. I was responsible for his child and his wife and he was responsible for my wife and child. It's not easy to carry such a burden.

One morning, we arrived at the cutting-room and the sound rolls were missing – sound rolls where we'd recorded masses of interviews which we hadn't used in the film. We had omitted them especially so as not to hand people over to the police, Party organizations or whatever. But that sound disappeared. Two days later it reappeared and I was summoned by the police and told that I had smuggled rolls out of Poland to sell them to Free Europe[10] for dollars. That's what they accused me of. But they'd organized it rather badly because I never heard of anyone ever broadcasting those recordings at Free Europe. I suspect it was just another provocation which proved unsuccessful and which probably didn't have anything to do with me but concerned somebody entirely different. I suspect it concerned somebody like Olszowski. Somebody was playing with someone but I didn't know what the game was. I didn't know what they were playing at and, to be honest, I didn't know who was playing with whom. I suspect that was one of the reasons why I grew sick of it all. I realized yet again how unimportant I was.

Curriculum vitae
ŻYCIORYS (1975)

I think that in the 1970s there were already a lot of people in the
Party who saw that it was going in entirely the wrong direction,
and that it was necessary to reform it, and adapt it to the needs of
the people. It's a generalization to say that Communists are bad
and the rest of us are fantastic – it's just not like that. Communists,
like us, are made up of those who are wise and others who are
foolish, those who are good and others who are bad. And it was
these people who agreed to, or even wanted me to make a film like
Curriculum vitae. That is, there was a faction in the Party in the
mid-1970s which tried to introduce some reforms into the Party.
They thought that with the help of such things as this film, for
example, it would be possible to sway the Party masses a little, to
show Party members that not all that the Party was doing was
wise, that the Party needed to be democratized.

Only when you describe something can you start speculating
about it. If something hasn't been described and a record of it
doesn't exist – it doesn't matter what form the description takes: a
film, a sociological study, a book, or even just a verbal account –
then you can't refer to it. You have to describe the thing or
situation before you can deal with it. If you understand that, then
you understand that certain anomalies, and even corruption, have
to be described. If you want to reform the Party, you have to say,
'It's got to be reformed because this, this and this are wrong with
it'. Now, where do you get the evidence that this, this and this are
wrong? From descriptions. It doesn't matter what sort. Of course,
they can take the form of Party reports or Party meetings. They
can take the form of discussions in the Press. But something like a
statement of fact has to come into existence. That's precisely
where *Curriculum vitae* fits in, although it wasn't commissioned
by anybody in the Party; the script and idea were mine. The film's
message is that this Party wasn't quite suited to meet people's
wishes, people's lives or their potential.

People saw *Curriculum vitae* at Party meetings and I attended
several of them because of this film. There were about seventy
copies made of it. I don't even know at how many different Party
screenings – restricted to Party members or even élite Party members – the film was shown. Then it was shown at the Kraków

Film Festival and even once on television, I think.

It was the most interesting thing one could do at the time – to be present at a session of the Politburo and make a film about it. The real decisions about life in Poland, about the state of the country, took place within the Party. They never let me in to any Politburo sessions so I made a film about the Party Control Committee,[11] which was quite a powerful organization in those days. They really did throw people out of the Party, accepted them or struck them off and really did destroy people. Often quite rightly so. Often these people were thieves. But often unfairly so. Like, for example, the hero of my film.

There are two ways of treating such matters. One way is to say: I hate them and I'll fight them until I die. And then you fight. But my attitude isn't like that. My attitude is quite the opposite. My attitude is: even if something is happening which isn't right, even if somebody is acting badly, in my opinion, then I have to try and understand that person. However good or bad they are, you have to try and understand why they're like that. I believe it's just as feasible an approach as the one of fighting.

I've always tried to understand people like these, too. Of course, I don't like the members of the Party Control Committee and I think that shows in the film. But even so, I try to understand how they work and why they act the way they do. If I see that people are acting according to some ideology – political, for example – through an inner conviction and not through the need for a comfortable life, then even if they are on the other side, I have a certain respect for them. But only up to a certain point, of course. I can't have any respect for someone who, say, believes that every-one should have their eyes gouged out, or that the best way of getting rid of your enemy is to slit his throat. That's something I couldn't try to understand. I wouldn't try to understand that and I think I can see quite clearly where the limits are. It's not a binding rule, but for me these limits exist. Of course, it might have been easier to show a dull-witted bureaucrat than a person who also has his reasons, but I was more interested in the latter. It's like that in many of my films, and I think that for me, as a film-maker, it's the only feasible way.

It's not a question of justifying these people. Understanding isn't necessarily associated with justification. Justification, in this case, would imply making the film through the eyes of the other side. I don't look through the eyes of the other side in my films. I always look through my own eyes. Although I did try to understand the other side, I didn't change my point of view because that would be false and insincere, and immediately obvious. But my point of view in no way precludes trying to understand the other side.

Curriculum vitae is a typical example of combining drama with documentary; this was something which interested me enormously at the time. I also used this technique in *Personnel*, which I also made in 1975, where the action – subtle, minimal, enigmatic action – is combined with documentary; with a certain state of affairs, people's minds, faces, hands, their behaviour. Everything concerning the Party Board of Control in *Curriculum vitae* was real, because it was a real Party Board of Control. Nobody was specially selected for it. I simply went to various Party Committees and asked them to give me the most enlightened, the most liberal, the most circumspect Party Board of Control in Warsaw. So they gave me this Board because it was the best. It was terrible. But I deliberately asked for the best because I simply knew how terrible the worst would be. I wanted the best in order to show that even the best Board disputes the lives of its members in this way, decides what a member is and is not allowed to do, decides how many minutes he should boil his egg for breakfast. Has he got the right to boil it for three minutes? It interferes in the most intimate, the most private aspects of life. So, everything about the Party Board of Control in the film is a true record of its authentic reactions and behaviour. Whereas everything that the main character brings in – that is, the man they're judging at this Party Board of Control – is fictitious: a life-history – made up of a combination of life-histories – written by me. The man was an engineer. He worked in telephones, constructing telephone lines or something like that. In real life, he'd had exactly the same problem with the Party, that is, he used to be in the Party, then he was thrown out. He'd been reprimanded and harassed by the Party. This was the sort of person I was looking for to play the part of the accused man, Antoni Gralak.

I very often used the name Antoni again. The main character in *The Calm*, for example, has the same name. I still use Antoni although it's not all that popular in Poland. There's even an Antek in *Véronique* – the Polish Weronika's boyfriend is called Antek. I don't know why I used the name. Probably because I liked Antek

26 'Everything concerning the Party Board of Control in *Curriculum Vitae* (*Życiorys*) was real.'

27 'Whereas everything that the main character brings in is fictitious.'

Krauze a lot. Then I liked Filip Bajon[12]; the main character in *Camera Buff* is called Filip.

As a result of what I managed to shoot for *Curriculum vitae*, I wrote a play also called *Curriculum vitae* (*Życiorys*). I don't know whether it really is a play; it's hard to call it that. It's simply a theatrical record of a sitting with a Party Board of Control. I can't bear to think about it now – that I made something like that. I decided to do it because some theatre director urged me to do something for the theatre. It wasn't my idea. He persuaded me and I did it. It's a terrible play, a complete mistake.

But the theatre itself was excellent. It was the Old Theatre in Kraków (Teatr Stary).[13] I had excellent actors; Jurek Stuhr,[14] Jurek Trela.[15] Anybody I wanted. Trela, who'd played all the heroes in the great plays of the Teatr Stary, and acted in Wajda's and Swinarski's[16] plays there, played the main character in my play. So I had all these excellent conditions. Unfortunately I had one thing which was poor; namely, the play – which I'd written myself.

I was given the small auditorium. I didn't want the big one anyway because it was a play which could only be shown on a small stage. What significance could the play have? Besides, it didn't run for very long – maybe a month. Then it was taken off, rightly so.

That experience was quite enough for me. I realized that theatre absolutely didn't suit my temperament. Sitting in one place for two months. Constantly repeating the same fragment of a play. It simply doesn't meet my needs. As it is, I haven't got much patience left and I'm losing it with age, but I didn't have any patience for theatre even then, although I was only thirty-something. Wajda kept saying to me, 'Listen, find a good play. One which someone else has written, Shakespeare or Chekov, for example, and you'll understand how beautiful working for the theatre can be. How wonderful it is to discover something which has already been written.' And he's probably right. He obviously loves discovering the possibilities within a text, but he's right about himself, and I'm right for me. And so I never did anything in the theatre again. Nor will I. That's for sure.

I probably make films through ambition. Everybody makes films for themselves, really. Film isn't a bad medium. It's a much more primitive medium than literature but it's not a bad one if you want to tell a story, and I do sometimes. Finding money doesn't necessarily entail a total lack of freedom in the way you think about the story you want to tell. But really I make films because I don't know how to do anything else. It was a poor choice I made in the past but I probably couldn't have made a better one then, that is, I couldn't have made any other. Today I know it was the wrong one. This is a very difficult profession; it's very costly, very tiring, and gives very little satisfaction in proportion to the effort expended.

First Love
PIERWSZA MIŁOŚĆ (1974)

When I was finishing film school I wrote a thesis called 'Reality and the Documentary Film' where I put forward the argument that in everybody's life there are stories and plots. So why invent plots if they exist in real life? You only have to film them. That's the subject I invented for myself. Then I tried to make films like that but I didn't make any – except for *First Love*. I don't think it's a bad film.

I had always wanted to make a film about a guy who wins a million złotys on the pools. That was a lot of money in Poland in the 1970s. A large villa cost something like 500,000 złotys; a car cost 50,000 or even 70,000. Anyway, it was a huge sum of money, and very few people in Poland had so much. So I wanted to make a film about a guy who wins a million and observe him right up until the moment the money disappears; you could describe it as butter on a frying pan. You put a bit of butter on a frying pan and it melts, disappears.

Another idea which I had was the one I used in *First Love*. It's the other side of the coin – it's the idea of rising dough. You put dough into an oven and it rises of its own accord even though you're not doing anything to it any more. In this case it was the idea of a woman's belly, which at a certain moment gets impregnated and we watch it grow.

We spent a long time with the couple – Jadzia and Romek. A year, because we met them when Jadzia was four months pregnant, and we stayed with them until the child was two months old. So that was almost a year.

There was masses of manipulation in this film, or even provocation, but you can't make a film like that any other way. There's no way you can keep a crew at somebody's side for twenty-four hours a day. No way. I say we took eight months to make it but I think there were no more than thirty or forty shooting days. So during those thirty or forty days I had to manipulate the couple into situations in which they'd find themselves anyway, although not exactly on the same day or at the same time. I don't think I ever put them in a situation in which they wouldn't have found themselves if the camera hadn't been there. For example, they wanted a place to live. They went to the housing co-op, so obviously I had to go there earlier with the camera. But it was their housing co-op. They were trying to get their own apartment and not some fictitious one, and I didn't write dialogues for them.

I wanted them to read a book called something like *Young Mother* or *The Developing Foetus*. So I bought them the book and then waited for them to read and discuss it. These situations were clearly manipulated. They had a tiny room at their grandmother's and they decided they wanted to paint it violet. Right, let them paint it violet. I came to film them while they were painting and – this is clear provocation – I sent in a policeman, who arrived and complained that they weren't registered,[17] that they were living there illegally and could be thrown out. I deliberately found a policeman whom I thought wouldn't cause much harm, although Jadzia was in her eighth month by then and the whole thing could have been quite risky – an unexpected visit like that could have induced labour. Everybody was frightened of the police in Poland at the time, especially if they weren't registered where they were living. It wasn't as easy as it is today.

There were a lot of situations like that but there were also some which resulted from life itself. Like the wedding, for example – we were there with the camera. The birth was the actual birth – we were there with the camera.

A birth, as we all know, takes place only once. For the next one, you have to wait at least a year. So we got ready for it very carefully. We knew Jadzia would give birth at the hospital on Madalińskiego Street, where my daughter was also born. I can't quite remember whether this little one was born before or after Marta but it was more or less during the same period. I used to stand outside the same window to see Maryśka, my wife, and I can't remember whether I went to the window and had the feeling of *déjà vu* because Romek had stood there before, or the other way around. I think Marta is a little older and I used to go there and then when Romek stood outside the same window, in the same yard, to see Jadzia, I had the feeling of *déjà vu*, that something was happening for the second time.

Here's a story of how you can organize yourself for a documentary film and how, despite all the good will and forward planning in the world, you can still lose. Of course, we knew in what room Jadzia would be giving birth. We set up the lights ahead of time, a week before she was due to give birth. The microphones were also set up. Misio Żarnecki[18] was the sound recordist but Małgosia Jaworska[19] recorded sound for that scene so there was a woman present, not a man. As many men were eliminated from the crew as possible. There weren't any electricians because the lights had already been set up and Jacek Petrycki,[20] who was cameraman, had a little chart showing him where the lights were so he could turn them on himself.

Jadzia and Romek didn't have a telephone and we worked it out that the moment Jadzia went into labour, Romek would phone 'Dziób'.[21] Dziób had a telephone and so did everybody who was to be there in the labour room. The rule was that at any one time somebody had to be at home, so if, for example, Jacek, the cameraman, had to go out for a while Grażyna, his wife, would know where he was so that she could get in touch with him and he could rush off to the labour room. We all knew it was a question of two hours and that was it. Or even half an hour. We couldn't be late. We'd already worked on the film for five or six months before the birth so it was obvious we couldn't lose this scene. So Dziób was to phone me, Jacek, Małgosia Jaworska and the production manager. We didn't need anybody else there.

We waited. We waited a week. No news. Every day I sent Dziób off to check if by any chance Romek hadn't forgotten to phone. Then one night, Dziób, who liked to have a drink, couldn't hold out any more and went drinking. He decided he couldn't hang around by the telephone for twenty-four hours a day any more. Off he went and got drunk, Lord knows who with. He didn't know where he went himself. And at four in the morning he landed up on a night bus going from Ochota to Śródmieście.[22] He was completely drunk. The night bus in Warsaw goes once every two hours if you're lucky. So Dziób gets on the bus and falls asleep, of course. Sits on the back seat, rests his head on his knees or arms and falls asleep. And makes his way along in this bus. It's four in the morning. Night. It was winter, I think. No, it was already spring but it was cold that night. Suddenly he feels somebody shake him by the shoulders. He wakes up. It's Romek who'd got on the same bus with Jadzia. She had gone into labour that very night. They hadn't been able to find a taxi. They'd phoned Dziób but there was nobody there, of course , because Dziób was already lying drunk on the bus. They'd got on the bus and the only person they saw was Dziób, blind drunk, who immediately sobered up. He jumped off the bus, rushed to a telephone box and phoned me, Jacek and Małgosia. Half an hour later we were all there in the hospital and managed to film the whole birth which, in the end, lasted eight hours so there hadn't been any problem really. But no one was to know. It's like that sometimes. A random incident – like, for example, a drunk Dziób – could have prevented us from filming what we needed.

I still keep in touch with Jadzia and Romek. They lived in Germany for a few years and now live in Canada. They've got three children. I met them not long ago. There was a retrospective of my films in Germany and I persuaded the organizers to show *First Love*. And since I knew that Jadzia and Romek were living in Germany at the time, I persuaded the organizers to invite the whole family to the screening. They all came. The little girl, whose birth we'd filmed, was already eighteen. Of course, everybody was in tears.

Nothing bad came of all this although I was afraid it might. I was afraid it might go to their heads. I was afraid they'd start thinking they were great stars. But then I realized this wouldn't happen. That's one of the reasons I chose that particular couple. I'd noticed that Jadzia, although she was only seventeen, knew exactly what she wanted and was clearly out to get it. And what she wanted was simply to have a child, get married, be a good wife, be a decent woman and have a bit of money. That was her goal, and she managed to get it all, of course. I knew she wouldn't have any pretensions which would change her attitude to life, make her think, for example, that she could be an actress, that she could perform. She knew perfectly well that that wasn't her world, and it didn't interest her in the least.

The film definitely didn't change them. They met with some very good reactions a week or two after it was shown on television. People recognized them in the streets and said hello or simply smiled at them. And that was nice. This only lasted for a short while. Everybody forgot about them afterwards, of course. Other films were shown on television, and other people were recognized in the streets. Other people were smiled at or pointed out. But they had that brief moment when people were friendly to them.

I think that something positive came out of this film. You had to wait years for a flat in Poland in those days – and you still do, in fact, up to fifteen years. They were waiting, too, because they'd only just got married. Romek was already registered at the housing co-op and had been waiting for two or three years. There's this scene in the film where they go to the co-op and ask when they can expect to get a flat and are told that maybe in five years' time there might be a chance for them to go on a list which one day might have results. So there was absolutely no prospect of a flat in the foreseeable future. They had that tiny room at their grandmother's which they'd painted violet and where they couldn't really live with a child. They couldn't move either to his parents or to hers. Their parents' flats were too small and conditions were a bit too complicated for them to move in there, particularly with a little child.

Then I came up with this very simple idea. I wrote a short treatment called *Ewa Ewunia*.[23] This was after their baby was born, when we already knew that she was a girl and that she'd be called Ewka. So this was called *Ewa Ewunia* and the idea was that I'd make another film which would start the day Ewa was born and carry on to the day she gave birth to a child of her own.

I wrote the proposal and submitted it. Since *First Love* was an hour-long film made on 16 mm for Television,[24] I also submitted this proposal to them. Television was – and still is – very powerful in Poland. They said it was great. This really was a long-term and pretty impressive project. It is impressive to make a film about one person over twenty years and I wanted to make it. I even started on it. There must be some footage in the archives of when the little girl was five or six.

So, I went to the Television head, who liked the idea, and I said, 'Right, but do you want this film to be optimistic?' He replied, 'Of course we want it to be optimistic.' I remember this conversation very well. I said, 'If you want this film to be optimistic, then we have to create optimistic facts since the facts, as they are, are pessimistic.' 'What facts?' 'They simply don't have anywhere to live,' I said. 'And if we make a film where Ewa's born in some sort of hovel and is brought up in some horrific backyard, amongst other dirty, poor, neglected children, we won't have an optimistic film. We have to create an optimistic situation.' 'So what would this optimistic situation be?' 'We have to find a place for them to live.' With the help of its influence in various places – the Party, the council or whatever, I don't care where – Television found a flat for them. Suffice it to say that when the little girl was a half a year old, they already had a flat. A large, decent, four-roomed flat.

They lived there for a while and I shot some footage for *Ewa Ewunia* there. And then I stopped because first of all, I'm not sure I'd have stuck it out. Maybe I would have done, if I filmed every two years or so. We wouldn't have had to film continuously. But something else happened. I just realized that I couldn't carry on filming this because if I did I might land up in a similar mess to the one I almost landed in later, in 1981, when filming *Station* (*Dworzec*). That is, I might film something which could be used against them, for example. And I didn't want that. So I stopped.

In my opinion, documentary films shouldn't be used to influence the subject's life either for the better or for the worse. They shouldn't have any influence at all. Especially in the realm of opinions, of one's attitude to life. And you have to be very careful there; it's one of the traps of documentary films. To a large extent, I've managed to avoid that quite well. I've neither crushed nor lifted up any of the subjects of my documentaries – and there have been quite a few.

Hospital
SZPITAL (1976)

Hospital, in turn, consisted of nothing but chance events. Satisfaction in film-making is rare, but in *Hospital* I had at least two occasions to experience satisfaction and evident pleasure at having a camera, lights, sound, and being able to film what was happening at that moment.

What happened in *Hospital* was like something out of a

textbook on documentary films. What is a documentary film? And how well do you have to get to know your subject or the people you're filming – this concerns documentaries, not feature films – in order to catch something which is important at a given moment?

The film wasn't going to be about doctors initially. It was to be about the fact that, in all this mess which surrounds us, in all this dirt, powerlessness, human impotence, this inability to finish anything, to do anything well, there is a group of people who manage to achieve what might today be called success. But what was important to me was the fact that they should be doing something calculably good, something worthwhile. I looked for all sorts of different people. There was a very good volleyball team who'd won a gold medal at the Montreal Olympics. I thought that this was such a group, for example. Then I thought that it could be a miners' rescue group who after an accident, toil for days on end in terrible physical hardship, to rescue somebody who's barely alive.

I looked all over the place for professional groups like that. Finally, I thought that perhaps they should be doctors. We started to look among doctors, then surgeons and finally I came across a hospital where there was an exceptionally pleasant and warm-hearted atmosphere among the doctors. The recce must have taken about a year before I decided. That doesn't mean I worked on it eight hours a day, every day, but we did recce every now and again.

I started to figure out how to film what they were doing, and straight away I made the decision never to show the patients. Then I had the idea to have the film follow the time of day. That is, that we'd show one hour after another, one hour after another – another textbook example. Initially, I thought I really would film at, say, midday sharp for the midday scenes and not at five past twelve, then it would be shown as being midday on the screen. I quickly realized how very stupid it was to hold on to such an authoritative assumption. Why deprive the viewer of something interesting which might be happening at five past twelve and throw something boring at him which happened at twelve? It's a fine assumption theoretically but practically it's idiotic.

In those days we had to write scripts for documentary films – quite rightly so. You never know what's going to happen in a film but thanks to the fact that we were forced to write a script, we were compelled to put our thoughts into some sort of order. So I asked the doctors about various important, dramatic details which they may have remembered from their profession, from their lives or from their work with patients. The orthopaedic surgeons told me that they always need a hammer for bone surgery. In normal hospitals everybody has surgical hammers, but they told me that in 1954 they had a hammer like the ones used for hammering nails into walls, and that while they were putting some man or woman together, this hammer split. So, in my script I wrote that the hammer splits during an operation.

Well, this was one of those particularly satisfying occasions. I don't know how many nights we'd been standing there. Once a week, they had 24-hours shifts; they worked their twenty-four hours then another seven, making thirty-one hours non-stop, and we'd go there for the thirty-one hours. We did this every week for about two or three months. Sometimes we'd wrap early because we just couldn't stand it. They had to carry on working with their bones but we could barely stay awake so we'd go home. But sometimes we'd also sit right through the night.

Our 35 mm camera was a huge, heavy thing which two or three men had to lug from one place to another, and there were several locations. There was the admittance room, the corridors, one other room, an operating theatre, another operating theatre and a small recovery room. You can see the doctors walking from one building to another in the film. We had to move too, of course, but it was impossible to move the camera three times in one night. We had to set it up in the operating theatre and that's where it had to stay all night. We could if necessary move it once, towards morning, and take it to the room where the doctors took an hour's nap and shaved. So there were about six or seven locations in the hospital where we'd set up the camera, the lights, of course, the microphone and so on, for the entire shift.

On one occasion the ambulance brought in the production manager's aunt, which was amusing. That is, it wasn't amusing that she'd broken her leg but the sequence of coincidences was. They brought her in and rolled her into the operating theatre where we were waiting with our camera – again through sheer coincidence. She'd broken her femur and in order to put a femur together again you have to hammer a sort of skewer, the thickness of a finger, into the bone near the knee. It's not really a skewer but a sort of tube through which a skewer is then passed. So they were

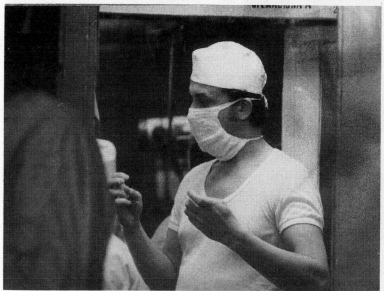

28, 29 *Hospital* (*Szpital*). 'They worked their twenty-four hours then another seven, making it thirty-one hours non-stop.'

30 *Hospital.* 'We became such good friends.'

hammering in that tube. The operation took about three hours and every now and again we'd turn on the camera. And what do I see? That they've got a hammer in that operating theatre – the sort of hammer they'd been telling me about. So I film this hammer, of course, because they were using it. If they'd been using a different one, I'd have filmed them using that. Well, you have to be lucky and perhaps have a bit of intuition to have the camera set up in the right place, to have the camera loaded, to have the tape-recorder loaded and, on top of that, to have switched the camera on twenty or thirty seconds before the hammer split. Because that hammer did split – during a take! So the situation described in the script repeated itself although it shouldn't have done so because the hammer had split previously in 1954. What's more, I'd described it in the script because they'd told me that story. Consequently everybody suspects that the hammer's some sort of trick. There's no trick behind it. It's just luck. One of those moments when you feel that you've filmed something really important.

The whole point of the film was to show that everything was becoming disconnected; to show the hard conditions, that people don't have cotton wool, that there are power cuts, that the cables don't work, that the lift doesn't work. That's just life. That's how it was.

But those doctors were so open and we became such good friends, that they felt as if we weren't even there. That's the whole point of documentaries taking so long to make, yet nobody knows this, especially television reporters these days. They come along, stick a microphone under your nose and tell you to answer some question; you'll answer wisely or stupidly but that doesn't reveal the truth about you.

I Don't Know
NIE WIEM (1977)

I've tried to be considerate towards the various main characters in my documentaries. But I know one man who bore me a terrible grudge because I'd filmed him even though he'd agreed to it himself. It was a one-hour film called I Don't Know, which never made its way to the screen, partly because I didn't want it to be shown for fear of harming him. He fought for the film not to be shown but instead of simply uniting his efforts with mine, he started to kick up a fuss at the Ministry of Arts and Culture, which was absolutely ridiculous. I don't really know what he wanted. He had no right to kick up a fuss since he'd signed a contract and accepted money for it. No great sum, but he had accepted money and in this way expressed his consent. Meanwhile I was also trying to stop the film from making its way to the screen.

The film is the confession of a guy who was the director of a factory in Lower Silesia. He was a Party member but he opposed the mafia-like organization of Party members which was active in that factory or region. And they completely finished him off. He looked like Edward Gierek – this was the Gierek era – a big guy with short, cropped hair, and was of the same class as the rest of those Party members but he thought that things were starting to go too far. Those people were stealing leather and debiting the factory account. They'd sell the leather, and drink vodka and buy cars with the money. Unfortunately he didn't know that people higher up – from the provincial police and Party Committee – were involved in the affair.

I met him and simply said that I wanted to make a film about his experience. Nothing more. He said, 'Certainly.' We met. I recorded his whole monologue on a tape recorder and then played it back so that he'd know what was there. Then I told him I wanted to film it. He agreed and signed the contract, but when we'd finished, I realized that if this was shown on screen then those people could cause him even greater harm than they had to date. I mean, on screen it really became far more risky than it had sounded while I listened to him talking, without a camera. So I erased all the names he'd mentioned; I covered them with the sound of a typewriter and made them incomprehensible. And still I thought the film shouldn't be shown.

Later, after 1980, Television tried to get hold of things like this[25] and desperately wanted to show the film but I still didn't agree. And, in effect, it's never been shown anywhere. Not even at festivals. I knew the main character had experienced deeply the very fact that the film had been made and, even though he'd signed the contract, he later realized that what he had said was very risky. Those who had destroyed him hadn't disappeared in 1980. People only behaved outwardly in a way which insinuated that there was more freedom than there really was. Nothing had changed really.

That's one thing. Second, I believe that if I do something in a film, sign my name to something, then I ought to stick to it and not change my mind because the situation may have changed. And that's what I do. For example, if I've agreed to certain cuts in a film – and I've agreed to cuts on numerous occasions – then I don't keep them in a wardrobe or under my bed counting on the fact that one day I'll be able to stick them in again and show the film in all its beauty. No, if I've agreed to the cuts and signed the version (if I've signed it, because there are many versions which I didn't sign and consequently the films were shelved for many years) then that's the final version. That's my ultimate decision. I won't go back to what I've cut out in order to show how fantastic the film had been before the censors had ruined it. I don't think that would be professional or masculine, as it were.

From a Night Porter's Point of View
Z PUNKTU WIDZENIA NOCNEGO PORTIERA (1978)

You never know how a film's going to turn out. In every film there's always a very narrow threshold which each of us can only cross according to our own discretion. At that point, I retreat. If, for example, I realize that Marian Osuch, the subject of my film *From a Night Porter's Point of View*, is going to be harmed because my film's going to be shown on television, then I retreat.

The porter – Osuch – saw the film and he liked it. Then the film won a prize at the Kraków Film festival and was shown as supporting programme to a Fellini film at the Confrontations.[26] A lot of people went to see it but there's a very specific audience which goes to the Confrontations. But in 1980, they really wanted to show it on television. And I did exactly the same thing as I had done before; that is, I absolutely disagreed because I thought that if the film was shown on television then it could cause the porter greater harm. His acquaintances, family, neighbours, daughter, son and wife would see it and would either make a laughing stock of him or humiliate him. I didn't need that, especially as I didn't have anything against him personally. I was against a certain attitude which he represented, but that doesn't mean that if he has such an attitude then he has to be driven to the wall, especially as he knew that I expected it of him, that I wanted him to say the

31, 32 *From a Night Porter's Point of View (Z Punkta Widzenia Nocnego Portiera).*

33   *From a Night Porter's Point of View (Z Punkta Widzenia Nocnego Portiera)*. 'The porter wasn't a bad man.'

things he did. He threw himself into it because he wanted to satisfy my wishes which he sensed instinctively.

The porter wasn't a bad man. I suspect he's quite an ordinary human being. He just happens to think that it would be a good thing to hang people publicly because that would make everybody else afraid to commit crimes. We've already met this point of view in history and he was merely a representative; it comes from his not too high level of intelligence, from a rather vulgar attitude to life and the environment he was brought up in. I don't think he's a bad man.

I might have suggested subjects to him. 'What do you think of capital punishment?' for example, or, 'what's your attitude to animals?' He says: 'I like animals . . . I used to keep budgies but they died, because my son went and let them loose in the room. So one, you know, fell into the soup and took a bath. Well, a creature like that's ill then, you know.' And so on. So I might have asked him, but I didn't write any dialogue for him. How could I ever invent something like that?

When I started work on the film I knew who I was looking for. I asked Dziób to find a particular kind of person. It took him a long time. For many years, I'd been reading all sorts of diaries which were published by the Ludowa Spółdzielnia Wydawnicza (The People's Publishing Co-operative) in Poland but which few people read. They were incredibly interesting, sociologically speaking. They were called: *A Month of My Life* (*Miesiąc mojego Życia*), or *The Most Important Day in My Life* (*Najważniejszy Dzień w moim Życiu*), or *Women's Diaries* (*Pamiętniki Kobiet*) or *Workers' Diaries* (*Pamiętniki Robotników*), or *Twenty Years on a Farm* (*Dwadzieścia Lat na Roli*) or *Peasants' Diaries* (*Pamiętniki Chłopów*). There were all sorts of titles, and in one of the books I found the diary of just such a porter. That is, a man who, to put it bluntly, had anti-humane or fascist opinions, and I thought I had to make a film about him. He was a porter in a factory, the man who'd written this diary. I met him and he turned out to be utterly impossible to film. He had so many shortcomings that it was absolutely impossible to make a film about him. But because I'd already thought this out and WFD (State Documentary Film Studios) had agreed to the idea, Dziób simply started to look for a man like that. He must have gone through about fifty factories in Warsaw and seen 150 porters, ten of whom he showed me. I chose this one.

Tolo and I used Orwo film specially.[27] We shot on Orwo so that the distortion of colour which is, as it were, inherent in this East German film stock, created a certain distortion of the world. This porter is a distortion of a human being and we wanted the colour to accentuate the grotesqueness of the world surrounding him. It was Tolo's idea and a very good one too.

All my films, from the first to the most recent ones, are about individuals who can't quite find their bearings, who don't quite know how to live, who don't really know what's right or wrong and are desperately looking. Looking for answers to such basic questions as: What's all this for? Why get up in the morning? Why go to bed at night? Why get up again? How to spend the time between one awakening and another? How to spend it in order to be able to shave or make yourself up peacefully in the morning?

Station
DWORZEC (1981)

When I think of *Station*, I see that there are several shots of such people: someone has fallen asleep; someone's waiting for somebody else. Maybe they'll come, maybe they won't. It's about people like that, people looking for something. It's not individualized in *Station* but that doesn't matter. We made the film to show these very people. We spent about ten nights filming them.

The idea of somebody watching all this, an observer, came to us later. I can't even remember whether it was in the script or not. We just thought that the story line was a bit weak. The film didn't really develop because there was nothing there to move things on. So we put in this guy who's watching all this, as if he knows everything about these people. He doesn't know anything really but he thinks he knows. However, the film wasn't about him.

An incident occurred, while we were making *Station*, which really was a final warning that I'd accidentally found myself where I didn't want to be. We were filming nights at the station and one night we were filming people's funny reactions to left-luggage lockers, which were a novelty in Warsaw at the time. Nobody knew how to use them. There was a long notice explaining that first of all you had to insert a coin, then you had to turn, find the number and so on. People didn't quite know how to go about the

34 *Station (Dworzec)*. 'People looking for something.'

whole thing, especially those from the country. With a half concealed camera – we'd hide it a little with our backs or we'd shoot from far away using a telephoto lens – we tried to observe people's reactions to these lockers. And we managed to get a few amusing portraits. That night, as usual, we were returning to WFD (the State Documentary Film Studios) at four or five in the morning and the police were there waiting for us. They seized all the footage, all the negative, which we'd shot that night. I had no idea what it was all about although I'd already had some experience of audio tapes being stolen when I was working on *Workers '71*. There had also been several other occasions of uneasiness when I'd been summoned by the police and interrogated because of films I'd made. But these weren't important. On the other hand, the *Workers '71* incident was very important to me because there I felt that I had abused somebody's trust. If I make recordings and promise secrecy or discretion and the film or tapes are stolen then I'm still responsible. Nobody had ever stolen film from WFD before. I therefore thought that this time maybe I'd filmed something politically improper and so they were confiscating the film, but they didn't want to tell me. Then they summoned me, very politely. We watched the material. Two or three days later they gave it back to us. There hadn't been anything on it which they'd wanted and nothing was missing. They didn't take anything.

We only found out later on, once they'd given the film back to us, that on that night a girl had murdered her mother, cut her to pieces and packed her into two suitcases. And, that very night, she'd put those suitcases into one of the lockers at the Central Station. Or they thought it was that night. So they took our film in the hope of spotting her. It turned out that we hadn't filmed the girl. She was later arrested. But what did I realize at that moment? That, like it or not, independently of my intentions or will, I found myself in the situation of an informer or someone who gives information to the police – which I never wanted to do. They'd simply confiscated the material and that was it. I had no say in it. Then they returned it.

Right, so we didn't film the girl. But if we had, by chance? We could have filmed her. If we'd turned the camera left instead of right, perhaps we'd have caught her. And what would have happened? I'd have become a police collaborator. And that was the moment I realized that I didn't want to make any more docu-

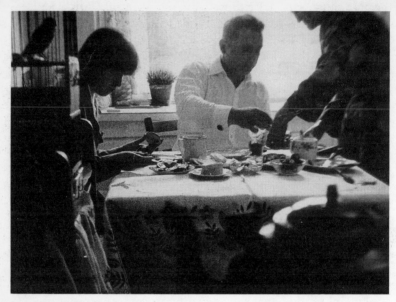

35   *Bricklayer (Murarz).*

36, 37   *Seven Women of Different Ages (Siedem Kobiet w Różnym Wieku).*

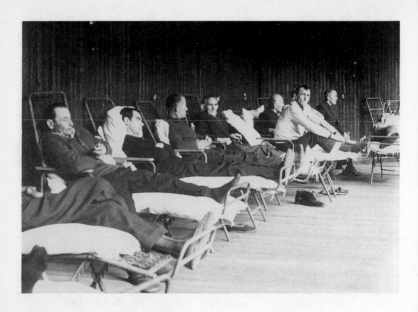

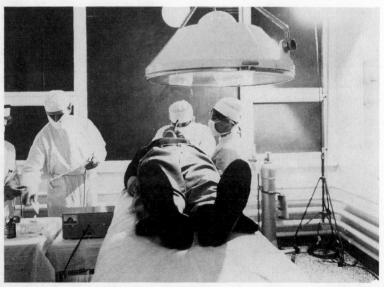

38, 39   X-Ray (Prześwietlenie).

40 *Refrain (Refren)*.

mentaries, a moment which in itself wasn't important because there hadn't been any repercussions, negative or positive. Nevertheless, all this made me aware again of what a small cog I am in a wheel which is being turned by somebody else for reasons unknown to me – reasons which I don't know and which don't really interest me.

Of course it's a different matter whether it's good or bad that a murderer is arrested. That's an entirely different question. There are people whose job it is to arrest murderers and they should do it. But I'm not one of them.

Not everything can be described. That's the documentary's great problem. It catches itself as if in its own trap. The closer it wants to get to somebody, the more that person shuts him or herself off from it. And that's perfectly natural. It can't be helped. If I'm making a film about love, I can't go into a bedroom if real people are making love there. If I'm making a film about death, I can't film somebody who's dying because it's such an intimate experience that the person shouldn't be disturbed. And I noticed, when making documentaries, that the closer I wanted to get to an individual, the more the subjects which interested me shut themselves off.

That's probably why I changed to features. There's no problem there. I need a couple to make love in bed, that's fine. Of course, it might be difficult to find an actress who's willing to take off her bra, but then you just find one who is. Somebody's supposed to die. That's fine. In a minute, he'll get up again. And so on. I can even buy some glycerine, put some drops in her eyes and the actress will cry. I managed to photograph some real tears several times. It's something completely different. But now I've got glycerine. I'm frightened of those real tears. In fact, I don't know whether I've got the right to photograph them. At such times I feel like somebody who's found himself in a realm which is, in fact, out of bounds. That's the main reason why I escaped from documentaries.

TRACKING:
41 Concert of Requests (Koncert Życzeń).

42 With Jacek Petrycki during filming of *Before the Rally* (*Przed Rajdem*).

43   *The Calm (Spokój)*.

BEHIND THE CAMERA:
44 *From the City of Łódź (Z Miasta Łodzi).*

45 With Jacek Petrycki during filming of *First Love* (*Pierwsza Miłość*).

46 With Witold Stok during filming of *Workers '71*.

47 *Workers '71.*

48 *The Calm.*

49 With Krzysztof Pakulski during filming of *Short Working Day*
(*Krótki Dzień Pracy*).

50 No End (*Bez Końca*).

CHAPTER 3

The Feature Films

In Order to Learn
PEDESTRIAN SUBWAY (PRZEJŚCIE PODZIEMNE) (1973)

I followed the most usual path in Poland – a compulsory one[1] – when I made my first feature, a half-hour television film. Various friends of mine avoided taking this path but I didn't. I wanted to take it because I didn't think I knew how to make full features. There was a rule that if you wanted to make feature films you had to make a half-hour film for television, then an hour film for television and only then a full feature. I knew something about documentaries but I didn't know anything about working with actors or staging. So I willingly made shorter films in order to learn.

That first film I made was called *Pedestrian Subway*. I shot it with Sławek Idziak.[2] The entire film takes place during one night in a pedestrian subway which had just been opened in the centre of Warsaw at the crossroads of Jerozolimskie and Marszałkowska Avenues. It was a fashionable place. There are ghastly Russian traders there now but it used to be an elegant place at one time. That was the beginning of the 1970s, in 1972. And that's where the action was located.

I wrote the script with Irek Iredyński.[3] That really was the only script I ever wrote with a professional writer. (Later I wrote another with Hania Krall,[4] but that was different because the script for *Short Working Day* was based on one of Hania's reports, whereas in *Pedestrian Subway* the idea that the action should take place underground was mine.) I took my idea to Irek and together we wrote the script. It was tough going because I had to arrange to meet him at six or even five o'clock in the morning since that was the only time he was sober. He'd take out a frosted bottle of vodka from the freezer. And we'd start to drink and write; we'd manage to write two, three, four or five pages before we got drunk. It wasn't a very long script. It was about thirty pages all in all so we probably met about ten times. And each time it was the same: at the break of day, a bottle of vodka from the freezer. Vodka, frozen and oily. Six o'clock in the morning and we'd knock it back. Knock it back. Knock it back. Knock it back. Knock it back. Until we were blind drunk. At least I was. I'd pick up what we'd managed to put together and go home.

Then I shot the film. We had ten nights; I shot the whole film in nine and on the ninth night I realized that I was shooting something idiotic, some nonsense which didn't mean anything to me. The plot didn't mean much to me. We would put the camera somewhere. The actors said some lines. And I had the impression that we were making a complete lie. And on the last night I decided to change it all. I only had one night left. I couldn't go over the allocated number of shooting days because they were strictly limited. In full features you have fifty days and can always do some manoeuvring. In a short television film like this, you have ten or twelve. You don't get any more – that's what professionalism is all about, among other things. Anyway, I had one night left and I decided on that night that we'd shoot the whole film from the beginning. And we did, using a documentary camera. We stopped only to reload the camera because I think we had 120-metre magazines, meaning we had to change the magazine every four minutes. It was a small camera which you could carry on your shoulders. The Arriflex BL2 or 3 hadn't been invented yet. We had to use it without sound, so we recorded the dialogue later. The actors knew the script very well. After all, we had been shooting the situations for the past nine nights. We still had enough film stock left. I bought a bit of stock myself from some assistant. Then I edited the film, using about twenty percent, if not more, from that documentary night.

In fact, I improvised. I said to them, 'Listen, this is the situation. You're a shop decorator.' Teresa Budzisz-Krzyżanowska played the woman and Andrzej Seweryn played her husband, who had come to Warsaw. She had left some small town where they used to be teachers, and was now a shop decorator. He'd come to Warsaw to look for her since he still loved her, and he tried to persuade her to come back to him. I can't remember any more of the script. They talk about something. Something happens. Someone comes to the night shop – the shop she's decorating at night. Someone wants something. Something takes place outside the shop window.

All sorts of things happen. I said to them, 'Listen, act it all out. Do it all the way you feel best. And I'll shoot it.'

I think that thanks to this rather desperate operation, the film took on a life of its own and became much more authentic. This was terribly important to me at the time, and still is, in fact – to make films authentic in reactions, and details.

It was my first experience with professional actors, apart from film school. I'd done some theatre for television but this was my first real feature film.

A Metaphor for Life
PERSONNEL (PERSONEL) (1975)

Personnel, my first longer film, was nearly one and a half hours long and made for television. It was that one-hour television film I was talking about, but it grew in length a bit. But with that, too, we'd already started shooting when I suddenly realized that I was shooting something absurd: inauthentic from start to finish. I phoned the then head of the production house, Staś Różewicz,[5] and said that I thought the whole thing was useless. He asked us to send him the footage we had already shot. We did. There was a break in production. After a few days, I phoned again and said I still thought the same as before. Actually, I thought I was going up some dead-end street and that production should be stopped while there was still time. Only a relatively small amount of money would have been lost at that stage. He replied, 'Then stop if you don't like it.' He behaved very wisely, of course, just like my father had done once when he'd sent me to the Firemen's College: 'You want to go to work? Fine, finish the Firemen's College. You'll be a fireman and working.' Staś Różewicz said: 'You want to stop? Then stop if you don't like it. That's fine. We've looked at the footage. I don't think it's all that bad, but if you want to stop, then stop tomorrow. Go back to Warsaw.' We were shooting in Wrocław. But it's precisely because he said what he did instead of cheering me up by saying it's not all that bad, that my ambition didn't allow me to stop. On the contrary. I resolved to finish the film.

I've managed to work like this many times. That's one of the reasons why I used to work on two films at the same time. So as to have the possibility of playing around with time, actors, money and so on.

The script of *Personnel* was more or less like the finished film, plus all sorts of things which happened on the way, of course. The action was very loose, very free. That is, it was very delicate and extremely enigmatic. A young man comes to the opera to work as a tailor. And suddenly he sees that his idea of the theatre, or art, is pretty naïve. Confronted with artists and people who run the theatre, his dreams are a mere illusion. In the presence of artists, singers, dancers and so on, he is pretty helpless. This world which had seemed to be so beautiful to him doesn't exist. People just sing their pieces to get them over with; they just dance to get it over with. There are constant quarrels, haggling, conflicting ambitions, shouting. Art, in fact, just dissolves away somewhere. You can retrieve it when you come to the theatre in the evening. Everything goes quiet, the curtain rises, and you experience something. But if you take part in it behind the scenes, then you see what sort of people, what trivial matters you've got to deal with and how uselessly it's all run.

Theatre and opera are always a metaphor for life. It's obvious that the film was about how we can't really find a place for ourselves in Poland. That our dreams and ideas about some ideal reality always clash somewhere along the line with something that's incomparably shallower and more wretched. And I think that that's the way this film works, more or less. The script was an outline of the action and it opened up possibilities for scenes which were improvised. We improvised for a very simple reason, and I made that film for one reason. Well, for several really – you can always find several reasons if you want to.

But first of all I wanted to find a way to pay back my debt to the College for Theatre Technicians, because I got to work a bit in the theatre – for a year or so. Some time after that, as I've said, I was a dresser at the Contemporary Theatre (Teatr Współczesny). It was a good theatre then; the best in Warsaw at the time. I was constantly dealing with brilliant actors who now appear in my films. We still like each other very much but the relationship is entirely different. The actors include Zbyszek Zapasiewicz, Tadeusz Łomnicki, Bardini, Dziewoński – many people who are now in my films. I used to hand them their trousers, wash their socks and so on. I used to attend to them behind the scenes and watch the performances – forever in the wings – because a dresser's got to work before the performance, after the performance and during the intervals, but during the actual performance he's virtually free. He can fold napkins and tidy things up but he can also go to the wings and watch the performance.

One of my teachers from the theatre college appeared in the film, too. She was probably the best teacher I ever had – Irena Lorentowicz, daughter of the great Polish painter, Jan Lorentowicz. She was an outstanding pre-war stage designer and taught me technical theatre skills. She was the stage designer in *Personnel*. She went to America during the war and lived there until about 1956 or 1957 and then returned to Poland. She did stage design for the Warsaw Opera and taught technical theatre skills at my college. Those were the debts I was paying off in *Personnel*: to various people, institutions, emotions that I used to have, discoveries which someone had led me to.

The second reason why I made the film was the feeling that when I made documentaries which were short and compact, I'd always have an enormous amount of material which I liked a lot but which I had to throw out. This material was only interesting when it was on screen for quite a long time; gossip, for example, and various observations about people's behaviour. When people started talking about this and that in a way which was amusing and moving, the documentary would grind to a halt, because the idea behind it had stopped unfolding. And then I thought that I'd use this sort of material in *Personnel* as a dramatic device. Consequently, there are a lot of scenes there, ten or more, which basically consist of expressing atmosphere, and showing people's various absurdities – in the good sense of the word.

I brought in my main character, played by Julek Machulski.[6] I brought in Tomasz Lengren who was a film director, and Tomek Zygadło, another film director; and Mieczysław Kobek, another film director, who played the manager of the workshop. But the rest of the tailors were real tailors at the Wrocław Opera. They just carried on making costumes while we moved around among them. When it came to the improvised scenes, I simply gave them some topic for the sort of conversation which always takes place in theatres and places like that. People are always sitting around and talking about something or other; about what's happened, about their dreams, what they're doing, who's been unfaithful to whom.

They gossip. And it's this atmosphere that I wanted to film.

So, in these scenes, my people didn't have much to do, because what I really wanted to photograph were the reactions of people who really were tailors and really were sewing. And everybody who worked in that theatre stayed in their places. We photographed them all the time, and against this background I shot the minuscule action of the disillusionment suffered by the boy who comes to work in the theatre with such high hopes. I knew my director colleagues much better than I knew any actors. Also, the effect was more authentic when I had real tailors, a director and a stage designer interacting with non-actors than it would have been had they been playing alongside actors, because actors are always playing a role whereas non-actors aren't. My film directors simply tried to enter the characters and then just be them.

Various little things turned up which testify to our schematic way of thinking. For example, we think that a tailor has always got a tape-measure around his neck. And what do we see on the screen? Sure, we see men with tape-measures around their necks, but they're only the people I brought in. Real tailors don't wear tape-measures around their necks. The real tailors really are sewing whereas my ones are only pretending. A non-actor and a film director playing somebody else is a better combination than a non-actor and an actor playing somebody else. I think that a director can enter into the spirit of the situation of those around him better and can adapt to the prevailing atmosphere. And that's how it was.

There's one man there who's an actor; he plays the singer and he's terrible. It was all right for this part but imagine what would have happened if I'd taken actors like him to play the tailors. Not only would you have tape-measures around their necks all the time but you'd also have a clash of inauthenticity in the manner of speech and thought because an actor like that would naturally want to stand out. The film directors didn't because they understood perfectly well that I didn't want them to stand out. Quite the opposite. The point was to have them stay in the background. And that's what we managed to achieve.

A Flawed Script
THE SCAR (BLIZNA) (1976)

My first feature for the cinema, *The Scar*, is badly made. Socio-realism *à rebours*. Socio-realism is an art movement which was in force in Soviet Russia from more or less 1930 up to Stalin's death (in 1953), and the mid-1950s in the Socialist bloc. It boiled down to making films which showed how things ought to be and not how they were. That's what socio-realism was about. And it's obvious how things ought to have been according to the people who funded films in Russia in the 1930s and in Poland after the Second World War. People ought to have been working, they ought to have been pleased with their work, they ought to have been happy, they ought to have loved Communism, they ought to have believed in the future of Communism, they ought to have believed that, together, they'd change the world for the better. That's socio-realism. They were extremely coarse films because an assumption like that means you always have to have a goody and a baddy in order to have a conflict. The goody's on our side. The baddy's on the other and is usually somebody who has something to do with the American secret service, or some old bourgeois habits. He's got to be defeated and since our side, the goodies, believe in their mission and in the future, they always beat the baddy. *The Scar* is a tiny bit of socio-realism *à rebours* – with some socio-realistic frills even. It all takes place in factories, workshops, and at meetings, in all those places where socio-realists loved to film, because socio-realism didn't consider private life to be all that important.

The Scar shows a man who not only doesn't win but is embittered by the situation in which he finds himself. He's got the feeling that while doing good he's also doing something extremely wrong. And he can't see or weigh up what's more important – the wrong he's done or the good. In effect, he has probably realized that he's harmed the people more than he's helped them.

There are many reasons why it's not a good film. No doubt the flaw, as with any film that doesn't work, began with the script. This was based on a report, which was simply a collection of certain facts, written by a journalist called Karaś. But I deviated from this report a great deal because I had to invent the action, a plot and characters, and I did it badly. With documentary films it

51–2   *The Scar (Blizna).*

53–4 *The Scar (Blizna)*.

varies, but with features the idea always comes first. Apart from two exceptions where my films were based on literary or pseudo-literary material (*The Scar* and *Short Working Day*), the idea always came first and the attempt to narrate something based on this idea came later; a simple affirmation or simple statement. Then slowly, slowly I'd find a form for it.

A documentary film unfolds with the help of the author's idea. Drama unfolds with the help of action. Well, I think that what has stayed with me is that my feature films unfold more with the help of the idea rather than the help of the action. And that's probably their chief fault. Because if you do something you should do it consistently, and I don't know how to narrate action.

In my seminars, we frequently analyse how close a film remains to its initial concept. There's an initial sense of why the film is being made, and then, after one, two or five years the final result appears. And it's only true to the first idea. It's not really identifiable with all that happens later because masses of things happen later. Characters are born, heroes, protagonists, action, the camera comes along, the actors, props, lights and a thousand other things on which you have to compromise. You have to agree to a thousand inconveniences. And it's never what you imagine while writing the script, while thinking about the film. Whereas that initial idea is really only the rudiment of an idea, or an intuition. It's very good to bear that in mind, to be able to summarize the film in one sentence.

How do I go about writing a script? I sit down on a chair. I pull out the typewriter – or computer now – and just try to hit the keys. The whole problem is to hit them in the right order. That's the only problem really.

I've got a formula which I worked out a long time ago and which works for me. I don't say it's the best formula for everybody but it does work for me. The spring-board formula. The high-jumper has to have a hard board in order to jump, right? He runs on a soft surface and at a certain point he has to have a hard spring-board. Well, I use the same principle. I always write the whole thing first, whatever it is. And I start from the shortest version of this whole – that is, a page or a page and a half. But it's the whole thing; I never concentrate on individual scenes, individual solutions, individual characters. The whole is my spring-board.

This system of writing, which I have to this day, was forced on me by rules prevailing in Poland. At the time when I started making films the system was such that the successive stages of script-writing had to be approved by the production house. This had a good side to it which we made use of, namely, we got paid for each stage of the script. Since we were making very little money, and could barely make ends meet, I willingly made use of all these successive stages, all these possibilities of earning money.

There were four stages in a film script. First we'd write the outline – that was a page – and for that we'd get 1,000 złotys. Then we'd write the 'novella' which should be about twenty or twenty-five pages. I still write these 'novellas' only now I call them 'treatments' because at the moment I'm writing for foreign productions. Next came the script. Then the shooting script.

It wasn't even a question of censorship, although the initial intention probably was to censor each stage of a production. But later, when I was signed up with a good production house where there was absolutely no question of censorship and we understood perfectly well what was allowed and what wasn't, I looked upon this process as a way of earning money. At the same time, I realized very quickly that this method suited me; not to play around with details, or break the thing up into little pieces.

Now I do it differently; I write a first version. I don't write a one-page outline. I write a sort of intuitive rendering of what the film's going to be about so that the producer knows what the proposal involves. This outline does not cover the scale of the production because that's not known at this stage yet. Usually it's just the idea that's put forward here. Then I write the treatment, so that the producer can see the scale of the production. This is exceptionally important for me because the treatment contains action or the seeds of action and a sketch of the characters. There's no dialogue yet. Or only scraps of it. Sometimes it's just descriptive. But at any rate, the treatment's another version of the whole. Usually I write two or three versions of a treatment, and only give the third one in. Then I write the script which is about a hundred pages long. A page a minute, more or less. I also write two or three versions of the script. I don't write a shooting script. Nobody pays me for it and there's no need to write it. I don't need it. Nobody needs it, in fact.

It seems natural that at some time I've got to write dialogue.

Somebody enters a room, looks around and sees somebody else. He walks up to him and has to say something. Well, now you have a wider space and write: name, colon . . . Then I think of what the character has to say in the scene and why. And why. And why. And how. I try to imagine the character and think how he'd express himself in just such a situation.

We used to assess each other's scripts in Poland. That was during the wonderful period when there was a group of us who were close friends. That was during the period of the Cinema of Moral Anxiety in Poland. We were friends – Agnieszka Holland, Wojtek Marczewski,[7] Krzyś Zanussi, Edek Żebrowski, Feliks Falk,[8] Janusz Kijowski, too, and Andrzej Wajda – who all had the feeling that we were giving each other something. We were of different ages, with various experiences, different achievements. We'd tell each other our ideas. We'd discuss the casting, all sorts of solutions and so on. So the script would be written by me, but it had a mass of authors; a lot of people gave me ideas, not to mention all those who gave me ideas without even knowing it, simply by having been in my life in the past or in the present.

We'd all show each other films before they were edited or in very rough cuts. This habit has remained with me to this day. Maybe the partnership's not there now and we're not so close. Besides, we're a bit scattered across the world. We've rarely got time. But to this day, in fact, I discuss every script with Edek Żebrowski or Agnieszka Holland. With the three new films, *Three Colours* (*Barwy*), which I wrote together with Piesiewicz, we did it more professionally. They agreed to be my script advisers and were paid for it. We'd spend two days on each script, more or less, talking about it. We sat at the first one for two days. Two days at the second. Then for over two days at the third. And I'll ask them again, many times.

Then the actors come along. Then the cinematographer. And they change a lot of things again. A lot of things are changed before filming. I write another version of the script before the shoot. Then masses of things are changed during the shoot. The actors very often change the dialogue, too; or they tell me that they want to appear in some other scene, because they think that they ought to do or say something else. I bring them in if I think they're right. They often say they don't want to do something; they don't think it works for the character. If they're right, I agree with them.

In Poland, we used to get a budget for each film.[9] We simply got the money and could spend it. Whether the film was screened or not was a different matter. The censor could hold it back. I was able to make such films often by deception, by working something out in the script and not explaining what I meant until the end, by putting in false scenes and then shooting slightly different ones to replace them, by changing the dialogue and so on. That was the normal thing to do. They weren't major deceptions but we'd always do little things like that. We'd also deliberately film a lot of scenes for the censors to cut out and in this way direct their attention from other scenes. I noticed that my colleagues didn't have to worry about money or the way the film was received. But I had to worry about political censorship and about Church censorship[10] too, which already existed then. Obviously I had to worry about the way the public received the film but I didn't have to worry about the thing which worries people in the West: the need to muster a budget and to ensure that there is a market for the film. I never had to worry about that in Poland during Communism.

I don't know how ideas come to me. I don't want to analyse it because I think you lose authenticity when you analyse and rationalize. They come of their own accord. And where do they come from? From everything you've ever touched. I don't invent plots. I invent a story but, above all, I think that I sense and understand something rather than verbalize it in anecdotes. Anecdotes come later. There's nothing seething inside me which I have to express or else die from anguish.

At some point, I get the desire to tell a particular story which has started to unfold in a specific way. It expresses a certain idea which I think is worth expressing and I know that in ten years' time it won't be relevant any more. Especially as I've had the experience of making films which directly relate to reality. I have a note-book, a so-called director's note-book. That's one of the things the Łódź Film School thought up during my time. I still keep one. And I always advise my colleagues – when I'm teaching younger film-makers – to keep one. It's where I note down various things, addresses, or what time a flight I'm supposed to take is leaving, or the time a flight someone's arriving on is landing. Sometimes I note down something I've noticed in the street. And sometimes I note down something which has just come to mind. To be honest, I don't often refer back to it. I suspect that if I looked back I'd see that a lot of subjects had occurred to me before.

That's how it is with subject matter, or thoughts. If they don't come to you, it means that you've forgotten them but there are reasons why you've forgotten them. Namely, other thoughts have come to you. You think something else is important. And it seems to you that if you were to narrate something, it would be through other means or other anecdotes or altogether different events or a different world. We note down various things precisely because we forget them, especially at night. It's often like that, that certain ideas and solutions come to you at night. I always thought that something ought to be invented so that you could note down what comes to mind at night without having to wake up, because they're very valuable things – they're fantastic solutions. And when you wake up in the morning, you don't remember them any more. All day long you keep thinking, 'God, how did I solve that? How did I solve such and such a problem?' And you can never remember. You die convinced that your ideas will never come back because they've disappeared from memory.

But I firmly believe that if you've got a really good idea, then it stays somewhere in your memory. And, basically, all those note-books aren't really necessary. Since all that is really valuable, all that you really want and all that you really have to do, stays in your head, and in one way or another will emerge at the right moment. You'll be reminded of it by some impulse coming from the outside. Something happens and suddenly you clearly see what you had once thought out, what had occurred to you as a good solution.

A 'Period Piece'
THE CALM (SPOKÓJ) (1976)

The Calm was made for television. It was based on a short story but I can't remember the author's name. It was about a man who's released from prison but I can't remember what happened in the story. Anyway, the script was obviously very different.

I chose that story because there was a character in it whom I immediately knew how to adapt to fit Jurek Stuhr, whom I'd met while working on The Scar. I thought I had to write a film for him because he's so good. I absolutely had to make a film specially for

55, 56 Jerzy Stuhr in *The Calm (Spokój)*.

him, so *The Calm* was made essentially for Jurek Stuhr. It's the best possible situation you can imagine.

The Calm hasn't got anything to do with politics. It simply tells the story of a man who wants very little and can't get it. He can't even get that much. The fact that a strike's depicted somewhere along the line is, of course, the reason why the film wasn't shown in Poland for some six or seven years. This was the first time that the existence of something like a strike was shown on screen in Poland, and it's probably the first time this was shown in a feature film. But it's not the story of a strike by any means. The strike's got nothing to do with it. It's a film about our country, about our system where you can't get what you want, even if all you want is a television and a wife. And he didn't want anything else – that lad didn't want anything else.

The main character's a guy who's just released from jail. A free man, he works on a small building site. Prisoners are brought in to help. Television[11] had reservations about this scene. The Vice-President of Television was a very intelligent and shrewd man. He sent for me. I knew why. As I was approaching the Television centre, I noticed prisoners – dressed in prisoners' uniform, surrounded by guards watching over them with rifles – working on the tramlines. I went into the Vice-President's office. He said that he liked *The Calm* a lot and gave me a very astute criticism of the film. He really had understood everything. He really did like the film. I was pleasantly flattered and waited for the next bit – I knew I hadn't been called in to listen to compliments. I was right. The Vice-President was sorry to inform me that he must insist that some scenes be removed from the film. He didn't think it would be detrimental to the film. On the contrary, the film would be more succinct. Among the scenes he wanted removed, he mentioned the one with prisoners on the building site. 'Because in Poland,' said the Vice-President, 'prisoners don't work outside prisons. The convention forbids it . . .' Here he gave the name of the international convention. I asked him to come up to the window. He did. I asked him what he saw. 'Tramlines,' he said. 'And on the tramlines? Who's working there?' He looked carefully. 'Prisoners,' he said calmly. 'They're here every day.' 'In that case, prisoners do work outside prison in Poland,' I remarked. 'Of course,' he said. 'That's exactly why you have to cut that scene out.'

That's more or less what those conversations sounded like. That

57   On set: *The Calm.*

one was quite pleasant. I cut out the scene with the prisoners plus a few others but the film still wasn't shown for a few years. When it was finally shown, it was a period piece. Things change quickly in Poland.

Fourteen years have passed since my conversation with the Vice-President. The other day, I was passing through a small town. I slowed down because of road works. As if from a bad script, the workers were dressed in prisoners' uniform. Guards with rifles stood next to them. Today I'm allowed to make a film about that.

A Trap
CAMERA BUFF (AMATOR) (1979)

I think I wrote *Camera Buff* for Jurek Stuhr, too. I definitely wrote *The Calm* for him because I'd just discovered him. Whereas I wrote *Camera Buff* when Jurek was already well known, having been a success in *Top Dog* (*Wodzirej*)[12] after *The Calm*.

There were actors in *Camera Buff* who played given characters but apart from that there were people who exist in real life, who have names and appear under these names. Krzysztof Zanussi is a film director in real life, who from time to time takes part in 'evenings with the director'[13] in small towns. And in the film *Camera Buff*, he's a film director in exactly the same way. He arrives at an evening with the director in a small town. There used to be a lot of evenings like that in the past. There still are some, from time to time. (Not long ago, Piesiewicz[14] and I were at an evening like that in some monastery in Kraków. It was held for young people in a church after a screening of *Decalogue*. There were about a thousand people there. They couldn't get in and stood in the street throughout. They even installed loudspeakers.)

The main character in *Camera Buff* has a kind of fascination with film which he suddenly discovers while making a home movie of his newly born daughter with an 8mm camera. It's terribly amateurish, such a fascination. I wasn't ever fascinated with a camera like that. Later on I made films because that was my profession, and I was too lazy or too stupid or both to change profession at the right moment. Besides, at the beginning, it seemed to me to be a good profession. It's only now that I know how hard it is.

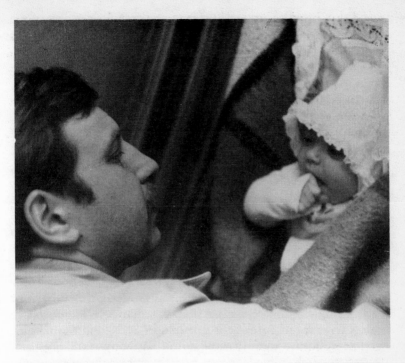

58, 59   Jerzy Stuhr in *Camera Buff* (*Amator*).

So I don't think *Camera Buff* is in any way a reflection of the dilemma of film or life, as film and life can co-exist. They can be reconciled – or at least you can try to reconcile them. It's difficult, of course. But, on the other hand, what's easier? Work in a textile factory isn't any easier. Forever being together with your family can end badly, too, just as rarely being together can. It's really not a question – or not only a question – of how much time we can devote to each other. Time and attention. You can probably devote more attention to your family if you work in a textile factory than if you work in films. But then, if you work in films, perhaps the attention you give to your family is more intense, more explicit. Because you feel – I feel – guilty that I don't give them enough time and attention. So when I do have the time, I devote it to family matters with exceptional intensity. I make up for the time I'm away and for not having enough patience by making tangible this feeling of guilt and living with my family. When I have a bit of time, I give it very intensely. So I don't know what's best in the end. I think both solutions – either forever or rarely being together – are possible and that love is possible in both just as a lack of love is possible in both, and harmony is possible in both – some general sort of harmony – and a general consent to such a fate; and in both solutions disharmony and hatred are possible.

Why does Filip, the camera buff, destroy the film towards the end? What does it mean? Always one and the same thing. He destroys what he's done. He doesn't give up because he turns the camera towards himself at the end. He simply realizes that, as an amateur film-maker, he's found himself in a trap and that, making films with good intentions, he might prove useful to people who'll use the films with bad intentions.

This didn't happen to me. I never actually destroyed any films. But if I'd known that they were going to confiscate my film the night we filmed those lockers while making *Station*, then, just like Filip, I'd have opened the cans and exposed the film before they could have got hold of it. Just in case, so that there wouldn't be any chance that the girl who'd murdered her mother would be there.

Chance or Fate
BLIND CHANCE (PRZYPADEK) (1981)

I don't really know why there wasn't any true description of Poland in the 1970s in the other arts. There wasn't even a proper description of it in literature and literature is easier to produce than film. It's not subject to censorship to the same degree although individual writers or individual books might be. Yet films offered the best description of Poland in the 1970s. At the end of the 1970s, I realized that this description was limited, that we had reached these limits and that there was no point in describing this world any further.

A result of this train of thought is *Blind Chance*, which is no longer a description of the outside world but rather of the inner world. It's a description of the powers which meddle with our fate, which push us one way or another.

I think its fundamental flaws lay in the script, as usual. I like the idea to this day; it's rich and interesting. I just don't think it was made adequate use of, this idea of three possible endings – that every day we're always faced with a choice which could end our entire life yet of which we're completely unaware. We don't ever really know where our fate lies. We don't know what chance holds in store for us. Fate in the sense of a place, a social group, a professional career, or the work we do. We've got much more freedom than this in the emotional sphere. In the social sphere we're greatly governed by chance; there are things which we simply have to do, or we have to be the way we are. That's because of our genes, of course. Those were the thoughts which pre-occupied me while I was making *Blind Chance*.

Witek, the main character, behaves decently in each situation. He behaves decently even when he joins the Party. At a certain moment, when he sees that he's been manipulated into a situation where he ought to behave like a bastard, he rebels and behaves decently.

The third ending is the one which means the most to me – the one where the aeroplane explodes – because one way or another, that's going to be our fate. It's all the same whether this happens in an aeroplane or in bed, it doesn't matter.

The film wasn't going all that well. I'd shot about eighty per cent. I edited it and realized that it was going in the wrong direction; it was equally inadequate in the way it was being filmed

60, 61   Bogusław Linde in
Blind Chance (Przypadek).

and in the way the idea of the three individual endings was being expressed. It was mechanical. It had been inserted into the film and didn't give the impression of forming an organic part of the whole. So I stopped shooting, and had a break for two or three months. Then I reshot about half of the material and another twenty per cent of new material which I needed. And there was a considerable improvement.

I often worked that way – and I still like doing this – that at some point I'd stop shooting and give myself a certain margin of freedom so that I could check in the cutting-room and on screen how various elements work together. Here, in the West, it's difficult to work in this way because there's a lot of money behind any project and it's terribly hard to play with this money. It was easy in Poland, at that time, because the money didn't belong to anybody, even though you had to take care not to make the films too expensive or unnecessarily extravagant. I was always very careful in this way. But you could play around with the money. You could manipulate it. And I often did.

The Communist Virus
SHORT WORKING DAY (KRÓTKI DZIEŃ PRACY) (1981)

I once wrote a script for one of my films with Hania Krall, a great friend of mine. It was a film based on one of her reports called 'Short Working Day' ('Krótki Dzień Pracy'). A terrible film. I made a complete hash of it but it was great writing it together. It's what you could call a typically political film: a film of its moment, which, had it been shown at the time, might perhaps have had some significance, but not necessarily. Reality changes and people don't care about it any more. They forget it ever existed. They don't remember what it was like. They don't remember why it was so painful. Rather than that, they try to remember all that was pleasant in that reality. That's probably why in all the Communist countries, there's this unexpressed – and probably nobody will express it – nostalgia for past times, although they were terrible. People are always joking: 'Commune, come back. Commune, come back', in Poland, in Bulgaria, in Russia, everywhere. People remember only the good things. Choices were pretty simple. You knew who was on your side and who was your enemy. You knew you could blame somebody and somebody was guilty – and he really was guilty. The system and those who worked for it were guilty of something, that's for sure. It was easy to blame them. They had their own membership cards, their own badges, their own tie colours, and it was all terribly straightforward. Now that's disappeared. Everything's become very complicated. To this is added nostalgia for times when we were younger, more energetic and had more hope. And that's how it is. Exactly the same goes for subject matter.

Short Working Day is a feature film for television, shot on 35 mm because they'd also planned to show it in cinemas. It's not been shown to this day – fortunately. First it was stopped by the censors. I managed to make *Blind Chance* and *Short Working Day* during a single production schedule and finished both of them in December 1981.

I suspect that the film didn't work because in the script we didn't try hard enough to understand the main character. It's a critical film about a Party Secretary, based on events in Poland. Rebellions and strikes had started up in 1976 because of price rises, and in a fairly large town 100 kilometres from Warsaw a large protest broke out. The protest ended up with people setting fire to the regional Party Committee headquarters, and the Secretary fled the building, at almost the last moment. He tried to stay right to the end but when the furniture started getting hot, the police, with help from their informers, somehow managed to get him out. Otherwise he'd probably have been lynched.

And I tried to make a film about this Party Secretary. The original report was called 'View from a first-floor window' ('*Widok z okna na pierwszym piętrze*') because his office was on the first floor. Then later, the film was called *Short Working Day* because that day he worked shorter hours than usual. He had to get out of the place at about two o'clock.

I had set myself a trap because in Poland at that time – and even more so now – there was absolutely no question of the public wanting to understand a Party Secretary. A Party Secretary had always been considered as somebody who belonged to the authorities; a moron usually. This particular Party Secretary wasn't too much of a moron and I was making a critical film about him. But I was in a trap created by ruthless public opinion. I didn't want to delve deeply into the Secretary's heart or soul, and I was a bit

62   On set: *Short Working Day (Krótki Dzień Pracy)*.

embarrassed to do so; a priest's or a young woman's maybe, but a
Party Secretary's? No, that wouldn't have been nice. Consequently, like it or not, the character is a bit schematic. He couldn't
be exploited in greater depth because of this political trap. Nowadays, it would be completely impossible to make a film about a
Party Secretary – in any depth.

Everybody from those Communist days is writing memoirs or
giving interviews now, in Poland. There are books everywhere.
Politicians, artists and television personalities are all writing about
how wonderful they were. You just don't know who was bad any
more. You can't find a single interview or read a single book where
someone admits to any degree of guilt. Everybody's innocent.
Politicians are innocent, artists are innocent. When you express
yourself publicly at any rate, you're always in the right from your
point of view. But it's a different matter altogether whether you
can sit in front of a mirror or face yourself and admit the various
mistakes you've made in your life. Yet I've never yet seen anybody
write publicly that something was their fault, that they'd done
something foolish or incompetent.

Various conversations appear in newspapers, books and on
television with people who, you'd think, had been responsible for
those forty years or at least a large number of those forty years of
Communism. Nobody says 'I'm guilty'; 'I was the reason that . . .';
'Thanks to my inefficiency, thanks to my foolishness, thanks to my
incompetence, this and this happened.' No, on the contrary.
Everybody says 'I saved this'; 'Thanks to me, we managed . . .' As
a result, nobody knows where the people are who were in any way
guilty. Where are the people who say 'Yes, it's me. I'm the one
who caused some injustice, pain, poverty'? There aren't any
people like that. Besides, that's why they write books, of course, to
justify themselves. It would be interesting to know whether they
write to justify themselves in the eyes of other people or in their
own eyes. That's what has always really interested me. But we'll
never find out. It's a fundamental question about evil. Where, in
essence, does evil lie? Where is it if it's not in us? Because it isn't in
us. Evil's in others. Always.

I'm not sure these people are lying. That's how it was, according
to their point of view. Or perhaps they just think that that's how it
was. Maybe their memory highlights only those fragments, actions
and situations in which they tried, in some way, to be better or

more decent than others. And that's the problem of relativism. Do absolute criteria exist? That's the question nowadays because everything's becoming so relative, isn't it?

Today, in the eyes of public opinion in Poland, all Party activists are simply a gang of thieves, swindlers, people with bad intentions. It wasn't like that. It's a fair opinion as regards some of them, of course, but not all. Like anybody else, the Communists are made up of intelligent and stupid people, lazy and hard-working people, people with good intentions and those with bad. Even among the Communists there were people who had good intentions. It's not true that they were all bad.

So it was impossible to make a film like that then and it's impossible now. And probably the fault of the film or my failure, to be more precise, lay in the fact that I didn't take the existence of such a trap fully into account. I made a film which isn't any good. It's boring, badly directed and badly acted.

I wanted to cast Filipski in the main role and the film would probably have been better but I was afraid of him. I was simply afraid of working with him. Filipski is an actor – he later became a director – who's very well known in Poland for his arrogance; insolent self-confidence, and feeling of superiority. He was very well known in Poland for his anti-Semitic proclamations, for his terrible relentlessness in this matter. He gave masses of anti-Semitic performances in the theatre then. But he was a very good actor, and a strong personality. And he should have played the Party Secretary. If I'd have cast him, the film would probably have been better because I'd have had to fight him all along. And I'd have had to be afraid of him all the time because I was afraid of him as a man. He simply hated me. Just like he hated everybody else. I didn't like him either, I must say – as a man, of course, although there's no doubt that he was a brilliant actor.

The film was shelved by the censors in 1981. It was entirely out of the question to show something like that even on television. I can't remember if Television sorted out its debts with the Production House. It was a big financial problem for the Production House. But I think they sorted out the accounts.

I finished editing *Short Working Day* and *Blind Chance* just before the introduction of martial law in December 1981. A hard winter had already begun in November and a month or a month and a half before martial law, it started to be bloody cold. It was

cold as hell in the cutting-room. I asked the man who represented
the trade union Solidarity in our studio, in the Wytwórnia, to see
to the heating because I thought that was the trade union's role. If
you're cold in a room because the radiators aren't working, then
it's the trade union's job to get somebody to mend them or to get
somebody to buy electric heaters and install them in the cutting-
room because people are freezing twelve hours a day. But he told
me that Solidarity had more important things on its mind. And
that's when I realized that this wasn't the place for me.

This is quite apart from the fact that I have grave doubts as to
whether a trade union is the best solution for artists. I don't think
it is. I think that a trade union is an exceptionally bad solution for
artists and for the whole industry which surrounds art and culture.
It's a disastrous solution. It always ends up with cleaners running
the library not librarians, because there are more of them. And it's
not the directors or producers or cameramen who run film-making
but technicians, electricians, drivers and so on. I think that a trade
union is contrary to an artist's nature, his nature to create something original and unique which, in essence, is what art should be.
It's contrary to that nature because the people who run trade
unions aim at something completely the opposite, at constantly
repeating the same things because that's easiest. The trade
unionists are very nice people. I've got nothing against them. On
the contrary, I love and respect all these people, but I don't see
why they should rule me. I can't agree to it.

I realized that this was simply another lie and swindle. What
does that mean, a swindle? That's the wrong word, of course. It's
not a swindle. Of course there were masses of good intentions,
that's obvious. But it makes me uneasy if you talk of a trade union
(because Solidarity was a trade union) but, in fact, are aiming at
something else. And this was pretty evident. Of course, they
couldn't say at the time that they were aiming at something else
because everything would have fallen apart. But I couldn't really
see myself living the lie which lay at the root of all this. I signed
myself out very quickly after that. Then, because of martial law, I
slept all the time. For about five months, half a year.

Right at the beginning of martial law I thought I was even
prepared to resort to different measures. Not with the help of a
camera but, for example, with a rifle, hand-grenade or something
like that. But it turned out that nobody in Poland was prepared to

do that. Nobody in Poland wanted to die. Nobody in Poland wants to die for the so-called rightful cause any more. This became clear more or less at the beginning of 1982.

I tried to be a taxi-driver because the only thing I can do apart from films is drive a car. But it turned out that I was too short-sighted, and that I hadn't held my driving licence for long enough. You had to have held it for twenty years or something. You couldn't work in my profession during martial law, and nobody counted on being able to work. But after some time, of course, we did start trying to do something.

Martial law was all so dramatic but it seems funny now. It was funny, in fact, but from the perspective of those times it looked dramatic. I thought it was something for which the people simply wouldn't ever forgive the authorities and that the people would do something about it. I immediately started signing petitions and letters in opposition to martial law. It was very hard for my wife to take because she thought that I was responsible for her, for our child. And she was right. But at the same time I thought I was responsible for something more. Well, that's precisely an example of a situation where you can't make the right choice. If you make the right choice from the social point of view, you make the wrong one from the point of view of the family. You always have to look for the lesser evil. The lesser evil consisted of my going to bed and sleeping, like a bear.

So they didn't want to show *Short Working Day* for a good few years. Now they very much want to show it. But I'm against it now. I censor it myself, as it were. I'm trying not to let them show it because I know how bad it is. There's another reason, too. Now, when Communism no longer formally exists, but the Communists are still installed everywhere and endless plans exist to move away from Communism and throw the Communists out of the body politic, as far away as possible from positions of influence, it seems deeply distasteful to me to kick somebody who's not really there any more. It seems morally unpleasant. I simply wouldn't want to do it. Those are sufficient reasons to try and stop the film from being shown; but they still want to show it. They keep looking for proof of how bad the Communists were. And *Short Working Day*, of course, is proof of this. That's true.

The problem of Communist files has now come up in Poland – who was a UB[15] agent and who wasn't, who was from the SB[16] and who wasn't. How easy it is to say, All you secret agents fuck off, and all you others go the other way, and now we'll simply divide you up: the bad ones and the good. How simple. But think of the people who at the time fell into a trap and simply couldn't act differently. Recently, I read a letter from a man like that. An ordinary man who isn't on any list and never will be because he's, I don't know, perhaps a barber or a clerk in some office or simply works as a labourer and unloads rail trucks. He wrote to a newspaper saying that he'd been forced to do what he did, that he didn't have any choice, and that there was absolutely no way out for him. He never gave any information to the UB, he never told the truth. On the contrary, he even suggests that he gave the police false information so as to make them waste their energies on dissolving non-existent underground organizations. A simple, ordinary man wrote: So what's going to happen to me? Am I one of the bad guys? I never did any harm. I never informed on anyone. I never handed over any information which might harm anyone. It's true that I signed a list at the UB. So what's going to happen to me? Is it a sin that that man signed a list of agents at the UB if he didn't do any harm? And the people who didn't sign any list of agents at the UB but were informers? Those who never signed, weren't collaborators, didn't take any money, but betrayed their colleagues? What's worse? What's the measure of this sin? I'd certainly think twice before passing judgement in a case like that, because, given the limitations of our knowledge and the imperfection of our intelligence, there's no way we can gauge the reality or the gravity of sin, the extent of guilt.

People adore passing judgement in Poland. They love to criticize, to categorize those they know and even those they don't know, and to label them. And I always ask, Excuse me, but who's passing moral judgement? Who's criticizing? What makes him or her a better judge than me? Why is he or she judging? How does he or she know the real truth? I really dislike this characteristic of the Poles which, unfortunately, is very often tied up with their aversion to those who are a bit better off than they are.

I'm very careful about judging people although I sometimes do so, of course. But I think I do it on a private level rather than a public one. I'm always amazed at the way people can throw labels and judgements around so easily. Of course, everyone's subject to being judged and that's normal. But this extraordinary aversion to one's neighbour is a national characteristic of the Poles. You can see it in the streets and shops. Nobody is polite to anybody. Nobody says 'Please' or 'Thank you'. You can see it when you drive, you can see it everywhere. It's a characteristic of individualists who can't really come to terms with other people. I'm an individualist, too, of course. I don't know, maybe it's a question of upbringing or a set of values, but I believe that a certain degree of hostility or aggression towards other people has to be held back. You have to try to hold it back or keep it to yourself. It's exceptionally common in Poland to be told that somebody's a secret agent, a son of a bitch, a Communist, or a crook.

There's a general bitterness there, which comes from the fact that hopes have been so frequently shattered. So many times a light which has appeared has been extinguished by somebody, by something or by history. I don't think it's just a matter of the past few years. I think it's a matter of centuries. And if you look at Polish classical literature, you'll find the same theme everywhere; Poles will very willingly and very easily drown another Pole in a glass of water.

There are also things which surprise me by their blatant shamelessness – such as changes of opinion about the present situation. This mostly concerns the politicians at present. But it surprises me in people who aren't in politics. There are people in Poland now in very high positions who took what the previous government offered them. They accepted jobs, and power, too.

There was a man called Waldemar Świrgoń and during martial law they made him Secretary of Culture.[17] He was a young, gifted politician, and even quite pleasant, although a bit forbidding. I met him twice, I think. He always offered me a drink first. When I'd tell him I was driving, he'd say that a driver would follow me and should the need arise he'd sort things out with the police. It didn't matter. So I asked that the driver shouldn't follow me, saying that I didn't particularly want to have a glass of vodka with him. But, of course, that wasn't the reason for the visits. They wanted to offer me a production house (zespół filmowy).[18] A production house held quite a bit of power in Poland in the 1980s, and in the 1970s. There were eight or nine of these houses. It was a good job both financially and as far as prestige was concerned. Of course, I didn't accept any production house from this man. I didn't want to accept anything whatsoever from him. But he summoned me on two or three occasions on the pretence of various things and, in the end, it always turned out that he wanted to offer me this production house. There were colleagues who did accept.

In every newspaper you open, you'll read accusations, people reproaching each other for having written differently before. But I don't have anything against these people because I know that you can do something and then change. You can even expiate guilt. And that's no problem until those people start accusing others for having done the same thing. Then I think it's wrong.

A lot of people who are active oppositionists today, many of them exceptionally wise and noble writers were fanatical advocates of Communism in the 1950s, and particularly after the war, in the 1940s, before the unification of the Party. I think I can understand why; I can understand this fascination. It wasn't a fascination with evil. It was a fascination with good. People didn't know at the time that it all had to turn to evil. Even if they knew that Stalin had murdered several million peasants in order to confiscate the land he'd previously given them, even if they knew this, they could still have thought that it would turn to good because the principle or the theory of Communism or socialism according to Marx and Engels, or even Lenin, is exciting. Justice, equality for everyone – there's something very exciting in it. You have to have great perspicacity to see that this isn't possible. And many people talk and write about it today; they try to justify themselves. Konwicki,[19] for example, Szczypiorski,[20] or Andrzejewski[21] in his previously unpublished works. Many people were simply fanatical advocates of Communism and they don't hide the fact. I don't think there's any shame in it. There's no disgrace. It's simply a mistake. It's a mistake based on the fact that you don't grasp, don't understand that this theory is impossible to realize in practice and that it has to lead to evil being done.

Communism isn't infectious although a lot of people have been infected by it at certain stages of their lives and throughout history. An enormous amount of people who seemed to be completely immune to the disease turned out not to be. I was lucky enough not to get infected, but I was exposed to it just like everybody else.

Communism is like AIDS. That is, you have to die with it. You can't be cured. And that applies to anyone who's had anything to do with Communism regardless of what side they were on. It's irrelevant whether they were Communists or anti-Communists or entirely uncommitted to either political side. It applies to everybody. If they've been exposed to the system as long as they have been in Poland – that is, for forty years – then Communism, its way of thinking, its way of life, its hierarchy of values, remains with them and there's no way of expelling it from their system. They can expel it from their minds, of course, they can say they're no longer sick. They can even say they've been cured. But it's not true. It stays inside. It exists, it remains and there's no way of getting rid of it. It doesn't particularly trouble me. I just know I've got it and know that I'll die with it, that's all. Not die of it, die with it. It only disappears when you disappear. The same as AIDS.

We All Bowed Our Heads
NO END (BEZ KOŃCA) (1984)

In September or October 1982, at the end of the first half-year of martial law, I decided to submit several film proposals to the WFD (State Documentary Film Studios). This was after *Station* so, to all intents and purposes, I didn't want to make any more documentaries but there was no question of making features at the time.

During martial law I thought I'd make a film about the guys who paint over graffiti on walls. Everybody was painting all sorts of graffiti on the walls: against martial law, against Jaruzelski,[22] against the Communists, and so on. 'WRON won za Don.' That was the main one. WRON was the Military Council for the Salvation of the Nation (Wojskowa Rada Ocalenia Narodowego). *Won* is the Russian for fuck off. *Za Don* means, beyond the River Don, therefore, get out of Poland. 'WRON won za Don.' There was graffiti like this and various other kinds, too; caricatures and so on. The army was fighting this graffiti. Special army or military brigades were allocated. I don't know who exactly. And I wanted to make a film called *Painter* (*Malarz*), about a boy, a young lad, who's in the army and paints over graffiti. Because they did paint over it, or wiped it off, or changed it to something else. They also changed the letters to make them read favourably for the Communists; it was terribly funny, all in all. I thought it would make an amusing film.

Apart from that idea, I wanted to make a film which would take place in the law courts. The courts, at that time, were passing many long sentences for trivial matters. They would pass sentences of two to three years for painting graffiti, for being caught with an underground newspaper, for strikes, or any sort of resistance. Sentences were being handed out to those caught after curfew, that is, after eight or ten in the evening. So I wanted to make a film which would take place entirely in the courts and there'd only be the faces of two people. The accuser and the accused. Meaning, the film would be about the 'guilty' – 'guilty' in inverted commas because these people weren't guilty of anything really – and about the accusers.

I didn't know the legal circle at all. I didn't know anybody. It was even harder in the early 1980s than in 1970, when we were working on *Workers '71*, to persuade anybody to agree to being filmed because people absolutely loathed Television by then. So I had to win the trust of people connected with the law.

First of all I had to get an agreement from the authorities. It took a very long time, about two months. But while we were sorting out this agreement – and banked on getting it – I was already trying to get through to influential people in this circle; lawyers mainly, people defending the accused who were later sentenced to two or three years for trivial matters, for nonsense. Hania Krall told me that she knew two young lawyers, who were forever defending people at these trials during martial law. They'd also acted for the defence before. They'd defended various organizations, including the Workers' Defence Committee (KOR)[23] and the Confederation of Independent Poland (KPN).[24] She said she didn't know which one would be better for me but said, 'Try and meet one of them,' and arranged for me to meet Krzysztof Piesiewicz. I explained to him what I wanted, what sort of film I wanted to make. He didn't trust me all that much, to be honest, but since I'd been recommended by Hania Krall and he'd seen some of my work somehow I managed to overcome his reluctance. They were clearly reluctant to allow anybody to note, film or show any of this at all. I managed to explain to Piesiewicz that I wanted to defend those who were being sentenced, and to expose those who were passing sentences, so that there'd be evidence of all this, of this nonsense which was going on.

Unfortunately, it took a long time before I got permission and it must have been November by the time we started shooting. We got permission to film in both public and military courts. I had got to know Krzysztof (Piesiewicz) by then. He knew more or less what I wanted and had agreed, in the names of some of his clients, to the filming. The moment I started shooting, something strange began to happen. The judges didn't sentence the accused. That is, they passed some sort of deferred sentences which weren't, in fact, at all painful.

There were two reasons for this. The first was that the law courts had become a bit less severe since martial law had already been in force for almost a year (this was in November 1982). And the second reason, which I found very interesting, was the plain human fear of the judges in front of the camera. I didn't realize this at the beginning, but later I caught on pretty quickly. The judges didn't want to be recorded at the moment of passing unjust sentences, because they knew that if I turned on the camera, then some time in the future, after three, ten or twenty years, somebody would find this film. And they'd see themselves. Of course, they appeared in all the documents, they signed papers; but it's one thing to sign a piece of paper and quite another physically to appear on screen at the moment of passing an unjust sentence. Those are two entirely different matters.

Then a very strange thing started to happen in court. Just as at the beginning nobody wanted to let us in on any trials – the lawyers, in particular, defended themselves against this, and the defendants – so later they were all begging us to film their cases. It got to the point where I had to hire a second camera in order to make it from one trial to another on time. When a camera was in the courtroom, the judges didn't pass prison sentences. So I didn't even load the second camera with film because there wasn't any need. They were simply dummy cameras which were only there so that through plain human fear, the judges wouldn't pass sentences.

I spent about a month or so moving back and forth from one courtroom to another. I don't know how many trials we attended – fifty, maybe more, maybe eighty. And I didn't film one single metre of all this since every time I switched the camera on – and I'd switch it on just as the judge was about to say: 'In the name of the

Republic of Poland, I sentence citizen . . .' – it would turn out that
he didn't sentence the citizen. So I'd immediately switch it off. I
didn't shoot any film; nothing came of it. I don't know, I filmed
maybe seven minutes, all in all, where you could see, on screen, the
camera starting and immediately stopping again. Starting and
immediately stopping. That's how I met Piesiewicz. He was the
first to catch on to what was happening.

Afterwards there was a very unpleasant affair connected with all
this. I still don't know how I managed to get out of it to be quite
honest. After the month or month and a half of filming – this was a
shoot, after all, and everybody on it was working; electricians,
assistants, everybody gave their time – I wrote a letter to WFD
(the State Documentary Film Studios) saying that, because I was
filming for over a month and various people were employed (here I
gave the names, including the production manager's) I'd be grateful if they would pay these people. The film didn't, in fact,
materialize because I couldn't get the material which I needed, but
these people did work, so please pay them their due. I gave up my
own remuneration of course because there wasn't any reason why
I should be paid – and I didn't want to. But I did want my
colleagues to be paid. Because of this I had to stipulate, in the
letter, what I didn't manage to get. The subject of the film was
there, the script had been submitted and I simply wrote that the
script assumed that the courts would pass sentences and that I'd
show the faces of the accusers and the accused, but, as it turned
out, no jail sentence had been passed at any of the trials which I
attended. That's what I had to write.

I gave the letter to the office at WFD where films were
approved. And literally the following day, the President of Television sent for me. He had been the Vice-Minister of Arts and
Culture with special responsibility for Cinematography, so I knew
him. I realized that he hadn't sent for me because he'd just been
made President of Television but because he wanted me to state on
television, that law courts in Poland weren't passing sentences
during martial law. Obviously, I refused because I'd written the
letter simply to allow a few people to get a few thousand złotys
and that was all. But that wasn't the end of it. The letter found its
way to Kiszczak,[25] who read it to a few Polish intellectuals who'd
come to ask him to intercede in some matter, saying: 'What are
you talking about? Here you are. Even your man, Kieślowski,

writes that the law courts aren't passing sentences during martial law.'

Obviously he'd only read them a fragment of the letter. The opinion of social groups was exceptionally powerful in Warsaw during martial law because there weren't any other channels of opinion. There weren't any newspapers, telephones weren't working, and so on. The only thing that existed really was public opinion. Suddenly, I realized that a strange vacuum was forming around me, that people were taking me for an informer or somebody working for, I don't know, the law courts or police or something.

Of course, I immediately took the letter to the people to whom Kiszczak had read it. That was Klemens Szaniawski[26] and Andrzej Wajda – the two most distinguished intellectual names in Poland at the time. I showed them the whole letter. They understood then, of course, that they'd become victims of Kiszczak's manipulation. I managed to get the whole thing back into perspective and win back my normal position – one which I had already begun to lose – my normal place in my circle, in my world. So these were dangerous games. I was really threatened with being ostracized by my circle.

But that's not all. The Secretary of Culture at the Central Committee, Waldemar Świrgoń, sent for me, too. He was the highest dignitary of cultural affairs in Poland. He was the one who really decided everything. He said that he'd willingly give me a production house or anything else I might desire. He said that I should take something. Of course, this was all tied up with the letter. They thought that if they gave me something, I'd tell, I don't know, the papers or television, that martial law is fantastic, that nobody passes sentences on anybody, that everybody's terribly nice and awfully polite.

It was very important for the authorities of martial law to have an opinion like that, especially in Western eyes. They wanted an opinion that martial law was lenient, subtle and didn't, in fact, infringe on anybody's private goods. And there's a little bit of truth in that. Umpteen or even scores of people paid for martial law with their lives but the scale of bloodshed was minimal compared to what could have happened. Of course, a lot of people suffered terribly through imprisonment, internment, separation from their loved ones, and so on. It was awful at the time. I thought they'd lock me up, too. Luckily, they didn't. Today, a lot of people think they would love to have been locked up because now this gives good credentials. I'm very pleased I wasn't, although they did look for me. At one moment, it looked as if they really did want me, but the caretaker where I lived warned me that they were looking for me and I simply didn't go home for two or three days and they stopped. That was at the very beginning of martial law, around 15 December 1981, obviously not during the affair with the letter.

Anyway, a short while after I had seen Świrgoń I was called to see the police, and this time they blackmailed me with the letter, and again with the sound recordings I'd apparently sent to Radio Free Europe. They wanted me to comment on the letter or allow it to be printed. Of course, they could print whatever they liked, but since I'd countermanded their efforts, the letter had lost its credibility. Theories about the letter construed by those who wanted to discredit me in the eyes of my social group were no longer feasible because people knew what the whole thing was really about.

Well, that's the story. That's when I met Piesiewicz. I can't even remember what the title of the film was supposed to be. *Faces* (*Twarze*)? No, not *Faces*, certainly not that. That's pretentious. I wouldn't use a title like that. I can't remember.

I spent a month and a half in those courtrooms; in the corridors, in the rooms. I met a lot of lawyers and judges, too, some of them very decent people. I wanted to film the atmosphere of the courtroom, of trial, of two distinct sides – and the division didn't by any means run between the accused and accusers. The lines of hatred ran somewhere else.

I thought at the time – and still do – that martial law was really a defeat for everyone, that everyone lost, that during martial law we all bowed our heads. I think that today we're reaping the results of bowing our heads. Because we lost hope, yet again, and the generation to which I belong never lifted its head again even though it did resume power in 1989. It tried to give the appearance of still having some energy and hope but I never believed in our generation's hope any more.

I decided that I wanted to make a film about this. I thought up a subject which was partly metaphysical – the metaphysical aspect was there at the outset. It was to be about a lawyer who's already dead and we only start filming at the moment of his death. When I got down to writing the script, I quickly realized that although I knew the atmosphere and knew a little about all this, I didn't know nearly enough about what was going on in the wings, or the real reasons why people behave the way they do, about real conflicts. I'd only observed scraps of conflicts and the effects in the courtrooms, and I hadn't observed their very essence. And so I took myself along to see Piesiewicz and proposed that we write the script together. This was the film *No End*. That's how we started working together.

The initial idea was for a film which takes place in a courtroom. About the lawyer who's dead, and about the woman he leaves behind who realizes that she loved him more than she thought when he was alive. I didn't know anything more about the film. The film is terribly diffuse, of course, since it is three films in one, as it were. And you can see that – the stitching's not very subtle. The film doesn't fuse together to form a whole. A part of it, the discursive part, is about a young worker. A part of it is about the widow's life (the widow is played by Grażyna Szapołowska). Then there's the most metaphysical part, that is, the signs which eman-ate from the man who's not there any more, towards all that he's left behind. And these three films don't really want to come together. Of course, they do mix all the time, threads and thoughts constantly interweave, but I don't think we managed to bring it together. Those are the film's flaws but I still like it despite them.

The most important thread for me was the metaphysical one. Unfortunately, I don't think it worked. Yet, for someone interested in telling a story and expressing a certain social or political idea – namely, that we are all lost and are all bowing our heads – then that aspect of the film was just as important. So this was a trap, too, in a way. Every film, in fact, is a trap. You want to say something yet at the same time you want to do something slightly different.

I'm trying to tidy up these problems more and more now. I'm trying to avoid them so that there's simply one clear driving force. The *Decalogue* was a good exercise in this. The films were short and consequently the driving force could be very clearly stated, defined, marked out.

On *No End* we shot masses of material with Jurek Radziwił-łowicz, who plays the dead lawyer. Masses and masses. Yet in the end he only appears four times as a ghost. The film wasn't written

63 Artur Barciś in *No End*.

64 Grażyna Szapołowska in *No End*.

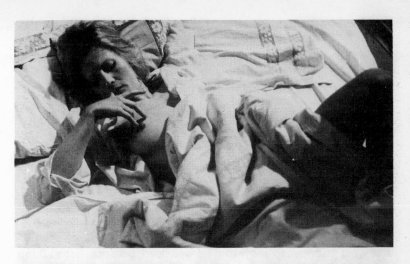

65–6   Grażyna Szapołowska in *No End*.

for him, but at a certain moment I realized that he ought to play the part. He was the actor who'd played in *Man of Marble*[27] and *Man of Iron*[28] for Andrzej Wajda and as a result had become a symbol of someone who's evidently morally pure, evidently honest. I realized I had to hire him simply so that it would be clear to the audience that this man is someone who is inwardly extremely clean, extremely pure, extremely clear. I knew that Jurek Radziwiłłowicz would work that way not because he's like that – though he really is like that in real life, too – but because of the associations he conjures up for people. It was an example of type-casting.

It was interesting, too, to try to find a way of showing a man whose conscience was clear, yet who couldn't do anything in Poland in 1984. That's when we were making the film. It seemed that we'd just have to show that he was dead, because that's taking the notion of the man's inability to do anything to its ultimate limit – he's just not there any more. He's dead. People like that, people with such clear consciences and such clean hands don't stand a chance any more. Now, how do you show that they don't stand a chance? You show that they're not there any more. They have to die. They're not made for these times. They're not in a state to survive these times. That their purity and clarity brought into collision with these times has to end with their disappearance.

The original title of *No End* was *Happy Ending* (*Szczęśliwy Koniec*), because the heroine walks off with her husband who's already dead. We see that they've found a world which is a little better than the one in which we're immersed. But it seemed too literal and coarse to call it *Happy Ending*.

I'm not in the least bit interested in taking part in seances of any kind. But I do think there's a need within us – not only a need but also a fundamental kind of feeling – to believe that those who have gone and whom we dearly loved, who were important to us, are constantly within or around us. I'm not thinking about calling up spirits; I mean that they exist within us as somebody who judges us and that we take their opinions into account even though they're not there any more, even though they're dead. I very often have the feeling that my father is somewhere near by. It doesn't matter if he's actually there or not, but if I wonder what he'd say about what I've done or want to do, that means he's there. My mother, too. I often wonder whether I should do one thing or another. And I think, What would my father say? If I think he'd probably say 'no', then I don't do it. I simply take his opinion into account, even though he's not there any more, because I do know what his opinion would be, more or less. It's an appeal to the good, decent side of us. It's some sort of ethical system which exists somewhere within. We can tell ourselves that it's a question of our father not wanting something and so we don't do it. But, after all, it's only our good side saying, 'No, don't go that way. Don't do that. That's not right. You shouldn't do that. It's best not to. Perhaps you should try it another way.' Whether we identify this with people for whom we've got a lot of respect or love isn't all that important. I think we're constantly taking into account opinions of people who can't give us their opinions anymore.

Personally, I hold quite an unpopular opinion. I believe that from birth people are basically good. It's in everybody's nature to be good. And then the question arises: Where does evil come from, if everybody's good? I haven't got any reasonable and logical answer to this, of course, but I think that, generally speaking, evil comes from the fact that, at some point, people realize that they're not in a position to bring about good. It comes from a certain kind of frustration. It's irrelevant whether they do it consciously or subconsciously. It's impossible to make any generalizations as to why they're not in a position to bring about good. There are so many different reasons, thousands of them.

There is a saying: 'Hell is paved with good intentions'. In a way, it's true, in the social, political or general sphere. But it's not true in the sphere of each individual life. My so-called defeatism, bitterness or pessimism with regards to life – quite evident in my case – comes precisely from this; that my intentions, which were always good, worked out as if they were bad. But I've always been of a pessimistic disposition. My father was, too, and no doubt my grandfather, whom I don't remember and never saw, was like that, too, and my great grandfather. Of course, my father was seriously ill. He couldn't support his family and I suspect his pessimism and feeling of senselessness were well founded. But I think that these reasons, the illness and everything that happened to him only confirmed his pessimism. The things that happened to me also confirm me in mine even though many good things have happened. I can't – and don't – complain about that. On the contrary.

No End wasn't shown for about half a year. Then, when it was, it was terribly received in Poland. Terribly. I've never had such unpleasantness over any other film as I had over this one. It was received terribly by the authorities; it was received terribly by the opposition, and it was received terribly by the Church. Meaning, by the three powers that be in Poland. We really got a thrashing over it. Only one element didn't give us a thrashing, and that was the audience.

The film was atrociously distributed on purpose. If a newspaper wrote that *No End* was being shown somewhere, then when you turned up at the cinema you could be sure that *No End* wasn't on. Some other film was showing. And when it was written that some other film was being shown, then it would be that *No End* was on. You couldn't find my film. It was on at various cinemas, usually those where I never wanted my films to be shown. There are certain cinemas where I don't want my films to be shown because I know that it's difficult to get to them, there's a different audience there, the people there are used to taking their children with them, or young people are used to going there to see entertaining American films. And I don't want my films shown there. Of course, that's exactly where *No End* was shown and always under a different title.

This has been a well-known method ever since A. Zajączkowski and A. Chodakowski made *Workers '80 (Robotnicy '80)*,[29] which alluded to our film *Workers '71 (Robotnicy '71)*. That film was always shown under the title *All performances reserved (Wszystkie seanse zarezerwowane)*. First there was the name of the cinema, colon, then: *All performances reserved*. That's where *Workers '80* was being shown, so people would flock to cinemas where *All performances reserved* was said to be showing.

Then *No End* suddenly appeared at one cinema, at the beginning of July. That is, exactly at the beginning of the holiday season. Throughout the entire two months, the film was shown in that one cinema. There was a full house all the time and the last day of August, when the holidays ended, they took it off and it wasn't shown any more. That's how it was exploited.

So one group of people didn't give me a thrashing. The public. Firstly, they went to see it. And secondly, never in my life have I received as many letters or phone calls about a film from people I didn't know as I did after *No End*. And all of them, in fact – I didn't get a single bad letter or call – said that I'd spoken the truth about martial law. That that was the way they experienced it, that's what it was like. There weren't any tanks or riots or shooting or anything like that. It was a film about the state of our minds and the state of our hopes rather than about the fact that it was cold outside and that we were being interned or shot at.

The authorities couldn't receive the film well because the film was against martial law. Martial law was shown as being the defeat of those who had imposed it and those whom it affected. And the film showed that. *Trybuna Ludu*[30] wrote that it was an example of anti-socialist sabotage, that it contained instructions for underground activists, and these were very serious accusations at the time. These instructions allegedly consisted of encouraging people to bide their time because that's what one of the lawyers in the film says: 'You have to bide your time . . . You have to surrender for the time being. Later on, we'll see. For the time being you have to surrender.' Quite a few Russian newspapers wrote something on the subject, too, and were immediately quoted in the Polish press. Instructions for the underground. A profoundly anti-socialist film.

Meanwhile, the opposition wrote exactly the opposite – that it was a film commissioned by the authorities, for the very simple reason that the film showed defeat. It showed the defeat of both one side and the other. The opposition didn't want to see itself in the loser's role. The opposition believed that either it had won or, at any rate, certainly would win. It was right, as 1989 proved. But what state was it in when it won? That's the question I always ask. What state were you in when you won? What state are you in, winning? Do you have enough energy, enough strength, enough hope, enough ideas, to lead the country in the right direction after having won?

The best and the wisest of us won. There's no doubt about that. But can you look to the future with hope, at the moment, living in Poland? I don't think so, despite the fact that they're our people, or even our friends, and that we don't doubt their good intentions. But that's not enough as it turns out.

I think that I'm just as worried about Poland as I used to be. Maybe even more so because we've been disillusioned yet again. This had to happen at some stage. We're disillusioned that this country can't be organized in the way we'd imagined – or the way I'd imagined – to make it decent, tolerable, wise – wise perhaps isn't

the right word – to make it not so foolish. I can see people full of
good intentions trying to do something and that's the way it's been
for ages. They try to organize this country, put it on its feet, make
it great, noble, yet nobody's succeeding. Each time, a naïve, vital
longing for order, for decency, for a reasonable life is motivated by
hope. I've been living for over fifty years and, of course, I've
frequently had such hopes; but the hope's getting smaller and
smaller. It gets smaller with every disappointment. It's all the same
whether the hope's been inspired by the Communists in 1956 or
1970, or the workers in 1981 or our new government in 1990 and
1991 – it doesn't matter who inspires the hope. Every time we see
that this hope was just another illusion, another untruth; another
dream and not a real hope. You keep pouring water into a glass.
You keep pouring, pouring, pouring, pouring, pouring and then
suddenly it runs over. The glass is full.

I don't know what free Poland means. A free Poland is completely impossible simply because the country is badly situated
geographically. But that doesn't mean that this country can't be
organized intelligently. It most certainly can, but unfortunately
there aren't any signs of this; in fact, it's being just as foolishly
organized as before, except that now it's us who are organizing it.
And that's the saddest thing about it all.

A great many relationships have fallen apart; friendships, personal relationships, professional relationships. To be honest, I can
count the number of friends I met in Poland over the last four or
five years on the fingers of one hand. Not because I don't have
time, but because I haven't got any real need to see them. And they
don't need to see me. These relationships have simply fallen apart.
At one stage, I was very, very close to Wajda and we'd meet every
day, but I haven't seen him now for four or five years. I met him
once at some première. We gave each other a hug and that was all.
'Phone me.' 'Phone me.' And that was it.

I keep in close contact with Edek Żebrowski. Maybe because we
work together or maybe because we like each other. I keep in close
contact with Krzysztof Zanussi, although we see each other far
less frequently, of course, because we've got less opportunity to
meet. I keep in touch with Agnieszka Holland because she's here,
in Paris, but I see her just as often in Poland. I see Marcel,[31] my
cameramen and that's basically it. So there's very few people I
keep in touch with. It all fell apart after martial law.

67   With Sławomir Idziak and Agnieszka Holland in Cannes, 1988.

68   With Edward Żebrowski in Switzerland.

Some people might bear me a grudge. I remember having some problems with a very close friend of mine from film school, for example. In 1968, his father, who held a high position in the Party, was thrown out.[32] He was later reinstated in another high position in a ministry, but he didn't work in the Party any more. His son, who was from the same street, so to speak, as Adam Michnik,[33] was having real problems. He'd finished film school but couldn't get any work.

I was making a documentary and asked this friend of mine to be my assistant. He didn't have anything better to do so he accepted.

Then this film won a prize at the Kraków Film Festival. Suddenly a young film critic came up to me and said I'd behaved like an arsehole; that I'd gone up to collect the prize by myself instead of calling my friend on to the stage with me. He thought I should have shared the prize. At the beginning, I thought he was acting on his own initiative but then I realized it was my friend's initiative, it was my friend's point of view. I couldn't understand it because I had made the film and I had written the script. It was true my friend was my assistant so we'd often discussed how to make the film. He'd even travelled around looking for men we could film, saying that one was more suitable than another and then we'd go to see the one he'd chosen. He performed the normal duties of a first assistant. There wasn't any reason for him suddenly to become co-author of the film. It turned out later – but this was also because of various other private misunderstandings between us at that time – that this friend of mine, to this very day, bears me a grudge. I couldn't help my friend much. I wasn't in a much better situation than he was. I was a young director. He was politically ostracized. What else could I do? Maybe there was more I could have done. But then again, I've never had any great ambitions to go out of my way to help every little sparrow. I helped this particular man because he was my friend.

I bear a grudge, or am bitter, towards the life which surrounded me, surrounds me and will surround me, and which is the way it is, where everything is wretched, where there's no truth, only illusion. I'm talking about the Poland to which I've been condemned and where, no doubt, I'll spend the rest of my life. I'm very bitter about this life, about the country which I've come from and from which I'll never escape because it's impossible. And I bear myself the same grudge for being part of this nation. It's not a grudge against the people. The nation's made up of individuals. The nation's made up of 38 million individual people. But the will of these 38 million individuals decides, at a certain moment, that life goes one way rather than another.

We, as Poles, have tried to negate our historical location several times; that is, our position between the Russians and the Germans, a place through which all new roads always pass. We always lost. When I think of what Poland and the Poles are now and of how beautiful and wonderful it is that our honour doesn't permit us to live in bondage or be subjugated, and I see Warsaw which is horrifically ugly and thoughtlessly planned with its idiotically designed network of public transport, architecture and so on; and when I think that it's like this just because we're the sort of nation we are, then I wonder whether it's a good thing to be the way we are. Perhaps it's better to be part of a different nation where, after the storm of the Second World War, the streets are well planned out, and stone houses from the nineteenth century still stand and will continue to stand for hundreds of years. Perhaps it's better to be a nation like the French, who received the Germans, warmly or not, but where nothing very dramatic happened and everything stands, while in Warsaw everything got destroyed because we behaved the way we did. I wonder, what's better? To put up with something, which is an obvious restriction of freedom and an obvious humiliation, for the sake of a certain comfort, or not to put up with humiliation and allow yourself to be killed? That's the basic choice. There isn't any other.

When I say that I bear a grudge against my country, I really bear a grudge against history, or perhaps against the geography which treated this country the way it did. No doubt, that's how it has to be – that we'll get thrashed, that we'll try to tear ourselves away from where we are and will never succeed. That's our fate. But it can be quite tiring. It is tiring for me.

I recently read something by the English historian, Norman Davies, about the Kraków School of History (Krakowska Szkoła Historyczna) which was just about the best Polish school of history. 'In their view,' writes Davies,[34] 'the *Liberum Veto* (the right of the individual to obstruct the will of the community as a whole), the *Liberum Conspiro* (the freedom to conspire against authority), and the *Liberum Defaecatio* (the right to vilify one's opponents) were all Polish traits in the same, unfortunate tradition.' For years in the Polish Seym,[35] any member of parliament or senator could oppose an Act through the *Liberum Veto*, and that Act could not then be passed, even if everybody else was in agreement. That was the principle of the *Liberum Veto* in Poland. Davies continues that the Kraków historians 'held that the destruction of the old republic had occurred in the natural course of events, and that all attempts to revive it were pointless.'

That was written by an English historian who is probably quite objective. He, too, noticed these Polish characteristics, which probably come from Poland's unfortunate geographical and political location, and which make positive government impossible. Whereas when there's a threat the Poles immediately unite. When they're defeated, they immediately unite. They unite in adversity and suffering, but when there's a chance of agreement, they can't achieve it. Even the most intelligent man would lose energy, patience, talent, everything he's got when placed in government because no reasonable consensus will ever be achieved.

That's the paradox of politics. Of course politics needs intelligent people but doesn't the law need them too? Maybe it does. Maybe art needs them. Maybe medicine, literature, cinema, the law, and hospital management wouldn't be able to evolve without these people. Of course, all the intelligent, good, wise, calm, righteous, honest, decent, energetic doctors could be put into the Ministry of Health but then who would take care of the sick? The same goes for everything else. In my opinion, for example, Wajda, who has spent a few years in politics, made a great mistake. He invested his talent where it wasn't worth investing. He didn't change anything. He didn't achieve anything. Even though he did thousands of things, he never actually achieved anything. There's only one result – in all that time, he didn't make any films, and now, if he does – and I sincerely wish him a beautiful film – I fear it's going to be tainted by the bitterness he acquired while trying to play at politics.

So, the opposition believed that I'd caused them great harm with *No End*, because I hadn't shown victory. I thought I'd shown the truth. And the Church, of course, received the film very badly because the woman commits suicide in the end, not to mention the fact that she takes her knickers off several times. She commits suicide, which is a mortal sin and she dies leaving a little child, so that was utterly unacceptable to the Church. Only then is she content. It's only after the suicide that, in one scene, I show her feeling light and happy. That she's found a better place for herself over there.

Decalogue
DEKALOG (1988)

While all this was going on, I happened to bump into my co-scriptwriter in the street. He's a lawyer, roams around, hasn't got much to do. Maybe he's got time for thinking. It's true that he has had a bit to do over the last few years because we had martial law and he took part in quite a few political trials in Poland. But martial law finished sooner than we'd all expected. And one day I bumped into him. It was cold. It was raining. I'd lost one of my gloves. 'Someone should make a film about the Ten Commandments,' Piesiewicz said to me. 'You should do it.' A terrible idea, of course.

Piesiewicz doesn't know how to write. But he can talk. He can talk and not only can he talk but he can think. We spend hours on end talking about our friends, our wives, our children, our skis, our cars. But we keep going back to what would be useful for the story we're inventing. It's very often Krzysztof who has the basic ideas; ones which, in fact, look as if they can't be filmed. And I defend myself against them of course.

Chaos and disorder ruled Poland in the mid-1980s – everywhere, everything, practically everybody's life. Tension, a feeling of hopelessness, and a fear of yet worse to come were obvious. I'd already started to travel abroad a bit by this time and observed a general uncertainty in the world at large. I'm not even thinking about politics here but about ordinary, everyday life. I sensed mutual indifference behind polite smiles and had the overwhelming impression that, more and more frequently, I was watching people who didn't really know why they were living. So I thought Piesiewicz was right but filming the Ten Commandments would be a very difficult task.

Should it be one film? Several? Or maybe ten? A serial, or rather cycle of ten separate films based on each of the Commandments? This concept seemed closest to the idea of the Ten propositions, ten one-hour films. At this stage, it was a question of writing the screenplays – I wasn't thinking about directing yet. One of the reasons for starting work was the fact that for several years I'd been deputy to Krzysztof Zanussi, artistic head of the Tor Production House. Zanussi was working largely abroad so he made general decisions while the day-to-day running of the Production House was left to me. One of the functions of the Production House is to help young directors make their first films. I knew a lot of directors like that who deserved a break and I knew how difficult it was to find the money. For a long time in Poland television has been the natural home for directorial débuts – TV films are shorter and cheaper, so less risk is involved. The difficulty lay in the fact that Television wasn't interested in one-off films. It wanted serials and, if pushed, agreed to cycles. So I thought that if we wrote ten screenplays and presented them as *Decalogue*, ten young directors would be able to make their first film. For a while, this idea motivated our writing. It was only much later, when the first versions of the screenplays were ready, that I realized rather selfishly that I didn't want to hand them over to anybody else. I had grown to like some of them and would have been sorry to let them go. I wanted to direct the films and it became obvious that I would do all ten.

We knew from the very beginning that the films would be contemporary. For a while, we considered setting them in the world of politics but, by the mid-1980s, politics had ceased to interest us.

During martial law, I realized that politics aren't really important. In a way, of course, they define where we are and what we're allowed or aren't allowed to do, but they don't solve the really important human questions. They're not in a position to do anything about or to answer any of our essential, fundamental, human and humanistic questions. In fact, it doesn't matter whether you live in a Communist country or a prosperous capitalist one as far as such questions are concerned, questions like, What is the true meaning of life? Why get up in the morning? Politics don't answer that.

Even when my films were about people involved in politics, I always tried to find out what sort of people they were. The political environment only formed a background. Even the short documentary films were always about people, about what they're like. They weren't political films. Politics were never the subject.

Even when, in *Camera Buff*, a man appears who represents the so-called other side, that is, the factory director who cuts out some scenes from the main character's film, he's also a human being. He isn't merely a representative of dull-witted bureaucrats who cut scenes out of films. He's also a man who's trying to explain why he intervenes. He is just like the censor in Warsaw who used to cut various bits out of my films. Through *Camera Buff*, I wanted to observe him and find out what lies behind his actions. Is he only dull-wittedly carrying out decisions? Is he aiming for a more comfortable life? Or maybe he's got reasons which I may not agree with but which are nevertheless reasons.

I'm sick of Polish realities because everything's running its course in spite of us, above us and there's nothing we can do about it. Piesiewicz and I didn't believe that politics could change the world, let alone for the better. Also, we'd begun to suspect intuitively that *Decalogue* could be marketed abroad. So we decided to leave politics out.

Since life in Poland is hard – intolerable, in fact – I had to show a bit of this in the films. However, I did spare the viewers many very unpleasant things which happen in daily life. First, I saved them from anything as horrible as politics. Second, I didn't show queues in front of shops. Third, I didn't show such a thing as a ration card – although many goods were being rationed then. And fourth, I didn't show boring and dreadful traditions. I tried to show individuals in difficult situations. Everything pertaining to social hardships or life's difficulties in general was always somewhere in the background.

Decalogue is an attempt to narrate ten stories about ten or twenty individuals, who – caught in a struggle precisely because of these and not other circumstances, circumstances which are fictitious but which could occur in every life – suddenly realize that they're going round and round in circles, that they're not achieving what they want. We've become too egotistic, too much in love with ourselves and our needs, and it's as if everybody else has somehow disappeared into the background. We do a lot for our loved ones – supposedly – but when we look back over our day, we see that although we've done everything for them, we haven't got the strength or time left to take them in our arms, simply to have a kind word for them or say something tender. We haven't got any time left for feelings, and I think that's where the real problem lies. Or time for passion, which is closely tied up with feelings. Our lives slip away, through our fingers.

I believe everybody's life is worthy of scrutiny, has its secrets and dramas. People don't talk about their lives because they're embarrassed. They don't want to open old wounds, or are afraid of appearing old-fashioned and sentimental. So we wanted to begin each film in a way which suggested that the main character had been picked by the camera as if at random. We thought of a huge stadium in which, from among the hundred thousand faces, we'd focus on one in particular. We also had an idea that the camera should pick somebody out from a crowded street and then follow him or her throughout the rest of the film. In the end we decided to locate the action in a large housing estate, with thousands of similar windows framed in the establishing shot. It's the most beautiful housing estate in Warsaw, which is why I chose it. It looks pretty awful so you can imagine what the others are like. The fact that the characters all live on one estate brings them together. Sometimes they meet, and say, 'May I borrow a cup of sugar?'

Basically, my characters behave much as in other films, except that in *Decalogue* I probably concentrated more on what's going on inside them rather than what's happening on the outside. Before, I often used to deal with the surrounding world, with what's happening all around, how external circumstances and events influence people, and how people eventually influence external events. Now, in my work, I've thrown aside this external world and, more and more frequently, deal with people who come home, lock the door on the inside and remain alone with themselves.

I think that all people – and this is irrespective of the political system – have two faces. They wear one face in the street, at work, in the cinema, in the bus or car. In the West, that's the face of someone who is energetic, the face of someone who's successful or will be successful in the near future. That's the appropriate face to wear on the outside, and the appropriate face for strangers.

I think integrity is an extremely complicated combination and we can never ultimately say 'I was honest' or 'I wasn't honest'. In all our actions and all the different situations in which we find ourselves, we find ourselves in a position from which there's really no way out – and even if there is, it's not a better way out, a good

69　*Decalogue I (Dekalog I).*

70   *Decalogue II (Dekalog II).*

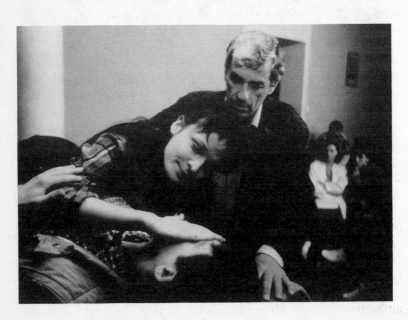

71   *Decalogue IX (Dekalog IX).*

way out, it's only relatively better than the other options, or, to put it another way, the lesser evil. This, of course, defines integrity. One would like to be ultimately honest, but one can't. With all the decisions you make every day, you can never be ultimately honest.

A lot of people who have seemingly been the cause of a great deal of evil state that they were honest or couldn't have acted any other way. This is another trap, although what they say might be true. It's definitely like that in politics, although that's no justification. If you work in politics, or in any other public sphere, you're publicly responsible. It can't be helped. You're always watched by others – if not in the newspapers then by your neighbours, family, loved ones, friends, acquaintances or even by strangers in the street. But, at the same time, there's something like a barometer in each of us. At least, I feel it very distinctly; in all the compromises I make, in all the wrong decisions I take, I have a very clear limit as to what I mustn't do, and I try not to do it. No doubt sometimes I do, but I try not to. And that has nothing to do with any description or exact definition of right and wrong. It has to do with concrete everyday decisions.

That's something we thought about a lot when we were working on *Decalogue*. What, in essence, is right and what is wrong? What is a lie and what is truth? What is honesty and what is dishonesty? And what should one's attitude to it be?

I think that an absolute point of reference does exist. Although I must say that when I think of God, it's more often the God of the Old Testament rather than the New. The God of the Old Testament is a demanding, cruel God; a God who doesn't forgive, who ruthlessly demands obedience to the principles which He has laid down. The God of the New Testament is a merciful, kind-hearted old man with a white beard, who just forgives everything. The God of the Old Testament leaves us a lot of freedom and responsibility, observes how we use it and then rewards or punishes, and there's no appeal or forgiveness. It's something which is lasting, absolute, evident and is not relative. And that's what a point of reference must be, especially for people like me, who are weak, who are looking for something, who don't know.

The concept of sin is tied up with this abstract, ultimate authority which we often call God. But I think that there's also a sense of sin against yourself which is important to me and really means the same thing. Usually, it results from weakness, from the fact that we're too weak to resist temptation; the temptation to have more money, comfort, to possess a certain woman or man, or the temptation to hold more power.

Then there's the question of whether we should live in fear of sin. That's an entirely different problem which also results from the tradition of the Catholic or Christian faith. It's a little different in Judaism; they have a different concept of sin. That's why I spoke about a God of the Old Testament and a God of the New. I think that an authority like this does exist. As somebody once said, if God didn't exist then somebody would have to invent Him. But I don't think we've got perfect justice here, on earth, and we never will have. It's justice on our own scale and our scale is minute. We're tiny and imperfect.

If something is constantly nagging you that you've done the wrong thing, that means you know you could have done the right thing. You have criteria, a hierarchy of values. And that's what I think proves that we have a sense of what is right and wrong and that we are in a position to set our own, inner compass. But often, even when we know what is honest and the right thing to do, we can't choose it. I believe we are not free. We're always fighting for some sort of freedom, and, to a certain extent, this freedom, especially external freedom, has been achieved – at least in the West, to a much greater extent than in the East. In the West, you've got the freedom to buy a watch or the pair of trousers you want. If you really need them, you buy them. You can go where you like. You've got the freedom to choose where you live. You're free to choose the conditions you live in. You can choose to live in one social circle rather than another, amongst one group of people rather than another. Whereas I believe we're just as much prisoners of our own passions, our own physiology, and certainly our own biology, as we were thousands of years ago. Prisoners of the rather complicated, and very frequently relative, division between what is better and what is a bit better and that which is a tiny bit better still, and what is a little bit worse. We're always trying to find a way out. But we're constantly imprisoned by our passions and feelings. You can't get rid of this. It makes no difference whether you've got a passport which allows you into every country or only into one and you stay there. It's a saying as old as the world – freedom lies within. It's true.

When people leave prison – I'm thinking about political im-prisonment in particular – they're helpless when faced with life and they say they were only really free in prison. They were free there because they were sentenced to live in one room or cell with one particular person, or to eat only this or that. Outside prison you've got the freedom to choose what you eat; you can go to an English, Italian, Chinese or French restaurant. You're free. Prisoners are not free to eat what they want because they only get what they're brought in a bucket. Prisoners are not free because they haven't the possibility of making moral or emotional choices, and they've got fewer choices because they don't have the day-to-day problems which fall on our shoulders every single day. They don't encounter love or can only experience longing. They don't have the possibility of satisfying their love.

Since there are far fewer choices to be made in prison, there's a much greater feeling of freedom than at the moment of leaving prison. Theoretically, when you leave, you've got the freedom of eating what you want, but in the realm of emotions, in the realm of your own passions, you're caught in a trap. People are always writing about this and I understand them very well.

The freedom we've achieved in Poland now doesn't really bring us anything, because we can't satisfy it. We can't satisfy it in the cultural sense because there isn't any money. There simply isn't any money to spare for culture. There also isn't any money for a lot of things which are more important than culture. So there is a para-dox: we used to have money but no freedom, now we've got freedom but no money. We can't express our freedom because we haven't got the means. But if that's all there was to it, of course, it would be relatively simple; some day money will somehow be organized. The problem is more serious than that. Culture, and especially film, had enormous social significance in Poland once and it was important what sort of film you made. It was the same in all the east European countries. And in a sense masses of people waited to see what film Wajda or Zanussi, for example, would make next because for a great number of years film-makers hadn't come to terms with the existing state of affairs, and they tried to do something which would express this attitude. The nation in general couldn't come to terms with the existing state of affairs either. In this sense we were in a luxurious and unique situation. We were truly important in Poland – precisely because of censorship.

We're allowed to say everything now but people have stopped caring what we're allowed to say. Censorship bound authors to the same extent as it did the public. The public knew the rules by which censorship worked and waited for a signal that these rules had been by-passed. It reacted to all these signs perfectly, read them, played with them. Censorship was an office and its workers were clerks. They had their regulations, books of injunctions and that's where they found words and situations which weren't allowed to be shown on screen. They'd cut them out. But they couldn't cut out words which hadn't been written in their regulations yet. They couldn't react to situations which their bosses hadn't described yet. We quickly learnt to find things which they didn't know yet and the public faultlessly recognized our intentions. So we communicated over the censors' heads. The public understood that when we spoke about a provincial theatre, we were speaking about Poland, and when we showed the dreams of a boy from a small town as being hard to fulfil, these dreams couldn't be fulfilled in the capital or anywhere else either. We were together, us and the public, in the aversion we had for a system which we didn't accept. Today this basic reason for being together doesn't exist anymore. We're lacking an enemy.

I have a good story about a censor. I have a friend in Kraków who's a graphic artist, a cartoonist mainly. His name is Andrzej Mleczko.[36] He's an extremely intelligent and witty man. Of course, he had constant problems with the censors. They kept bothering him. They'd take his drawings. Recently, they abolished censorship. It doesn't exist. One day, Mleczko sent for a carpenter because he had to level out his banisters. And who should come along? The censor, of course. He gets hold of the plane and works the banister with it. Mleczko approaches and says, 'I won't let that pass.' So the censor planes the banister a second day. Mleczko watches him: 'I won't let that pass.' The censor went bankrupt.

The fact that we had censorship in Poland – which even worked quite well although it wasn't as intelligent as it could have been – didn't necessarily entail tremendous restrictions of freedom since, all in all, it was easier to make films there then than it is under the economic censorship here in the West. Economic censorship means censorship imposed by people who think that they know what the audience wants. In Poland, at the moment, there's exactly the same economic censorship – audience censorship – as there is in the West, except that audience censorship in Poland is totally unprofessional. The producers or distributors are in no position to recognize the public.

When I had written all the screenplays for *Decalogue* I presented them to Television and was allocated a budget, but I realized that we were still short of money. We had two sources of finance in Poland at that time. One was Television. The other was the Ministry of Arts and Culture. So I went along to the Ministry; I took a few of the *Decalogue* screenplays with me and said, 'I'll make you two films very cheaply, on the condition that one of them will be number five' – because I really wanted to make number five – 'but you choose the other one.' So they chose number six, and gave me some money. Not much but enough. I wrote longer versions of the screenplays. Later on, while shooting, I made the two versions of both films. One for the cinema, and the other for television. Everything got mixed up later on, of course. Scenes from television went to the cinema version, from the cinema version to television. But that's a pleasant game in the cutting-room. The nicest moment.

What is the difference between films made for television and those made for cinema? First, I don't think the television viewer is less intelligent than the cinema audience. The reason why television is the way it is, isn't because the viewers are slow-witted but because editors think they are. I think that's the problem with television. This doesn't apply so much to British television which isn't as stupid as German, French or Polish television. British television is a little more predisposed to education, on the one hand, and, on the other, to presenting opinions and matters connected with culture. These things are treated far more broadly and seriously by British television, especially the BBC or Channel 4, and this is done through their precise, broad and exact documentary films and films about individuals. Whereas television in most countries – including America – is as idiotic as it is because the editors think people are idiots. I don't think people are idiots and that's why I treat both audiences equally seriously. Consequently, I don't see any great difference in the narration or style between films made for television and those made for cinema.

There is a difference in that you always have less money when making a television film, so you have less time. You have to make

TV films faster and a little less carefully. The staging has to be simpler, shots are closer rather than wider because in a wider shot you'd have to set up more scenery. That's where the principle of television close-ups came from. When I see films on television where there are very wide shots, even American large budget films, they're very watchable on the small screen. Perhaps you can't see everything in such detail but the impression is much the same. The impression is equally one of size. What doesn't pass the test on television is *Citizen Kane*, for example, which doesn't look right on television because it requires greater concentration than is possible on the small screen.

The difference between the cinema and television audience is very simple. The cinema-goer watches a film in a group, with other people. The television viewer watches alone. I've never yet seen a television viewer hold his girlfriend by the hand, but in the cinema it's the general rule. Personally, I think that television means solitude while cinema means community. In the cinema, the tension is between the screen and the whole audience and not only between the screen and you. It makes an enormous difference. That is why it's not true that the cinema is a mechanical toy.

It's a well-known theory that film has twenty-four frames to the second, and that a film is always the same; but that's not true. Even though the reel might be exactly the same, the film's entirely different when it's shown in a huge cinema, to an audience of a thousand, where a certain tension and atmosphere are created in perfect conditions, on a perfect screen, and with perfect sound. It's a completely different film when shown in a small, smelly cinema in the suburbs, to an audience of four, one of whom might be snoring. It's a different film. It's not that you experience it differently. It *is* different. In this sense, films are hand-made; even though a film can be repeated because the reels are the same, each screening is unrepeatable.

Those are the main differences between television and cinema films. But, of course, there are also characteristics specific to television films which are mainly based on the fact that television has got people used to certain things. I'm not talking about stupidity – God forbid – but it has got people used to certain things. For example, to the fact that every evening or once a week the same TV characters will pay them a visit. That's one of the conventions when you make a serial, for example, and people have grown used to it, have grown to like these visits, like their family visiting them on Sundays or having Sunday lunch with their friends. If they've got any sympathy for the characters, that is. The Americans try very hard to make their characters likeable even though you might have reservations about them.

So television films have to be narrated in a way to satisfy the viewers' needs to see their friends and acquaintances again. That's the general convention and I think that's where I went wrong in *Decalogue*. *Decalogue* was made as a number of individual films. The same characters reappear only now and again and you have to pay great attention and concentrate very hard to recognize them and notice that the films are interconnected. If you watch the films one a week, you don't really notice this. That's why wherever I had any influence on how the films would be shown on television, I always asked that they be shown at least two a week, so that the viewer would have a chance to see what brings the characters together. But that means I made an obvious mistake in not following conventions. I'd probably make the same mistake again today because I think there was some sense in the films being separate – but it was a mistake as regards the viewers' expectations.

Talking about conventions, one more thing has to be mentioned. When you go to the cinema, whatever it's like, you always concentrate because you've paid for the ticket, made a great effort to get on the bus, taken an umbrella because it's raining outside, or left the house at a certain time. So, because of the money and effort spent, you want to experience something. That's very basic. Consequently you're in a position to watch more complicated relationships between characters, more complicated plots, and so on. With television, it's different. When you're watching television, you experience everything that's going on around you: the scrambled eggs which are burning, the kettle which has boiled over, the telephone which has just started to ring, your son who isn't doing his homework and whom you have to force to his books, your daughter who doesn't want to go to bed, the thought that you've still got so much to do, and the time you have to get up in the morning. You experience all this while watching television. Consequently – and that's another mistake I made with *Decalogue* – stories on television have to be told more slowly, and the same thing has to be repeated several times, to give the viewer who's gone off to make a cup of tea or gone to the loo a chance to catch up with what's happening. If I were to make the films again today, I still probably wouldn't take this into account even though I consider it a mistake.

The best idea I had in *Decalogue* was that each of the ten films was made by a different lighting cameraman. I thought that these ten stories should be narrated in a slightly different way. It was fantastic. I gave a choice to the cameramen I'd worked with before, but for those whom I was working with for the first time, I sought out ideas, or films, which I believed would, in some way, suit and interest them and allow them to make best use of what they had: their skills, inventiveness, intelligence, and so on.

It was an amusing experience. Only one cameraman made two films; all the others were made by different lighting cameramen. The oldest cameraman must have been over sixty, and the youngest about twenty-eight – he'd just finished film school. So they came from different generations, had completely different experiences and approaches to the profession. Yet these films are, all in all, extremely similar visually, even though they are so different. In one the camera is hand-held, in another a tripod is used. One uses a moving camera while another uses a stationary one. One uses one kind of light, another uses something different. Yet despite everything, the films are similar. It seems to me that this is proof, or an indication, of the fact that there exists something like the spirit of a screenplay, and whatever resources a cameraman uses, if he's intelligent and talented, he will understand it, and this spirit will somehow get through to the film – however different the camerawork and lighting – and determine the essence of the film.

I've never given lighting cameramen as much freedom as I did in *Decalogue*. Each one could do as he pleased, albeit because my strength had run out. Besides, I counted on the competence, on the energy which results from freedom. If you impose restrictions on someone, he won't have any energy. If you give him freedom, then he'll have energy because there'll be lots of different possibilities for him and he'll try to find the best. So I gave my lighting cameramen a tremendous amount of freedom. Each one could decide how and where he put the camera, how to use it, how to operate it. Of course, I could disagree but I accepted nearly all their ideas concerning operating, structure and staging. And despite this, the films are all similar. It's interesting.

I know a lot of actors in Poland but there are a lot I don't know and I met a great many of them for the first time when making *Decalogue*. Some actors I didn't know and I might as well go on not knowing them because they're not my actors. It often happens that you meet an actor whom you think is fantastic then, when you start working, it turns out that he simply doesn't understand, work, or think on the same wavelength as you. And, consequently, your work together simply becomes an exchange of information, an exchange of requests. I ask him to play like this or like that. He plays like this or slightly differently and not much comes of it. On the other hand, I met a lot of actors whom I didn't know before and I really ought to have known; experienced actors of the older generation and young actors whom I used for the first time.

The films kept overlapping because of the actors and because of various things to do with organization and production. It was all carefully planned. People knew that if, on a particular day, we were going to be filming a corridor in a building which was going to be used in three films, then three cameramen would come along, light it and we'd do their three successive scenes. This was simply because it was easier to bring in three cameramen, and even change the lighting, rather than hire the same location three times, demolish everything three times and set it up again.

This is how we worked. The lighting cameraman would be informed ahead of time that he'd have to come on a certain day because a bit of his film was going to be shot, a bit of his scene in a given interior. So he'd come along. We often made breaks in the shoot. Why, for example, did we interrupt the filming of *Decalogue 5*? We began it, shot half, and made a break. Sławek, the cameraman, was probably busy, working on some other film. So we shot more or less half of it and then took a break of two or three months. Meanwhile we made two other *Decalogues* and then returned to number five. Of course, it's more difficult in the West because the money involved belongs to somebody in particular: the money's not nobody's, that is, it's not State money as it was in Poland. So it is harder, but I do try this stratagem. *Decalogue* was a typical example of this. I could manoeuvre all the time. If something didn't seem right in the cutting-room, I'd simply shoot another scene. Or reshoot it. I'd change it. And I'd know why I was changing it and how. It was much easier.

In fact, I just keep shooting these tests all my life. Then suddenly the tests are finished and a film's got to be cut from them. I always work like this and always have done. It's difficult for me to write a film on paper the way it will look in the end. It never ends up looking like that. It always looks a bit different.

Decalogue took a year to shoot with a break of a month, so eleven months in all. I even went to Berlin during that time because I was giving seminars there. Sometimes I'd go on a Sunday or in the evening. I'd go in the evening, for example, and come back in the morning, to shoot.

I often used to catch flu or a cold or something but I don't get ill when I'm shooting. I don't know why. Energy accumulates, from some past time in your life and that's when you use it – because you're in dire need of it. I think it's like that in general. If you really need something, really want something, then you get it. It's the same with energy and health while filming. I can't remember ever being ill while shooting. My own energy kept me going, plus something like – for example in *Decalogue* – curiosity to know what was going to happen because a new lighting cameraman was coming the following day, with different actors and so on. What's going to happen? How's it going to turn out?

I was shattered by the end, of course. But I remembered everything accurately; how many takes I had, how many retakes of a particular take in film 4 or 7 or 3 or 2 or 1, right up until the very end of the edit. I didn't have any problems there.

There's this guy who wanders around in all the films. I don't know who he is; just a guy who comes and watches. He watches us, our lives. He's not very pleased with us. He comes, watches and walks on. He doesn't appear in number 7, because I didn't film him right and had to cut him out. And he doesn't appear in film 10 because, since there are jokes about trading a kidney, I thought that maybe it's not worth showing a guy like that. But I was probably wrong. No doubt I should have shown him in that one, too.

The guy didn't appear in the screenplays initially. We had a very clever literary manager,[37] Witek Zalewski, at the time in whom I had and still have immense trust and, when we'd written the *Decalogue* screenplays, he kept saying to me, 'I feel there's something missing here, Krzysztof. There's something missing.' 'But what, Witek? What do you feel is missing?' 'I can't say, but there's something missing. Something's not there in the scripts.' And we talked, talked, talked, talked and talked and in the end he told me this anecdote about a Polish writer called Wilhelm Mach. This Mach was at some screening. And Mach says, 'I liked the film very much. I liked it and especially that scene at the cemetery.' He says, 'I really liked the guy in the black suit at the funeral.' The director says, 'I'm very sorry but there wasn't any guy in a black suit.' Mach says, 'How come? He stood on the left-hand side of the frame, in the foreground, in a black suit, white shirt and black tie. Then he walked across to the right-hand side of the frame and moved off.' The director says, 'There wasn't any guy like that.' Mach says, 'There was. I saw him. And that's what I liked most in the film.' Ten days later he was dead. So Witek Zalewski told me this anecdote, this incident, and I understood what he felt was missing. He missed this guy in a black suit whom not everyone sees and who the young director didn't know had appeared in the film. But some people saw him, this guy who looks on. He doesn't have any influence on what's happening, but he is a sort of sign or warning to those whom he watches, if they notice him. And I understood, then, that that's what Witek felt was missing in the films so I introduced the character whom some called 'the angel' and whom the taxi-drivers when they brought him to the set called 'the devil'. But in the screenplays he was always described as 'young man'.

The Polish ratings for *Decalogue* were good, or rather, the so-called ratings. They're counted in percentages by a special office. It started with 52 per cent for film 1 and went up to 64 per cent for film 10. That means about 15 million viewers, which is a lot. The critics weren't bad this time. They had a few digs at me but rarely below the belt.

A Short Film about Killing
KRÓTKI FILM O ZABIJANIU (1988)

This is a story about a young boy who kills a taxi-driver and then the law kills the boy. In fact there's not much more you can say about the film's narrative since we don't know the reason why the boy kills the taxi-driver. We know the legal reasons why society kills the boy. But we don't know the real human reasons, nor will we ever know them.

I think I wanted to make this film precisely because all this takes place in my name, because I'm a member of this society, I'm a citizen of this country, Poland, and if someone, in this country, puts a noose around someone else's neck and kicks the stool from under his feet, he's doing it in my name. And I don't wish it. I don't want them to do it. I think this film isn't really about capital punishment but about killing in general. It's wrong no matter why you kill, no matter whom you kill and no matter who does the killing. I think that's the second reason why I wanted to make this film. The third reason is that I wanted to describe the Polish world, a world which is quite terrible and dull, a world where people don't have any pity for each other, a world where they hate each other, a world where they not only don't help but get in each other's way. A world where they repel each other. A world of people living alone.

People are very lonely in general, I think, regardless of where they live. I often see this because I work abroad. I'm in touch with young people in various countries; Germany, Switzerland, Finland and many others. I see that what really troubles people most and what they deceive themselves about most – because they won't admit to it – is loneliness. It's the fact that they haven't got anybody to talk to about really important matters. It's the fact that through the increasing ease of everyday life what used to be so important has, as it were, disappeared; conversation, letter-writing, true contact with another person. Everything has become far more superficial. Instead of writing a letter, we phone. Instead of travelling, which used to be quite romantic and quite an adventure, we arrive at an airport, buy a ticket, fly and alight at another airport which is much the same.

I get the impression, more and more, that, although people are lonely, many of them, paradoxically, want to get rich to allow themselves the luxury of being alone, of distancing themselves from others. To allow themselves to live in a house away from anybody else, to be able to go to a restaurant which is so large that nobody sits on top of them or listens to their conversation. On the one hand, people are terribly afraid of loneliness. When I ask: 'What are you really afraid of?', I often hear the reply, 'I'm afraid of being alone.' Of course, there are people who answer that they're afraid of death but in the majority of cases, now, people say, 'I'm afraid of loneliness. I'm afraid of being alone.' And yet, at the same time, there's this urge to be independent. Each of the main characters in *A*

Short Film about Killing lives alone and is, in fact, incapable of doing much. He can't decide about anything other than his own fate.

I don't know what the Poles want. I know what they're afraid of. They're afraid of tomorrow because they don't know what might happen tomorrow. What would happen if somebody were to murder your prime minister tomorrow? What would happen in England? Let's say it was the IRA even. Let's say they succeeded in killing him. Would anything change in your lives? You'd take the same bus or the same car to go to the same office in the morning. Your colleagues and boss would be waiting there. Everything would be the same. You'd probably go to the same restaurant for lunch. Whereas, in Poland, if the prime minister were killed, everything would change the very same day. I don't know whether I'd still have a production house. I don't know whether the telephones would be working. I don't know if my money would be worth anything – it may be worth nothing, since they would have changed it overnight. And so anything can happen in Poland and everybody's terribly afraid that something bad will happen. So they make the most of life today. And that's very dangerous.

A Short Film about Killing takes place in Warsaw. The city and its surroundings are shown in a specific way. The lighting cameraman on this film, Sławek Idziak, used filters which he'd made specially. Green filters so that the colour in the film is specifically greenish. Green is supposed to be the colour of spring, the colour of hope, but if you put a green filter on the camera, the world becomes much crueller, duller and emptier. Everything was shot with filters; it was the cameraman's idea. He made 600 filters because he had to have a different filter for close-ups, and for medium close shots, a different filter if there are two heads, a different filter if there's sky and a different filter for interiors. Usually there were three filters in the camera. They once fell out. What an effect! There's a scene in the film where the boy beats the taxi-driver over the head with a stick and the taxi-driver's false teeth fall out. Very cheerful. Anyway, we had to film these false teeth. So the cameraman leaned over with the camera. I threw those damn teeth into the mud fifteen times. I kept missing. Finally, I got it right and at that very moment the filters fell out. First we saw it on the screen, then we saw what we were doing. There was a perfectly normal set of false teeth lying in normal mud once the filters fell out. But before, you couldn't see anything. You couldn't see either the teeth or the mud. I realized then that we were doing something horrific. I think that the cameraman's style, the style of camerawork in this film, is very apt for the subject. That city's empty; that city's dirty; that city's sad. And the people are the same.

These are technical methods which demand precision when making copies. If you spoil the copying process then the effect of these filters suddenly appears like dirt. If you watch the cinema version of *A Short Film about Killing* on television, for example, you'll see that it looks as if there's a technical fault. If you record it and watch it on video, you'll see the filters start to form circles. Why? Because contrast increases on television, so that what is light becomes slightly lighter and what is dark becomes slightly darker. Instead of being graduated these filters look as if a window had been cut out in them, which gives an awful effect, of course. Whereas film 5 of the *Decalogue* (*A Short Film about Killing*) – the television version of the film – was, of course, made on a much softer internegative and the copy was much softer. Consequently, the contrast wasn't so great, so that when seen on television with increased contrast, it looked more or less like the film copy on screen.

There are two murder scenes in the film. The boy murders the taxi-driver for approximately seven minutes and then for five minutes the law murders the boy. An American, an expert on horror films, told me that I had beaten the record for the longest murder scene in the history of cinema. It's thirteen or sixteen seconds longer than the previous one, which had been made by the Americans in 1934.

There was a problem in that we couldn't get a drop of blood from under the blanket which covered the taxi-driver's head. We kept on having problems with some pipes through which the blood was supposed to run but didn't. Since the crew didn't much like the actor who was playing the taxi-driver, they kept on persuading me to shove him under that blanket. Then blood was sure to run. But we didn't go that far.

The execution scene was really difficult since it was, in fact, shot in one take. This is what happened. I wrote the scene, built the prison interior in a studio, and hired the actors. They learnt what they had to say and do. The cameraman lit the scene. In other words, everything was ready and I asked them to have a rehearsal.

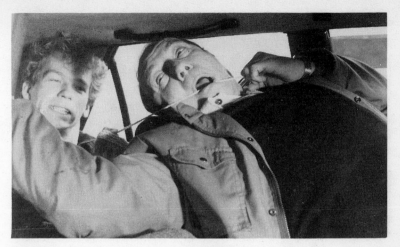

72–3 Mirosław Baca in *A Short Film about Killing* (*Krótki Film o Zabijaniu*).

74–5   Mirosław Baca in *A Short Film about Killing* (*Krótki Film o Zabijaniu*).

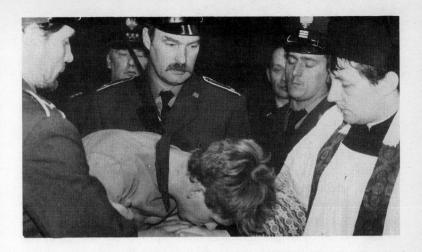

76 Mirosław Baca in *A Short Film about Killing* (*Krótki Film o Zabijaniu*).

And as they ran through the rehearsal I noticed that everybody was growing weak at the knees, including me. It was simply unbearable. Everything had been constructed by us but the electricians' legs gave way under them, the stuntmen's, the cameraman's and mine. Everybody's. This was about eleven in the morning. I had to stop filming. We shot it the following day. The sight of the execution is simply unbearable, even if it's only pretence.

The film was an indictment of violence. Inflicting death is probably the highest form of violence imaginable; capital punishment is an infliction of death. In this way, we link violence and capital punishment and the film is against capital punishment as a form of violence.

The truth is that the film was released quite by chance at the moment when debates about capital punishment were taking place. It was impossible to foresee this when we were writing the screenplay. You weren't even allowed to talk about the subject at the time. Then this debate arose and the film, of course, found its place. And the fact is that the new government of 1989 suspended executions for five years.

A Short Film about Love
KRÓTKI FILM O MIŁOŚCI (1989)

I probably changed A Short Film about Love in the cutting-room more than any other film I've ever made. We shot an enormous amount of material with Witek Adamek, the lighting cameraman – all sorts of scenes depicting so-called ordinary life – and this outside world forcing its way on to the screen really was a serious fault. Then, when I trimmed the film of all this surrounding reality, I liked it much more.

The film is very short. I think it's coherent. What I find interesting in it is the perspective. We're always looking at the world through the eyes of the person who is loving and not through the eyes of the person who is loved. First of all, we look at it from the point of view of the boy, Tomek, who's in love with the woman, Magda, but we don't know anything about her. We only see her as he sees her. There's a moment when we see them together, then the perspective changes completely. When Magda

77   Grażyna Szapołowska in *A Short Film about Love* (*Krótki Film o Miłości*).

78   Olaf Lubaszenko in *A Short Film about Love*.

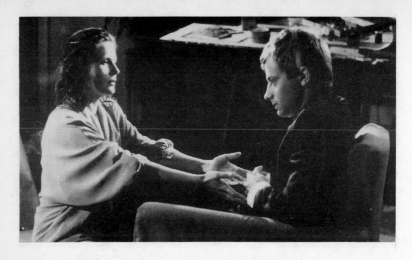

79　G. Szapołowska and O. Lubaszenko in *A Short Film about Love*.

starts feeling something for him – at the beginning it's pity, later, perhaps, pangs of conscience and then maybe some sort of affection too – we start to look at the world through her eyes. And we don't see him anymore. He disappears because he slashes his wrists and is taken to hospital. We're never in the hospital with him. We see everything only from her point of view.

This change of perspective two thirds of the way through the film – because it takes place more or less at the second turning point – is an interesting structural intervention. We watch from the point of view of the person who is loving and not the person who is loved. The loved one is merely in shreds, an object. This love is difficult both for the boy and also, later on, for the woman. So we're always looking at this love through the eyes of the person who is suffering because of this love. And this love is always tied up with some sort of suffering, some sort of impossibility. Tomek spies on Magda. Then Magda tries to find Tomek. This is because of guilt but also, no doubt, because she's reminded of the fact that she was like him at some stage, too. When she was his age, or maybe younger, she was like him. She was pure and believed that love existed. Then she probably got burnt. She touched something hot which hurt her very badly and decided never to love again because she realized that the price was too high. Then this surfaced. Whether this construction works or not is a different matter altogether.

The main problem was with the actress, with the leading role. I decided only at the last moment that it ought to be Szapołowska and nobody else. In fact we offered her the role only three days before the shoot. Szapołowska and I weren't on wonderful terms after No End so I wasn't sure whether I wanted to work with her. But when I looked through all the screen tests which we'd shot, at all the actresses available in Poland at that time, I realized that Szapołowska would be the best. She was by the sea at the time so I sent an assistant there with the script. He brought it to her on the beach, she read it and accepted.

When we knew she was going to play the main role, it became obvious that Lubaszenko should play the boy. He's the son of Edward Lubaszenko, a very good actor from Kraków. He seemed very interesting to me. His voice was decidedly too low for his age – he was nineteen and spoke in a bass or baritone – but it turned out not to be a problem. They definitely made a good pair.

Then when we were starting to shoot, Szapołowska told me she had reservations concerning the script. She thought that when people went to the cinema nowadays they wanted to see a story. She had an intuition that before long people would need, or already needed, a story. Not necessarily a happy ending, but a story. She thought that we ought to introduce some sort of convention which would make it clear that this wasn't merely harsh documentary truth about life but that this was also, as happens in stories, truth, or a concept, contained within a convention. A story is always associated with some very well-known convention. It always begins with 'a long time ago, there was a king', and so on and so on.

Certain things, solutions in certain films, aren't necessarily thought of by an actor or cameraman but evolve from the fact that an actor or cameraman throw doubt on something or put across an idea which later on is either used quite literally – and that happens very often – or recreated in some way. I thought that Szapołowska had good intuition. She's a woman and, like all women, has much better intuition than we do. So I believed in it and because of this Krzysztof Piesiewicz and I thought up this story-like ending for the cinema version of *Decalogue 6* which seemed to me to have a certain charm. I also liked it because it reminded me a bit of the ending of *Camera Buff*, where Jurek Stuhr turns the camera on himself and starts to run the whole film from the beginning, as it were. Possibilities are open, in the cinema version. The ending is such that everything is still possible, although we already know that nothing is possible. You could say that it's a far more optimistic ending.

The television ending is very dry, laconic and also very simple. Magda goes to the post office and Tomek tells her: I don't spy on you any more. And we know that he really won't spy on her ever again and maybe he won't spy on anybody. And when somebody spies on him, he'll hurt her the same way as Magda hurt him. The television ending is far closer to the view I have of how things really are in life.

While making this film I had an acute sense of the absurdity of my profession. Basically, the film is about a guy who lives in one flat in a block of flats and a woman who lives in the block opposite. Reading the script or looking at it from the audience's point of view, how were we to make the film? We'd rent two flats

– one his, the other hers – and a bit of staircase. To all intents and purposes, a very cheap film. Whereas, in actual fact, in order to shoot this film we used seventeen different interiors and these seventeen interiors give the impression that there are two flats opposite each other. Once or twice, Tomek or Magda goes out on to the street or to the post office and that's all. There are practically no other scenes.

Well, one of those seventeen interiors, namely Magda's flat, was in one of those hideous prefabricated houses which you can see 20 or 30 kilometres from Warsaw. The worst possible kind you can imagine. It's as if a chunk of some huge block had been taken and put somewhere in a field. That's the sort of villa that we found had very similar windows to the windows on the estate where we shot all our locations. And that's where we set up Magda's flat. So Magda's flat wasn't in a block but was some 30 kilometres from Warsaw in a tiny one-storeyed villa.

In order to shoot this flat from Tomek's point of view – we watch it from two perspectives, first his, then hers – we had to build a tower because the idea was that the boy lives one or two floors higher than Magda. And because Magda's flat was on the ground floor, we had to build a tower so that the difference in height that we see on location appeared to be from Tomek's perspective – when he looks down a little through the telescope, we also look down a little when we see Magda's flat. And that two-storeyed tower had to be far enough away from the little house to give the impression that, shooting with a long lens – we used a 300 and sometimes even a 500mm lens – we were looking through a telescope.

We'd arrive there at about ten in the evening because we needed silence and this was after all, a night shoot, and we'd climb up that tower. The whole crew went to neighbouring houses which the production had rented and either slept or watched pornographic videos while Witek Adamek and I were stuck up there on that tower like a couple of morons for six or eight hours until dawn. And dawn didn't break until about seven. It was bloody cold, below freezing. And because the distance between the tower and the house was about 60 or 70 metres, there was no other way of communicating with Szapołowska except through a microphone. I had the microphone while Szapołowska had a speaker set up in the house.

So there we were hanging around at night for a week in the bitter cold, alone – there was the cameraman's assistant, of course, and one of my assistants, too – in this absurd situation, in some dark suburban estate where there was one blazing window and two idiots on some two-storeyed tower one of whom was repeating into a microphone: 'Lift that leg higher! Lower your leg! Now go up to the table! Go on, pick those cards up!' I kept giving orders through the microphone but only during rehearsals, not when the camera was running because we shot in sync.

When I left that place for a while to get something to eat or whatever, the whole absurdity of the situation dawned on me. A small villa pretending to be a huge skyscraper, ablaze with light – because we were using long lenses and they have low apertures and need a lot of light – the only spot alight while everything else was in darkness; nobody around; night; and some absurd two-storeyed tower. I can imagine myself standing up there shouting into a microphone – 'Lift that leg higher!' Of course, the microphone didn't work properly and I had to shout in order to make myself heard through the speaker in the house.

All through that week I had a really acute sense of idiocy, of the complete absurdity of my profession.

Pure Emotions
THE DOUBLE LIFE OF VÉRONIQUE
(LA DOUBLE VIE DE VÉRONIQUE)
(PODWÓJNE ŻYCIE WERONIKI) (1991)

I often have the title of a film first of all and know exactly that that's what the film's going to be called, and it doesn't change. Like *The Calm* or *Blind Chance*, for example. Or *Camera Buff*. That's what the films were called right from the beginning. Those were the titles when the screenplays were written.

With this film we kept thinking about the title right from the moment we started working on the screenplay. It was much easier in Poland if you didn't know at first what the title would be. Publicity around a film wasn't all that important so I'd find a title once the film was edited. At least, by that time, I'd know what it was about, which made things easier. Here, a title's got to be found as soon as possible and the producer was quite rightly cross with me for not being able to decide. The screenplay was called 'Choir Girl' ('Chórzystka') – not the greatest of titles, let's say, although it accurately describes the main character's profession – she is a choir girl. However, it turned out that this had bad connotations in France. Somebody, having read the title, said, 'Oh God, another Catholic film from Poland.'

The main character's called Weronika/Véronique and, right from the beginning, her name seemed to me to be a good title. But it was impossible. The ending of the name in French – 'nique' – describes, not very elegantly, an activity which occurs every now and then between a man and a woman. So, again, we abandoned it. The producer's a jazz fan, so he kept finding poetic titles of jazz numbers – 'Unfinished Girl', 'The lonely together' – which seemed somewhat pretentious to me, so we abandoned them. I had about fifty titles in my note-book and I didn't like any of them. The producer was pressing me. Everybody was involved in looking for a title. My wife and daughter suggested all sorts of words. The assistants read Shakespeare's sonnets because they thought that the Bard had a pretty good brain. Travelling across the city, reading posters, announcements and newspapers, I caught myself constantly looking for an intelligent title. I also announced a competition among people working with me, with a good money prize. In the end, we decided on *The Double Life of Véronique*. It doesn't sound bad in Polish, French or English, is quite commercial before you see the film and renders its contents quite accurately after you've seen it. It has one fault – neither I nor the producer are really satisfied with it.

The film is about sensibility, presentiments and relationships which are difficult to name, which are irrational. Showing this on film is difficult: if I show too much the mystery disappears; I can't show too little because then nobody will understand anything. My search for the right balance between the obvious and the mysterious is the reason for all the various versions made in the cutting room.

Véronique is a typical example of a film about a woman because women feel things more acutely, have more presentiments, greater sensitivity, greater intuition and attribute more importance to all these things. *Véronique* couldn't have been made about a man. But I don't divide people up like that – into men and women. They used to criticize me terribly in Poland saying I portrayed women as one-dimensional characters, that I didn't understand the essence of womanhood. It's true that in my first films the women were never the main characters. There weren't really any women in *Personnel*, there weren't any in *The Calm*, *Camera Buff*, or *The Scar*. And if there were, they were very badly drawn. The women in *Blind Chance* were really only life-companions for the main characters. Maybe that's why I thought to myself, through ambition, 'Right, I'll make a film about a woman, from a woman's point of view, as it were, from the point of view of her sensitivity, her world.' My first film about a woman was *No End*. Then in *Decalogue* I think I distributed it evenly. There are films about men and films about women. There are films about boys and films about girls. There are films about old men. In the triptych of films, *Three Colours*, it's also evenly distributed. The first film is about a woman, the second about a man, and the third about a man and a woman.

I didn't have an actress for *The Double Life of Véronique*. It was the first film I was making in the West so I didn't have any idea about how the casting system worked. It was pretty difficult. But I imagined that anybody could play the girl. And I thought of an American whom I still like immensely called Andie MacDowell. I wanted to cast her in this. We met. She also wanted to play in it. The contract, in fact, was ready to be signed, but my producer, who hadn't had any experience, reckoned that if the contract was ready, then it could simply wait and we'd be able to sign it later. But that's not the way things turned out because, being a European film, the contract was low budget. It was too low for the Americans. Yet in spite of this, the agent had agreed. My producer neglected to sign the contract. I was furious with him at the time, of course, because I believed that if a contract had been drawn up where he'd managed to negotiate half the money the actress's agent had originally demanded, then he ought to fly out immediately that day and sign it. He thought, we're all in the same trade, after all, so they're bound to keep their verbal agreement; whereas nobody stuck to any verbal agreement and Andie was offered a film from a big studio. She immediately accepted, or her agent immediately accepted because it was an American film and she's American; it's her world, her kind of money, her life, and it seemed obvious to me that she should accept. The producer wrung his hands and cried, because he's of Italian descent and is, therefore, allowed to cry. But, on the whole, I was pleased that things turned out the way they did. I was pleased because I'd realized, by that time, that I shouldn't have an American play a French role. I don't think it would have been right. I think the French would have been furious and quite rightly so. They'd say, 'What? Don't we have any French actresses that an American has to play a Frenchwoman? What's all this about? Have we got a desert in this country?' They've got a very strong sense of nationality, like the English, in fact. In this respect the nations aren't any different; each regards the other as a bunch of idiots, more or less to the same degree. Then I just started looking for an actress, in the usual way, with screen tests and so on.

I decided on the leading role. It would be Irène Jacob; she was twenty-four but looked even younger. She's not tall and is slim. She was born and brought up in Switzerland, which I like, so that was a good sign for me. I asked experts what her French was like. 'If she plays a girl from the provinces, she'll be all right,' the experts said. She had played in small, short films; films made for a pittance, on a grant or something. She had also played a minor role in a very beautiful film, which I still love, *Au revoir, les enfants* by Louis Malle – that was the role I remembered her from. That's why I invited her for a screen test.

Andie MacDowell was thirty when we started *Véronique* and Irène Jacob was twenty-four. I was afraid she'd be too young, but then it turned out she wasn't. I always thought this should be a young woman while Irène is still a girl really – at least, in this film she's a girl. Later, when it all started to fall into place, I realized that it's a film about a girl and not a young woman.

The male lead in *The Double Life of Véronique* was to be played by the Italian director Nanni Moretti. I like him and his films very much. He's masculine yet very delicate. He's not an actor and only plays leading roles in his own films. But here, strangely enough, he agreed very willingly. I met him long before shooting started and I think we had a good meeting. We arranged the dates and the kind of jacket he was to wear in the film, which, incidentally, was his own jacket. We talked about more important things, too. But then I got bad news from Paris. Nanni couldn't play. He was ill. He'd be replaced by Philip Volter, a French actor whom I liked in Gérard Corbiau's *The Music Teacher* (*Le Maître de Musique*). It was very good of him, considering that I wanted Moretti.

Then I had talks with more actors. I didn't know the market. We discussed life, and sometimes they read fragments from the roles. Production had put me in an office, behind a desk. I didn't feel right behind a desk, but where else was I to sit? I couldn't work in a café, it was too noisy. I tried to get rid of the desk but then I didn't have anywhere to put my papers, notes, script. So I stayed in this stupid place and the actors who arrived no doubt felt they'd come for an exam. So at each talk, I had to get rid of this barrier first. If I asked them what they had dreamt of that night, I also told them my own dreams. I really wanted to know them and not merely to find out what they looked like and what their technique was. So the conversations often moved into unexpected and interesting territory. A thirty-year-old actress told me that when she was sad she'd go out into the street to be with people. I'd heard stories like this several times in France already. They sounded like literary fiction to me. So I asked for details. Why did she go out? What could possibly happen to a sad girl in the street? A concrete example. She remembered an event from six years previously. She was going through some breakdown and went out. She caught sight of the famous French mime artist, Marcel Marceau, in the street. He was now an old man. She walked past, turned to give him another glance. He also turned and suddenly smiled at her. He stood there for a few seconds, smiling and then walked on. 'He saved me then,' the actress said, and here literary fiction ended because she was completely serious and I believed her. We pondered for a while whether Marcel Marceau really lived only to save the young French actress. Maybe everything he'd done, all his performances and the emotions which he'd stirred in people through them, were nothing compared to this fact. 'Did he know how important he was for you?' I asked. 'No,' the actress answered. 'I never saw him again.'

I was looking for an actor who was under thirty. One came along – very tall, over six foot, handsome. I explained that the role was a teacher. He nodded, fine, why not? We read an excerpt from the text; he was obviously good. He asked if by any chance we were talking about a PE teacher. I confirmed this. He nodded again. I added that it was a PE teacher from a provincial town, that we were going to shoot in Clermont Ferrand. This time he smiled. I asked him what was so amusing. 'Because I was a PE teacher in a school in Clermont Ferrand for three years,' he answered. Immediately after him, I met an excellent, old actor. I knew him from Bertrand Tavernier's beautiful film *A Sunday in the Country (Un Dimanche à la campagne)*. I wanted him to play a music teacher, so I asked him whether he'd had anything to do with music, whether he played the piano, whether he read music. 'Yes,' he answered calmly. 'I'm a conductor by profession and I was the director of the Opéra in Marseilles for ten years.' With such coincidences, I had the impression that the film must work. I wondered whether this would prove true this time.

In the evening, on television, I saw my PE teacher from Clermont Ferrand. He was persuading me of the merits of a new deodorant. I thought, with regret, that he was too tall for little Irène. I wouldn't be able to use him.

When we were looking for a profession for our heroine, a profession, passion or whatever – a world for her – we remembered *Decalogue 9* and the girl who appeared on screen for half a minute or a minute. It's a shame she was only there for such a short time because it was a fine role, a fine character in general. But there wasn't any reason for her to appear any longer because the film was about something else. So she only appeared as a sort of window, as a contingency for the main character. But since we'd already invented the character, she already existed and it was easy to transfer her desire to do something, her desire to sing. She's conditioned by her illness because sickness sets limitations on her and she can't do what she really wants, although hypothetically she can because she sings beautifully. So we introduced this into *Véronique* as the heroine's profession, as her passion.

Véronique is a film about music, too, in principle. Or about singing, let's say. Everything was very carefully written down in the screenplay. Where the music would go, what the music would be like, what the concert would be like, the nature of it and so on. All this was carefully described but the fact that it was described didn't really change anything because a composer has to come along, in the end, and make something of what's been written in a literary language. How can you describe music? That it's beautiful, for example, sublime? That it's memorable? That it's mysterious? You can write all this down but the composer's got to come along and find the notes. Then the musicians have to come along and play these notes. And all this, in the end, has to

80 With Zbigniew Preisner in Paris.

remind you of what was written down in literary language. And Zbigniew Preisner simply did it wonderfully.

Preisner is an exceptional composer in that he's interested in working on a film right from the beginning and not just seeing the finished version and then thinking about how to illustrate it with music. That's the rule, right? You show the composer your film and then he fills the gaps with music. But he can have a different approach. He can think about the music right from the start, about its dramatic function, about the way it should say something that's not there in the picture. You can describe something which perhaps isn't there on the actual screen but which, together with the music, starts to exist. It's interesting – drawing out something which doesn't exist in the picture alone or in the music alone. Combining the two, a certain meaning, a certain value, something which also determines a certain atmosphere, suddenly begins to exist. The Americans shove music in from beginning to end.

I always dreamt of making a film where a symphony orchestra would play. The first time I managed it was with *Blind Chance*. I hired Wojciech Kilar. Before that, I usually used ready-made music. The music in *From a Night Porter's Point of View* was from Zanussi's film *Illumination* (*Illuminacja*). Very beautiful. But the music had already been written and I simply took it and used it to illustrate my film. So, the first time I managed to get an orchestra together was for *Blind Chance*. Then the next film I made was with Preisner. That was *No End*, and since then we've always worked together. We have just made *Three Colours* together. The first of these three films, *Blue* (*Niebieski*), is exceptionally musical, even more so than *Véronique*.

We used some of Dante's poetry as lyrics to the music in *The Double Life of Véronique*. That wasn't my idea; it was Preisner's idea. The words have nothing to do with the subject. They're sung in old Italian and even the Italians probably can't understand them. But it was important for Preisner to know what the music he was writing was about, what the words really meant, because he had a translation. And what those words meant, what the text was about, probably inspired him to write the music. We thought a lot about the music. For Preisner, instrumentation is just as important as the melody. But the sound of old Italian is also beautiful. The French bought 50,000 copies of the disc.

The boyfriend Alexandre's profession came about by pure chance because we had no idea what profession to give him. But one of us, I can't remember whether it was Krzysztof Piesiewicz or myself, had seen a fragment of a puppet show on television which was fascinating. It was only about thirty seconds long, maybe a minute. I'd come into some room or other, or he'd come into a room, and saw a fragment of this show, maybe two or three years before writing *Véronique*, and forgotten about it but the moment we needed it, the incident came back to us. We started to figure out what show it was, how come it had been on Polish television. And it turned out that Jim Henson who'd invented the Muppets had made a television series about puppeteers who create their own puppet theatres, and one of the people whom he interviewed and of whose performance he'd shown some fragments was Bruce Schwartz. I asked production to find all the cassettes for me. I went through them and the best was Bruce Schwartz.

We phoned Bruce Schwartz and it turned out that he wasn't working with puppets any more because he couldn't make a living out of them. He was forty-seven. What has this moronic world we live in come to? A man who's the best in the world in his profession can't make a living out of it, because this profession only consists of moving puppets. He had to give it up and now hangs paintings. But when I told him all this he said, all right, he'd read the script and if he considered it something worth returning to the profession for, he'd come back. We sent him the script, he read it and agreed.

We'd written that there'd be a puppet show, a ballerina breaks her leg, something like that. And what happened? Bruce Schwartz already had a puppet ballerina. He makes the puppets himself. He had all the puppets we needed. He suggested a story with a butterfly in it, because he had a puppet butterfly.

Schwartz came and joined us. He made one more puppet of Irène Jacob, of course, because we needed that for the last scene; that is, he made two puppets of her. Production have kept one of them because the contract stipulated that Schwartz would take one and production would keep the other. Then he came and joined us at the shoot. Well, all he had to do was pull those dolls out and we immediately realized what had already been so obvious when we'd seen that video.

He animated those dolls and immediately, within the space of a second, a whole new world appeared. He's exceptional in that unlike most puppeters, who usually hide their hands in gloves, or use strings, sticks or whatever, he does the opposite; he shows you his hands. And, after a second or two, you forget that those hands exist, because the doll lives its own life, even though you can see his enormous paws all the time. Yet you don't notice them; you only see the dancing, the puppet dancing beautifully. That was something which I thought was absolutely necessary. That Alexandre's hands should be there, too, the hands of someone who's manipulating something.

It was extremely moving. We shot this sequence in Clermont Ferrand, in a school, and the whole point of the scene was that this was simply a show hired by the school from a travelling puppeteer who moves from town to town with his little theatre. The whole school comes to the show. 'It's a problem,' said Schwartz, 'because I've never performed for children in my life. I've always done shows for adults. I'm terribly nervous and apprehensive.' He's an exceptionally sensitive and delicate man, this Bruce Schwartz. He'd always performed to tiny audiences of thirty or forty people. We brought in about 200 children, and the whole event took place in an enormous school sports hall. He was convinced that nothing would come of it. Well, of course, it turned out that the children understood him a hundred times better than the adults.

We shot the show several times because first we had to film the audience, then the stage, then the stage a little closer, then the details, then close-ups of the audience and so on. So it all lasted quite a long time. We did the first show as if with a documentary camera, concentrating on the children's reactions, so the camera was only on the children. We tried to pick faces which expressed something. There were some beautiful reactions. Beautiful. I had to cut them out later on because the scene couldn't take it, couldn't be that long. Wonderful material. Very beautiful faces and wonderful reactions. When we finished shooting that there was a break. The children immediately surrounded him and I saw a happy man. At that moment, Bruce Schwartz was really absolutely happy. He'd come back to his profession after many years, suffering enormous stage-fright and afraid that children wouldn't understand him at all, that children weren't interested in this sort of thing any more, that they were only interested in computers and Barbie dolls, and suddenly it turned out that this romantic, delicate story, about a certain tragic ballerina, had moved the children immensely. Some of them started to cry. For half an hour those children asked Schwartz all sorts of questions – technical questions, artistic questions. They also told him what they'd understood of the story because the story doesn't use words. The performance was much longer than it appears on screen and lasted about ten minutes. (There are only three minutes on screen.) They understood absolutely everything. Everything he'd wanted them to and even more. Suddenly I saw a truly happy man.

They're very gratifying, moments like these. The man was meant to come, animate his puppets and leave. But that's not the point. The point is that he came and suddenly rediscovered a past, a joy or happiness which he'd once had in the past and which he'd lost. He thought it would never come back, but with our film, it returned for a while. That's terribly important.

Theoretically, you'd still experience the scene in the same way if I'd shot it without the children, but in actual fact it's not true. All the small details, maybe the whole atmosphere, the feeling of the scene in general hangs on things such as the simple fact that Bruce Schwartz was happy that day because his audience had understood him.

I imagine Véronique doesn't spend her life with Alexandre. At the end, you see her crying. She's crying when he suddenly reads her his book and the way she looks at him isn't in the least bit loving, because, in effect, he's used her life. He's used what he knows about her for his own purposes. I think she's much wiser at the end of the film than at the beginning. Alexandre's made her aware that something else exists, that the other Weronika did exist. He's the one who found the photograph. Véronique didn't even notice it among the dozens of photographs she had. He's the one who noticed it, and perhaps he understood what she couldn't understand herself. He understood, then used it. And the moment he used it, she understood that he probably wasn't the man for whom she was waiting so desperately, because the moment this came out into the open, something she possessed, something which was so terribly intimate as long as it wasn't disclosed, was automatically, or almost automatically, used. And when it was used, it stopped being hers; and when it stopped being hers, it was no longer mysterious. It was no longer personal. It had become a public secret.

81 Irène Jacob in *The Double Life of Véronique* (*La Double Vie de Véronique. Podwojne Życie Weroniki*).

82 Philippe Volter in *The Double Life of Véronique.*

83, 84   I. Jacob in *The Double Life of Véronique*.

Of course, we shot a whole lot of scenes showing that she has a heart condition, but I thought that these were, more or less, in proportion, that this was the right number of allusions. We didn't need any more. We know Véronique's got a heart condition and the shoelace alludes to this. The point is that when your heart stops, the line on the ECG monitor goes straight. And at one moment Véronique pulls the shoelace straight and suddenly she realizes what it means. She lets it go. I think that was Sławek's idea. So Irène got the idea, for example, that, as the Polish Weronika she'd keep on having problems with her shoelaces. And she did. Later on, I cut out those incidents because it all became too long. But it was an excellent idea. Those are exactly the sort of things which get the imagination working and it doesn't matter whether they appear on screen later or not. They simply show that we're all thinking together. And Irène thought up this idea of constantly having problems with her shoelaces. The first thing she does when she has a heart attack is to untie her shoelace, not clutch at her heart. When she falls into a puddle of water when she's running, her shoelaces immediately come undone.

Véronique's constantly faced with the choice of whether or not to take the same road as the Polish Weronika, whether to give in to the artistic instinct and the tension instrinsic in art or to give in to love and all that it involves. That, basically, is her choice.

The Polish part of the film is livelier because the heroine is livelier. There's a different style of narration in general. In the Polish part, the narrative goes from episode to episode. A year or year and a half of the heroine's life is told very clearly in short signals over half an hour, or twenty-seven minutes to be exact, and then there's the turning point. That's the way it should be in a film of this length: one hour thirty-five minutes in all. So with the help of these twenty-seven minutes, I describe quite a large chunk of the Polish Weronika's life, omitting everything else. I describe only those umpteen essential scenes which lead to her death, and nothing else.

The Polish part of *Véronique* is narrated synthetically, if you like. It's the synthesis of a certain period of time. The French *Véronique* is narrated differently. First, she's far more focused in on herself, for several reasons. One of the reasons probably is that the other Weronika is dead and the French Véronique has sensed something to do with her death, something unnerving, which tells her to focus in on herself. Second, the whole French part is narrated analytically, conversely to the Polish part which is a synthesis. It's an analysis of Véronique's state of mind, and it can't be narrated in individual groupings, or sequences of scenes. It's narrated in long scenes. A glimpse of a passage, a corridor, someone running, ambience and there's another long scene.

That's why, among other things, I had to look for uniformity in the visual image, so that, in spite of everything, these two entirely different styles would merge. The French part is, I believe, too long by about five or six minutes. Unfortunately I didn't have time to cut it down. There are flaws in the script, too, which were bound to emerge in the finished film – especially in the French part. There are a lot of mistakes like that. For example, it's an obvious mistake to have introduced one particular, very short, secondary plot, which I had to leave in the film. It's short in the film but it was long in the script and I shot a lot of scenes for it. It's the plot about Véronique's friend, a very broad plot in the script. It seemed quite well constructed and we thought it would be a driving force for about one third of the film's action. Then it turned out that it wasn't a good driving force after all, and that it should be cut out. I threw it out of the film completely but then it turned out that the heroine no longer had her feet planted on the ground, she was always somewhere a few inches up in the air. Only the soul existed for her, only premonitions, only a certain magic. I simply had to reinsert that divorce plot so as to pull Véronique down to earth, to have her agree, for example, to appear in court, bear false witness against someone and in this way become a normal human being again. It fulfilled its purpose. Nevertheless, it's a completely artificial thread in the film. But at least for a moment you feel that Véronique could be your friend, she could be your neighbour; she isn't somebody whose head is forever up in the clouds.

We used one fairly basic filter in *Véronique* – a golden-yellow one. Thanks to it the world of *Véronique* is complete. It's whole. You can recognize it. Filters give uniformity, and that's very important. The fact that Sławek used filters for exteriors in *Véronique* isn't all that important, but it is extremely important in *A Short Film about Killing* where because of the filters, because of that different, very cold colour, the world becomes far crueller than it really is, and Warsaw even more disgusting. The same principle applies to *Véronique* but with the opposite effect. Here the world appears far more beautiful than it really is. Most people think that the world in *Véronique* is portrayed with warmth; this warmth comes from the actress, of course, and the staging, but also from the dominant colour, namely, this shade of gold.

I always have to bear in mind people who treat the world normally. The film's meant for everybody. If I need to say something, make something understood or give some sort of indication, then I have to use all sorts of devices relating to dramatization, actors and also filters. The whole problem lay in choosing these appropriate devices. Maybe there are people who are annoyed by the filters. It's very possible but, on the whole, they certainly help to express what the film's about.

In the morning, shooting; in the evening, editing. Production had an editing table delivered to Clermont Ferrand. Jacques Witta, the editor, came too. He was a very pleasant, calm, good man. That was important – I was going to spend three months of my life with him, day in day out. It was clear from the beginning that there'd be a language problem. Jacques didn't speak English; I didn't speak French. During this intimate work of editing, we needed a translator. Marcin Latałło, who did this very well, is young, and after a full day's shooting he would nod off in the cutting-room. It's interesting that, although they drank so much orange juice and ate so much fruit and vegetables when they were little, all these young people don't have much endurance. Their generation's more beautiful, better educated and healthier than my war generation yet we can work longer, endure more. Who knows, maybe every generation should experience a bit of discomfort, poverty and suffering? Or maybe it's just a question of character.

At one stage we had the idea of making as many versions of *Véronique* as there are cinemas in which the film was to be shown. In Paris, for example, the film was to be shown in seventeen cinemas. So we had the idea to make seventeen different versions. It would be quite expensive, of course – especially at the last stage of production – making internegatives, individual re-recordings and so on. But we had very precise ideas for all these versions. What's a film? we thought. Theoretically it's something which goes through a projector at the speed of twenty-four frames a second and, in fact, the success of cinematography depends on repetition. That is, whether you project in a huge cinema in Paris or a tiny cinema in Mława or a medium-sized cinema in Nebraska, the same thing appears on screen because the film passes through the projector at the same speed. And so we thought, Why, in fact, does it have to be like that? Why can't we say that the film is hand-made? And that every version's going to be different? And that if you see version number 00241b then it'll be a bit different from 00243c. Maybe it'll have a slightly different ending, or maybe one scene will be a tiny bit longer and another a bit shorter, or maybe there'll be a scene which isn't in the other version, and so on. That's how we worked it out. And that's how the script was written. We shot enough material to make these versions possible. It would be possible to release this film with the concept that it was, so to speak, hand-made. That if you go to a different cinema, you'll see the same film but in a slightly different version, and if you go to yet another cinema, you'll see yet another version, seemingly the same film but a little different. Maybe it'll have a happier ending, or maybe slightly sadder – that's the chance you take. Anyway, the possibility was there. But as always, of course, it turned out that production absolutely didn't have the time, and that, in fact, there wasn't any money for it either. Perhaps the money was less important. The main problem was time. There wasn't any time left.

As it is there are two versions of *Véronique* because I made a different one for America. We see a man emerge from a house which we already know and he calls, 'Véronique! It's cold. Come inside.' 'Dad!' Véronique says and runs to him. And cuddles up to him. That's the ending for America. It's obvious that that's her family home. You know that the man's her father. But as I've said, it hadn't been clear to the Americans before that he was her father. Maybe it was some other man fiddling around with the timber. How can you know? And the film's doing well in America. It's made a lot of money – for the producer, of course.

What can you draw an audience with? What is commercialism? What draws an audience? Either the story you're telling or an actor who's well known and brings people in to see the film, right? What advantages did I have in the case of *Véronique*? I had a completely unknown French actress who had played a tiny role in a film by Louis Malle and nothing else. Nobody knew who she was or even that she existed. And I had a weak and vague storyline, and that's the way the story stayed – not very clear to everybody – a story about feelings, about a certain sensibility, a certain sensitivity which is really impossible to express in a film. What did I count on? Money? Commercialism?

Of course, I had some idea of how I'd narrate the story. That's why a compromise was necessary. I had to tell the story in such a way as to make it comprehensible to the audience. Whatever aspect of a film I'm thinking about – casting, script, the solution of individual scenes, dialogue, music, whatever – I always think of the audience. That's fundamental. Of course I thought about the audience all the time when making *Véronique* so that I even made a different ending for the Americans, because I thought you have to meet them halfway, even if it means renouncing your own point of view.

I play on pure emotions in *Véronique* because it's a film about emotions and nothing else. There's no action in it. If I make a film about emotions then obviously I play on them. People also told me that I was playing on emotions in *A Short Film about Killing*, because both the murder and then the hanging scene last for such a long time. Of course I'm playing on emotions. What else should I play on? What else is there other than emotions? What is important? Only that. I play on them so that people should hate or love my characters. I play on them so that people should sympathize with them. I play on them so that people should want my characters to win if they're playing a good game.

I think that if you go to the cinema, you want to give in to emotions. But I'm not saying that everybody has to like *Véronique*. On the contrary. I think it's a film for a very limited group of people. I don't mean an age group or a social group but a group of people who are sensitive to the sort of emotions shown in the film. And such people can be found among the intelligentsia, among workers, among the unemployed, among students and among old-age pensioners. I don't think it's a film for the élite, by any means, unless we call sensitive people élite.

The film's doing very well at the box-office in Poland, too, surprisingly. I've always had conflicts with film critics in Poland and, no doubt, always will to the day I die. Before, during the Communist era, I always accused the critics of not being authentic. I accused them of writing what was demanded of them. I had the right to say this because we didn't make the sort of films which were demanded of us. We made our own films, but critics wrote as

they were told to. Pieces like that keep appearing in the newspapers. Various meetings, various reminiscences of politicians
where they admit to having manipulated, frankly controlled the
critics. In the art world, too, and also in films. So I was right to
accuse them of that, and since I was right it hurt them terribly.
Consequently, it was impossible for them to like me. But I really
can't complain at the way the critics received *Véronique*, although
even when they liked it, they'd write: 'It's such a beautiful film – it
seems a bit too beautiful.' Or, 'it's such a moving film – I'm not
sure if it's not a bit too moving.' Or, 'Something stinks of commercialism here', 'It's too beautiful', 'Too moving', 'The heroine is too
good', 'The actress is too good'. Those were the feelings of serious
critics, alongside a certain resentment that the film wasn't about
Polish things, Polish history and Poland at present – that I didn't
show the situation in Poland.

When you look at something from a provincial point of view,
you always want it to be about the provinces, about your pro-
vince. If you're a hairdresser and go to see a film about a hairdresser then you get terribly annoyed if the actor doesn't hold the
scissors properly. It doesn't matter to anybody else. But you can't
watch the film because that's not the way the actor should be
holding his scissors. 'Such important elections were going on in
Poland, different political parties are forming, the Communists
have fallen, and the film doesn't make any reference to any of this
at all. How come?' they'd say. It's not pure chance that I'm not
concerned about all this in the film. On the contrary, it's well
thought out. I'm not concerned about Polish politics because they
don't interest me in the least. Elections, governments, parties,
whatever.

But I'm not complaining about the way the critics generally
received *Véronique*, and quite the opposite as far as the public is
concerned. I'm very happy that the film played to full houses for a
couple of months in Warsaw. I don't know how big the audiences
were there but the distributors at any rate didn't lose on it; on the
contrary – they made a bit of a profit. So, what else could I want?
The Church didn't pay much attention to the film. I think it was
too busy retrieving property which the Communists had confiscated from it after the war. And apart from that, it was busy
worrying about abortion and religious instruction in schools. It
hasn't got time for films at the moment, luckily.

But I'm never satisfied. I believe that if you achieve a third of what you want, it's enough. That's how much I reckon I achieved with *Véronique*. It's as if a third satisfies your ambition and then that's fine. You have to get used to not achieving more.

In France *Véronique* just managed to rise above a certain mediocrity. That's what a director's ambition is based on these days; to rise above the flood of other films; somehow, for some reason, to stand out. And there's no doubt that this film did stand out. I think it's a film which appeals to a certain generation – younger rather than older.

French critics like to like something. That's extremely important because a section of the public can depend on this. The public wants to see what the critics like. But I don't divide critics into French or non-French. To be perfectly honest, I don't read French reviews because I don't understand French. Sometimes somebody will translate a word or a sentence for me, and I can see that French critics have good intentions. Critics like these believe they're vital in promoting a film, for example. Polish critics don't feel this at all. Polish critics describe something and know beforehand that it hasn't got any significance at all. In the past, when the *Trybuna Ludu*[38] praised something, the public knew it wasn't worth seeing. If the *Trybuna Ludu* said that something was bad, then there was a good chance it would be good. So it had exactly the opposite effect. The public, the reader, didn't believe in anything that was written, and the critic knew that what he was going to write wasn't going to have any influence on the reader or future audience. This created a situation where the critic in Poland knew, while writing, that he wasn't important. On top of that the critics lied, didn't say what they thought but repeated the lies they were told so it was terribly hard to trust them, of course.

I don't have any sort of strategy that if I do something in a certain way the critics will understand what it's supposed to mean, and so I'm giving them what they want. I never think like that. I never really think where I put the camera. It comes naturally to me. I don't analyse and I don't contrive. If you haven't got your own compass within yourself which clearly points you in a certain direction then you won't find it. And it doesn't depend on any film school or anything you might learn in a film school.

I do weigh things up a bit when writing the script, of course, bearing in mind all sorts of needs – dramaturgical and financial needs, needs relating to actors. If I know that I've got such and such an actor then I have to – and want to – write in such a way as to make things easier for him, but if I don't have him, then I simply write something general which later on, during filming, acquires substance through a particular actor. If I don't have money for a certain scene, then I don't write it. What's the point of writing a scene if I won't be able to shoot it? I look for another way of doing it. I knew, for example, that I wouldn't have 50 million francs to shoot the last scene in one of the *Three Colours* films. I didn't have the money and I didn't want to have it. Above all, I didn't want to have it. I don't want to use this sort of money. I simply consider it immoral to spend so much money on a scene or film.

I think there's more freedom in making a low budget film than a big budget one. I think there's something deeply unethical in laying out money you can't know will make a return. If, for example, a film like *Terminator* 2 makes, say, a $100 million profit, then you know that some of this money will be used for something. Some of it will probably be foolishly spent, but some of it will be used for something, maybe to make other films, including one which might be worthwhile, or maybe it'll be used by some institute to discover a vaccine which some day will prove useful, or in the form of taxes, grants, subsidies or whatever. If a film makes a profit, it means that a lot of people have wanted to see it. If they wanted to see it, then maybe it's given them something, I don't know, maybe even a moment of forgetfulness. I don't care what. But I, personally, don't want to make films which cost $100 million, not because I'm afraid that they won't make a profit but I'm afraid of the terrible restrictions big money brings with it. I don't want that. Why should I?

It's much harder, at the moment, to find money in Poland than in France and it's particularly difficult for me. It's not even right for me to try to find money there because the Poles quite rightly believe that I can get money elsewhere. There's a theory or notion which I've had for a long time. Namely, that there's a given quantity of goods, a given quantity of everything in the world. Similarly, there's a limited amount of money to spend on films in Poland, and if I take the money then somebody else certainly won't get it.

I always think on a small scale, and I certainly don't want to make a film about things on a macro scale, on a global scale. That doesn't interest me in the least because I don't believe societies exist, I don't believe nations exist. I think that there simply are, I don't know, 60 million individual French or 40 million individual Poles or 65 million individual British. That's what counts. They're individual people.

I don't film metaphors. People only read them as metaphors, which is very good. That's what I want. I always want to stir people to something. It doesn't matter whether I manage to pull people into the story or inspire them to analyse it. What is important is that I force them into something or move them in some way. That's why I do all this – to make people experience something. It doesn't matter if they experience it intellectually or emotionally. You make films to give people something, to transport them somewhere else and it doesn't matter if you transport them to a world of intuition or a world of the intellect.

For me, a certain sign of quality or class in art is that when I read, see or listen to something, I suddenly get an acute, clear feeling that somebody's formulated something which I've experienced or thought; exactly the same thing but with the help of a better sentence or better visual arrangement or better composition of sounds than I could ever have imagined. Or, for a moment, gave me a sense of beauty, joy or something like that. That's what differentiates great literature from average literature. When you read great literature, you'll find a sentence or two which you think you've either said or heard. It's a description, an image which deeply concerns you, which deeply moves you and is your image. On some page, you keep finding yourself in the same situation, or you find somebody completely different but who thinks like you once thought or sees what you once saw. That's what great literature's about. That's what great film-making's about too – if something like that exists. For a brief moment, you find yourself there; but whether you find yourself there and treat this emotionally or start to argue about it intellectually, comparatively, analytically, doesn't, in fact, matter.

A lot of people don't understand the direction in which I'm going. They think I'm going the wrong way, that I've betrayed my own way of thinking, that I've betrayed my way of looking at the world. I really don't have any sense of having betrayed my own point of view, or even of having deviated from it, for whatever reason – comfort, money or career. I don't feel that. I don't have any sense of having betrayed anything whatsoever within myself by making *Véronique*, *Three Colours*, or *Decalogue*, or *No End*. I absolutely don't feel that I've betrayed any of my opinions or my attitude to life.

The realm of superstitions, fortune-telling, presentiments, intuition, dreams, all this is the inner life of a human being, and all this is the hardest thing to film. Even though I know that it can't be filmed however hard I try, the simple fact is that I'm taking this direction to get as close to this as my skill allows. That's why I don't think *Véronique* betrays anything I've done before. In *Camera Buff*, for example, you also have a heroine who knows that something bad is going to happen to her husband. She knows it. She feels it. Just like Véronique feels things. I don't see any difference. I've been trying to get there from the beginning. I'm somebody who doesn't know, somebody who's searching.

I haven't got a great talent for films. Orson Welles, for example, managed to achieve this at the age of twenty-four or twenty-six when he made *Citizen Kane* and, with his first film, climbed to the top, to the highest possible peak in cinema. There are a few films like that. *Citizen Kane* will always be in the top ten. A genius immediately finds his place. But I'll need to take all my life to get there and I never will. I know that perfectly well. I just keep on going. And if somebody doesn't want to or can't understand that this is a lasting process then obviously he or she will keep on saying that everything I do is different, better or worse, from what I've done before. But for me it isn't better or worse. It's all the same only a step further, and, according to my own private scale of values, these are small steps which are taking me nearer to a goal which I'll never reach anyway. I haven't got enough talent.

This goal is to capture what lies within us, but there's no way of filming it. You can only get nearer to it. It's a great subject for literature. It's probably the only subject in the world. Great literature doesn't only get near to it, it's in a position to describe it. I suspect there are a few hundred books in the world which have managed to achieve a full description of what lies within us. Camus wrote books like that. Dostoevsky wrote books like that. Shakespeare wrote plays about that. The Greek dramatists, Faulkner, Kafka, Vargas Llosa, whom I love, wrote books like that. *Conversation in The Cathedral* by Vargas Llosa, for example, is a book which, I think, has achieved this goal.

Literature can achieve this, cinema can't. It can't because it doesn't have the means. It's not intelligent enough. Consequently, it's not equivocal enough. Yet, at the same time, while being too explicit, it's also too equivocal. That means that when I film a scene with a bottle of milk, for example, somebody suddenly starts to draw conclusions which never even crossed my mind. For me, a bottle of milk is simply a bottle of milk; when it spills, it means milk's been spilt. Nothing more. It doesn't mean the world's fallen apart or that the milk symbolizes a mother's milk which her child couldn't drink because the mother died early, for example. It doesn't mean that to me. A bottle of spilt milk is simply a bottle of spilt milk. And that's cinema. Unfortunately, it doesn't mean anything else.

I keep explaining to all my younger colleagues whom I teach that when you light a cigarette lighter in a film it means the cigarette lighter's lit, and if it isn't lit, it means the lighter doesn't work. It doesn't mean anything else; and it'll never mean anything else. If once in 10,000 times it turns out to mean something else, that means that somebody's achieved a miracle. Welles achieved that miracle once. Only one director in the world has managed to achieve that miracle in the last few years and that's Tarkovsky. Bergman achieved this miracle a few times. Fellini achieved it a few times. A few people achieved it. Ken Loach, too, in *Kes*.

I say a cigarette lighter – an idiotic example, of course – but what I mean is the literal nature of film. If I have a goal, then it is to escape from this literalism. I'll never achieve it; in the same way that I'll never manage to describe what really dwells within my hero, although I keep on trying. If film really means to achieve anything – at least, this holds true for me – then it's that somebody might find him or herself in it.

There's a beautiful story which an American journalist told me. He read a novel by Cortazar where the main character has the same name, surname and exactly the same life as the journalist. The journalist didn't know whether this was coincidental or not. He wrote to Cortazar, that he'd read the book and suddenly had found he was reading a book about himself. He wrote to Cortazar saying he really does exist, and Cortazar wrote him back a beautiful letter. The journalist told me about this letter which said how beautiful it is that something like that had happened. Cortazar had never met the journalist. He'd never seen him. He'd never heard of him. And he was happy that he'd invented a character who really did exist. An American journalist told me this in connection with *Véronique*.

That's one thing. Then there's something which is, perhaps, more general. In the business I work in, as in many other businesses, other walks of life let's say, other branches of culture – if not all – you can't be clean to the end. It's impossible – at least I don't know of anyone who is – simply because of the rules of the game in this profession. It's not merely making films. You spend so much time on it that it's a large part of your life, demanding all sorts of compromises and all sorts of departures from your own point of view. Here, in the West, the reasons are usually to do with money, commercialism, and with what seems to be an apt name – public censorship, that is, taking the public's taste into account to such a degree that this taste becomes a sort of censor. I've got the impression, which isn't perhaps well regarded, that public censorship is even more restricting than the political censorship which we were subjected to in Poland during Communism. But there's no Communism in Poland any more.

So, you can't be completely clean in this business. But I don't consider myself a professional opportunist. In private, personal matters, of course, we're all opportunists. Surely trying to understand someone doesn't mean you're an opportunist. My work is not motivated by opportunism, it's motivated by the fact that I really want to understand, that I really want to see why things are the way they are. I've always asked myself that question and am still asking it.

There were three ways a film-maker could go during Communism. One way was not to make any films; that was possible, of course. To be honest, I don't know of anyone who quit making films for idealistic reasons. Maybe there were people like that but I don't know of any. Another way was to make films which were approved of; that is pro-Party, pro-Russian, pro-Lenin and pro-military. That was the second way. The third way was to back away and make films about love or nature or about the fact that something's beautiful or very ugly. And there was also a fourth way: to try to understand. I chose the fourth because that's in keeping with my temperament. That's what I did during film school and that's what I do today.

Apart from the film *Workers '71*, which we cut in a specific way, submitting to a certain pressure, I've never had the feeling of having crossed the boundary indicated by my own inner compass. I've never crossed it and because of that a great number of my films have been shelved for five, seven or ten years and some weren't shown at all. And that's fine. I've come to terms with that. The same applies here. People aren't in a position to be completely clean.

There's another aspect to all this. I, personally, believe that these compromises which you have to make and this agreement to relinquish your own convictions in certain matters – some better, some worse, of course – are healthy. Because absolute freedom only leads to great works if you're a genius. If you're not, it very often leads to pretentiousness, inferiority and something even worse, which is spending money and making films exclusively for yourself and your nearest friends. Restrictions, necessary restrictions and necessary compromises give rise to a certain ingenuity, inventiveness, and inspire energies which enable you to find original solutions and ideas within the script.

Initially, I came to Paris while filming *The Double Life of Véronique*. We were shooting so it was *en route* as it were. I shot in Poland and then in Clermont Ferrand. Then I came to Paris. It was simply another film location, nothing more, and then, gradually, the filming came to an end. I stayed on because I had to do the editing here, work and finish the film. I was busy working all the time. I didn't have time to live. I don't have enough time – or curiosity – for that certain something which once made me roam around, observe, look, watch. I don't think I have enough patience either. I've come to know what I could know, and what I didn't, I'm probably too old to know. I don't know the French language, for example, and won't ever know it. I know English a little but I learnt English for fifteen years, although the way I speak it, it sounds as if I've only been learning it for three months. I've got an obvious lack of talent for languages. That's a field I simply don't know and am making no effort to know, although I could do. After all, I do keep hearing the language around me all the time. I'm constantly talking to the French through an interpreter and could, therefore, be constantly trying to understand. I know what a phrase sounds like in Polish and I know what it sounds like in

French. I hear what it sounds like in French and then the interpreter translates it into Polish for me. So I know both versions, as
it were. I keep hearing them. Day in, day out. Every day. Many
times over. And yet I don't make any effort to learn the language. I
don't think it's just laziness, although there's a bit of that, too. It's
also that when I'm writing a screenplay or generally doing something, when I'm giving of myself, I'm in no state to take things in
as well. If I had a lot of free time, which I no longer imagine I ever
will, maybe I'd learn the language.

Someone adapts the French dialogue for me and that's it. Of
course, we sometimes discuss what would sound better with the
interpreter, or the man who adapts the dialogue, and the actors.
What would sound better to express accurately what I want to say.
But we only discuss it for a while. We find a solution, then act it
out. As for the tone, I have to rely on the actors, whom I trust in
such matters. If I've cast them properly then there's no problem. If
I've cast them badly, then there is a problem. But then, if I've cast
them badly, there's a problem in Polish, too.

My misgivings about working in France turned out to be
unnecessary and premature. The people in the crew wanted to
work and knew their profession. They were pleasant and surprised
that I was the first to arrive on set together with the lighting
cameraman and that later, when we'd wrapped, I didn't go off in a
car but tried to help to load the lorries. They didn't let me. They
believed that there's a strict division of labour. I have a completely
different attitude. I know that we're all making the film and, of
course, everybody is responsible for his part but we're also all
responsible for the whole.

There's another thing, and it's slightly embarrassing. Everybody's got something on set. The cameraman's got a camera and
lightmeter, the soundman's got a microphone, the electricians
have got lights and so on. I haven't got anything. I hand my
screenplay over to the script-girl straight away in the morning and
walk around with empty hands. It gives the impression – otherwise quite right – that I haven't got anything to do. Of course, I
direct. I talk to the cameraman, I say something to the actors, I
give some orders, I change something in the dialogue, sometimes I
even think of something. But I've got nothing in my hands. I was
recently working with an elderly, Polish cameraman – I was
making *Decalogue 1* with him. He watched me. We were working

together for the first time and it was going well. He once said, 'The
director's a guy who helps everyone.' I like that simple definition. I
repeated it to the French stage-hands who'd been protesting when
I carried boxes to their lorry after the wrap. They nodded, and
agreed to the boxes.

Several Italian journalists arrived. They wanted to know what
the difference was between making films in the East and here, in
the West. They shook their heads unhappily when I told them that
there weren't any great differences. So I found a difference, to the
disadvantage of the French. I don't like the hour-long lunch break
which distracts everybody in the middle of the day. They noted
that down with satisfaction. Maybe they don't have a break in
Italy? Or maybe they wanted something to be better in the East?

I don't have any problems in Poland either really. Of course,
people do sometimes rebel. They don't want to stay on into the
night or things like that. They've got their affairs, their families. I
make a film once in five years but they make films all the time.
They go straight from one to another and you've got to understand their attitude. There's a different attitude to work in general,
in Poland. Work is considered something terrible. The fact that
you have to work is simply terrible. For over forty years, people
were spoilt by the system they were living under, and besides that
there's this national feeling that we're created for something
altogether better than cleaning toilets or seeing that the streets are
tidy or decently laying tarmac or ensuring that the water pipes
don't leak, and so on. Poles aren't created for any of this at all.
These are embarrassingly down-to-earth activities. We're created
for greater things. We're the centre of the universe. People always
blamed Communism but I'm convinced that the Poles' attitude to
work is, to a large extent, the result of an absurd and totally
unfounded sense of superiority. Work, in fact, isn't important to
them. In France the people are more disciplined; the scheduling's
better, the organization of time, of hours, is more precise. There's
much more improvisation in Poland.

The same goes for collaboration with the lighting cameraman.
We discuss things in the evenings. Besides the basic ideas involved
in making the film, of course, we discuss what we're going to do
the following day. In Poland, the lighting cameraman isn't a
technician hired out to do the photography as he is here. This
results from a tradition which we created in Poland ourselves. It

existed before, but I think that we, that is our generation, raised the level of co-operation with the cameraman. He's a colleague who's there right from the very beginning of the script, in fact, from the initial idea. As soon as I have an idea, I go to the lighting cameraman. I tell him my idea, and we start to discuss it. When I write the screenplay I show him the first, second and third versions, and together we work out how to make the film. The lighting cameraman isn't someone who only does the lighting. He also has a certain influence on the staging. He makes comments about the actors and he's got the right to do so. I expect it of him. He has ideas as to how to resolve scenes. It's our joint concern. And because such a system of work has developed and we've got Polish lighting cameramen brought up in this way, used to it and, what's more, liking it, we all get a great deal out of it. A cameraman working in this way has the feeling of being co-author of a film, and he's right. Later on, of course, one always has to acknowledge that he's the co-author. Not only because it makes him feel good and predisposes him well for the next film but, above all, because it's true.

Credit is due to those who bring something into a film. At least I always try to credit them. So many people bring in all sorts of things. Of course, I'm the one who, at a certain moment, has to say, I'll take this, leave that. Someone's got to decide, and that's the director, of course. But the whole point is to motivate people to think together, to solve things together. And that's how I work with lighting cameramen, soundmen, composers, actors, grips and stage-hands and script-girls and everybody. I keep believing and expecting that someone will come up with a solution which is much better than mine, because he's got a mind of his own, he's got a brain of his own. Besides there's something like intuition which always varies a little from person to person. It can inspire much better solutions and very often does. I take these solutions and claim they're mine, but when the right moment arrives I always remember that these solutions came from somebody else. At least I hope I'm loyal in these matters. It's very important to me.

I try to leave everyone a lot of freedom in general. I don't know whether I really do. I think I do, but maybe, if you were to ask them, they'd say it's not like that at all. I'm under the impression that I give them a great deal of freedom and that, in fact, they can change nearly everything they like. The actors, too. This also is a result of an experiment I did in Poland right at the very beginning – when I was writing *The Calm* for Stuhr. I planned to write the dialogue with him from the start. He is a good actor and intelligent man and I counted on him having his own views as to how the character should express himself, what sort of words he should use, what syntax, what sayings and so on. So I sketched in a dialogue in the script, of course, but the real dialogue was written with Jurek Stuhr just before shooting, always in the evenings. That's my system – in the evenings, to go through what's going to be shot the following day. It was only then that the real dialogues came into being – from his ideas, my ideas.

I try not to tell the actors too much. To be honest, I try to give them one or two good sentences, no more, because I know that they simply listen to everything you say, especially in the initial stages of the film, and if you tell them too much then they quote you later on and you can't get out of it. So I say as little as possible. Everything's written in the screenplay. We talk for hours but about other things. How are you? Did you sleep well? And so on. Or rather I listen to them.

I've noticed a certain dangerous phenomenon among young directors – I've got the right to say that, now my hair's grey. So there are young directors and I see that they take the camera, which they have attached to a monitor, and sit in front of the monitor. The action's over there but they sit and bite their finger-nails over here. They're happy or worried if something goes wrong but they've got absolutely nothing to do with the people who are playing. Actors have got a fantastic ability of sensing all the director's nuances. They know exactly when something's right or something's wrong. Or rather, to be more precise, they know whether the director likes it or not. But how can they sense this if the director's sitting with his back to them, watching the monitor? I try to stay close by.

I love actors a lot, to be honest. They're such strange people. They'd do anything for me. It often happens to me that they bring their views, feelings, their attitude to the world. I make use of this, I simply take it. I love them for it. And if you love someone, you try to be close to them, you want to see everything just as it is. Besides, it pays dividends. They repay me in like manner. They're prepared to give more than just their skill and glycerine.

I really only make films to be able to edit them. Yet I couldn't be an editor because an editor's simply someone who puts films together. Editing, in fact, is a sort of assignment; the editor is assigned to stick together material which somebody else has shot. I could never do that because I don't think I'd be capable of getting through to this other person's world seriously or deeply enough to be able really to edit and not merely stick the film together. To edit is to build, to create some sort of order. I wouldn't be able to do that. I'm the editor of my own films to a certain extent, but only my own films and nobody else's. I must admit that of all my colleagues I give the editor the least amount of freedom simply because I really do like editing. I can't give him too much freedom because then I'd be handing over something which I like myself. No doubt, while I'm shooting, I've got a picture in my mind of how the film should be edited. Then a number of other possibilities become apparent and the whole trick lies in discovering these new possibilities. Maybe I'm wrong. Maybe if I gave the editor more freedom, he'd find these possibilities.

I think that a film really only comes into existence in the cutting-room. To shoot is only to collect material, create possibilities. I try to go about it in such a way as to ensure myself as much freedom to manoeuvre as possible. Of course, editing means sticking two pieces of film together and, on this level, there are a number of principles and rules which you have to follow and sometimes break. But there's another level to editing and it's the most interesting one. That is the level of constructing a film. It's a game with the audience, a way of directing attention, distributing tension. Some directors believe that all these elements are written down in the script. Others believe in the actors, the staging, lights, photography. I believe in that, too, but I also know that the elusive spirit of a film, so difficult to describe, is born only there, in the cutting-room.

That's why, during the shooting of *Véronique*, I sat there in the evenings and on Sundays and later on, after the shoot, I'd be there as long as possible. I was trying to get the rough cut ready as quickly as possible without paying any attention to details. This version was consistent with the script or the changes which I'd made on set while filming. After screening the first version, it became apparent how many blunders, repetitions and super-ficialities there were in the script. So I made the next version as quickly as possible, resolutely shortening scenes, throwing them out and changing the sequence. Usually, it turned out that I'd exaggerated. The third version, in which I often came back to what I'd got rid of, began to resemble a film. It still didn't have a rhythm or cuts, but there was a shadow of some sort of order. During this period, I'd have a screening every other day or sometimes even every day to check all sorts of possibilities and play around with the material. In this way seven or more versions were made which were, in fact, entirely different films. A fairly clear picture arose from these changes and frequent screenings, and the film took shape. Only then did we start to work in detail, look for cuts, a rhythm, atmosphere.

I'm one of those directors who parts very easily with whole chunks of material. I don't regret losing good scenes or beautiful ones or ones which were expensive or difficult to shoot. If they're superfluous to the film, I throw them out ruthlessly – with a certain amount of pleasure even. The better they are the easier it is for me to part with them because I know that they're not being discarded because of their bad quality but only because they're unnecessary.

Absolutely everything which isn't necessary has to be discarded. I usually shoot more scenes than there are in the final film. Later on, I throw them out with pleasure when I see they're not necessary. The editor even cries sometimes, 'Such a beautiful shot! She played so beautifully in that scene!' But when I see it's not necessary I really do cut it out without any qualms whatsoever. That's another problem with young directors. Namely, the way they're attached to their own materials. Everything has to be used. Everything I've done is wonderful, they think – while, usually, most of it is completely useless. We all make these mistakes. The difficulty lies in being able to understand what is unnecessary.

I feel a kind of freedom in the cutting-room. Of course, I have only the rushes I've shot at my disposal but these rushes, in fact, give boundless possibilities. I don't feel the pressure of time and money, of the actors' moods, the urgency of schedules, the frustration of faulty camera equipment – even if it is the best – nobody has hundreds of questions to ask me every day, I don't have to wait until the sun has gone down, or they've set up the lights. Slightly excited, I await the result of every action on the cutting table.

CHAPTER 4

'I Don't Like the Word "Success"'

I haven't backed out of filming in Poland. I still film there. Of course co-production is something different; it offers me better conditions.

I don't like the word 'success', and I always fiercely defend myself against it, because I don't know what the word means at all. For me, success means attaining something I'd really like. That's success. And what I'd really like is probably unattainable, so I don't look at things in these terms. Of course, the recognition I have won, to a certain or even large extent, satisfies an ambition which every film-maker has. I'm certainly ambitious and no doubt I behave the way I do through ambition. There's absolutely no doubt about that. But that's got nothing to do with success. That's very far from success.

On the one hand, my ambition's satisfied. Yet, on the other hand, recognition only helps you to satisfy ambition because it'll never be completely satisfied. You can't ever completely satisfy ambition. The more ambitious you are, the more impossible it is to satisfy your ambition. Recognition makes certain things easier which is very good in resolving everyday matters. Obviously it's better if you can find money easily rather than if you have to fight for it. The same goes for actors or anything else you might think of. But, at the same time, I'm not sure that making things easier is a good thing in itself. I'm not sure whether it isn't better if things are difficult. I'm not sure if it's not better to suffer than not to suffer. I think it's sometimes better to suffer. Everybody ought to go through it. That's what makes us. That's what makes human nature. If you've got an easy life then there's no reason for you to care about anybody else. I think that in order really to care about yourself, and particularly somebody else, you've got to experience suffering and really understand what it is to suffer, so that you hurt and understand what it is to hurt. Because if you don't understand what pain is, you won't understand what it is not to be in pain and you won't appreciate this lack of pain.

I'll never tell you about the time I suffered most; nor will I tell anybody. It's what's most painful and most hidden. So, first of all, I don't talk about it and, secondly, I very rarely admit it to myself, although it probably does emerge somewhere. No doubt, it comes out somewhere and you could find it, if you really wanted to.

Of course I feel I'm running away but that doesn't bother me. Sometimes, if you want to survive, you have to run away. I think I escaped from the Polish situation too late. I think that I allowed myself to be needlessly taken in yet again in 1980. I needlessly suffered yet another blow. I should have realized and run away much sooner. Unfortunately, I was too foolish.

Generally speaking, you run away from yourself, or from what you think you are. It hasn't caused me any problems, to be honest. Isolation hasn't caused me any problems either because, like everybody else, I think I'm the one who's right and not everybody else, whatever their reasons. And to this day I'm convinced I was right. The only thing I did wrong and foolishly, was to have turned away from it all so late. But that's the way it was meant to be, no doubt.

There are many reasons why America doesn't attract me. First, I don't like America. It's too big. There are too many people. Everybody runs around too quickly. There's too much commotion, too much uproar. Everybody pretends too hard that they're happy there. But I don't believe in their happiness, I think they're just as unhappy as we are, except that we still talk about it sometimes but they only say that everything's fine, that it's fantastic. It gets on my nerves on a day-to-day basis, and unfortunately directing is life on a day-to-day basis. You have to spend half a year in a place, in a country, in order to do something. And if I were to be confronted for a whole year with people saying that everything's fantastic then I simply couldn't stand it.

When Americans asked me 'How are you?', I said 'So-so.' They probably thought somebody in my family had died. But I simply had jet lag because I'd been flying for seven hours and didn't feel particularly well. But it was enough for me to say 'So-so' and they immediately thought that something tragic had happened. You can't say 'So-so'. You have to say 'Well' or 'Very well'. The most optimistic thing I can say is 'I'm still alive.' So I'm not cut out for America for that reason. Second, they don't allow directors into the cutting-room – at least not in the big studios. The director

directs the film; that's his job. There, one person writes the script,
another directs and yet another edits. No doubt, one day I'll direct
somebody else's script because it'll be much better than my own,
and far more beautiful and clever. But I'll certainly never give up
editing. So I can't go to America for that reason either. Of course, I
can't go to America because they don't allow cigarettes, so there
certainly are enough reasons for my not being attracted to
America.

I'm afraid of America. Whenever I'm in New York I always
have the feeling that it's going to cave in and all I can think about
is how to avoid being there when that happens. The same goes for
other places in America. You don't get all those people and all that
noise in the streets of California as you do in New York but, in
turn, there's a huge number of cars going to and fro and I always
have serious doubts as to whether there are any Americans inside.
You know, who's inside? I've always got the impression that those
cars drive themselves. So I'm simply frightened of that country,
and I always have the feeling that I'm on the defensive when I
arrive there. I've even been to small provincial places there and I'm
still frightened and always escape. I close myself in. I simply run
away to my hotel, and usually sleep, if I manage to get to sleep,
that is – I don't fall asleep as easily as I used to. But if I manage to
fall asleep, that's what I do.

I had this adventure. It was silly really. I was hurrying to some
screening. I think it was the first screening I had at the New York
Festival. *No End*, I think it was, in 1984 or 1985. I was in a
terrible hurry. I got into a taxi. It was raining. The taxi-driver hit a
cyclist. My journey took me through Central Park. It's like Hyde
Park in London where the roads cut across except that in Hyde
Park everything is on one level while in Central Park the roads are
lower down, not in a tunnel but a sort of gully. Well, that's where
my taxi-driver knocked over a cyclist. It was dusk already or even
dark. No, it was dusk. Raining. And he simply hit him. The cyclist
jumped off and fell and the taxi-driver ran over the bike. He
simply ran over the bike. The road's narrow there; that is, one line
of cars can go in one direction and one line in the other, no more.
The cars there are terribly big and wide so maybe two French cars
would fit but only one American. Well, when he knocked over the
cyclist, he stopped, and got out. We started to help the cyclist up. I
also helped, because he was lying there with his leg bleeding. Well,

car horns started beeping. An enormous river of cars had stopped behind us. A gigantic traffic jam, a couple of miles long, had formed. And they started to beep their horns and flash their lights and shout and beep and so on and so on.

Since it was literally five minutes before the time I was to appear at the Lincoln Center, I gave the guy what I owed him, five or six dollars, I can't remember exactly how much, and I started to run. You can guess what the taxi-drivers coming up in the opposite direction thought. A taxi's standing and some guy is running away from it. Of course they thought that I'd done something to the driver. Mugged him, robbed him, killed him or something. I ran like hell because, on top of that, it was raining and I wanted to save my suit from becoming soaked before I reached the Lincoln Center. So I pelted along. I saw the taxis coming to a halt in the opposite direction, and they started signalling. Guys jumped out of the taxis. I simply started to run away, I started to run away from them, not to the Lincoln Center any more but away from them. I started to climb up the sides of the gully, jumped into the park but it turned out that there were taxi-drivers standing in front of the gully, too, and they'd also noticed a taxi and this guy running away. So they simply started chasing me through Central Park with these great big baseball bats. You know, those huge, long sticks. You get it with one of those and your skull's cracked open. And I saw the guys waving these sticks above the cars and chasing me across Central Park in their cars. I barely escaped. The trees were pretty dense there and they couldn't get through with their cars; that's the only reason why I escaped. Covered in mud, I went and explained at the Lincoln Center why I was late – I was five or ten minutes late. But that's not why I don't like America. That was just an amusing adventure.

That's what comedy's about, I reckon. You have to put the character in a situation which wouldn't be funny if you were in it yourself, but when you look at it from the outside, it's terribly funny. I don't make comedies like the ones which used to be made with comedians such as de Funes, for example, but I have made a comic film.

There are many films I regret not having made, but it wasn't my fault. The films simply didn't get made for various reasons. I had various ideas or scripts, for example, which I never realized. There are a lot of documentaries which I wanted to make but didn't, but

that's not true of full-length features. Maybe there is one I didn't
make; however, I've made all the ones I've written. I don't have
any drawer full of scripts which I dream of making but haven't
been able to make for various reasons. There's nothing like that. I
don't have any scripts which I wrote and never made; except one
that was written fifteen years ago.

At one stage, for example, I wanted to make a film with Jacek
Kaczmarski,[1] who sang beautiful songs. He once played a very
small role in *Blind Chance*. He now works in Munich. I once
thought that he was somebody who should have a film written for
him; that is, a role written for him. He had so much energy, so
much strength; there was so much truth in the way he behaved, yet
so much discretion, too. A film should absolutely have been written for him, but I didn't write it. To be honest, I couldn't write it
because he left the country and never came back. Now he's an
elderly gentleman, not the Jacek Kaczmarski he'd once been.

One of the documentaries I wanted to film – and I think if I had
done, it would be very useful now – was of various long talks with
politicians who have since died; with Communists, that is. I submitted the subject to the State Documentary Film Studios (WFD)
proposing between twenty or thirty hours of interviews with
Gomułka, Cyrankiewicz,[2] Moczar. And I must say that the
Studios even started making moves in that direction and probably
managed to get hold of some of these people, but they didn't get an
agreement. That was in the mid 1970s, after *Workers '71*. I
thought that something really had to be recorded on film about
these people. Just talking heads, nothing else. Not to do anything
else at all. I even proposed that we make the film and hide it in the
archives without showing it to anybody. Simply keep it in the
archives as a historical document. I suspect those people might
have said something, some truth, if I'd have been clever.

There were many documentaries which I didn't make. I managed to put a few of them into *Camera Buff*. The film buff makes
them as amateur films. A documentary about pavements, or about
a dwarf. Filip makes them.

I think that I made a few films completely unnecessarily, both
documentaries and full features. I don't know why I made them
any more. One such film is *The Scar*. I think I must have made it
because I wanted to make a film. That's the greatest sin a director
can commit; to make a film simply because he wants to make a

film. You have to want to make a film for other reasons – to say something, to tell a story, to show somebody's fate – but you can't want to make a film simply for the sake of it. I think that was my biggest mistake – that I made films I no longer know why I made. While I was making them I told myself I knew why but I don't think I really believed that. I made them simply for the sake of making them. Another such completely unnecessary film was *Short Working Day*. I've absolutely no idea why I made it. I made a lot of unnecessary documentaries, too.

Another mistake was that I realized too late that I had to move as far away from the world of politics as possible. As far away as possible so that there's no sign of it even in the background of my films. Of course, you could, no doubt, call my going to film school the biggest mistake I ever made.

The film industry is in a bad condition the whole world over. It's very nice to celebrate a silver wedding but it's good only if the married couple feel well, still love each other, want to kiss or go to bed with each other, but it's bad if the couple have had just about as much as they can take and aren't interested in each other any more. And that is more or less what's happened with the film industry; the industry's not interested in the public and the public, in turn, is less and less interested in film.

But it has to be said, we don't give the public much of a chance. Apart from the Americans, of course. They care for the public's interests because they care about their wallets; so that's a different sort of caring really. What I'm thinking of is caring also for the audience's spiritual life. Maybe that's too strong a word but something which is a little more than just box-office. The Americans take excellent care of the box-office. And while doing so they make the best, or some of the best, films in the world anyway, also on the spiritual level. But I reckon that this realm of higher needs, of something more than just forgetting about everyday life, of mere recreation, this realm of needs has been clearly neglected by us. So the public's turned away from us because they don't feel we're taking care of them. Maybe these needs are disappearing. But I willingly take part of the blame myself as director.

I don't know whether I've ever watched a film I've made. I once went in to a screening for a moment during some festival, in Holland I think it was. But that was for just a few minutes when I went in to see whether *Personnel* had aged. I decided it had aged a bit and left. I never watched any film of mine after that.

The audiences I like most are those who say that the film's about them, or those who say that it meant something to them, those for whom the film has changed something. I met a woman in a street in Berlin who recognized me because *A Short Film about Love* was being publicized at the time. This woman recognized me and started crying. She was fifty. She thanked me profusely because she had had a conflict with her daughter for a good many years; they weren't talking to each other although they were sharing a flat. The daughter was nineteen at the time. The woman told me that she and her daughter hadn't spoken for five or six years, apart from informing each other about where the keys were or that there was no butter or what time they'd be home. The previous day, they'd been to see my film and the daughter kissed her mother for the first time in five or six years. No doubt they'll quarrel tomorrow again and in two days' time this'll mean nothing to them; but if they felt better for five minutes – or at least the older woman felt better – then that's enough. It's worth making the film for those five minutes. The daughter had probably been in conflict with her mother for some reason and that reason lurked somewhere in the contents of *A Short Film about Love*. And when they saw the film together, the daughter or older woman probably understood what had been the real reason for the conflict, and the daughter kissed her mother. It was worth making the film for that kiss, for that one woman.

Many people, after seeing *A Short Film about Killing*, asked me: 'How do you know that that's what it's like?' Similarly, I got a lot of letters after *Camera Buff* from people asking, 'How do you know what it's like to be a film buff? It's a film about me. You made a film about me.' Or, 'You've plagiarized my life. Where do you know me from?' I got a lot of letters like that, after many of my films. The same thing happened after *A Short Film about Love*. I got a letter from a boy who claims that the film's taken from his life. There's something very pleasant when you make something without really knowing exactly how it'll go – because you never really know – and then it turns out that you've hit on somebody's fate.

Or take this girl, for example. At a meeting just outside Paris, a fifteen-year-old girl came up to me and said that she'd been to see *Véronique*. She'd gone once, twice, three times and only wanted to say one thing really – that she realized that there is such a thing as a soul. She hadn't known before, but now she knew that the soul does exist. There's something very beautiful in that. It was worth making *Véronique* for that girl. It was worth working for a year, sacrificing all that money, energy, time, patience, torturing yourself, killing yourself, taking thousands of decisions, so that one young girl in Paris should realize that there is such a thing as a soul. It's worth it. These are the best viewers. There aren't many of them but perhaps there are a few.

CHAPTER 5

Three Colours

EDITOR'S NOTE: This chapter on *Three Colours* (*Barwy*) is based on conversations I held with Krzysztof Kieślowski in Paris in June 1993 when he was still editing *Blue*, *White* and *Red*. A rough cut had already been made of *Blue*, but the other two films were nowhere near ready. I based my questions about *White* and *Red* on the scripts I read and the stills I saw. Obviously, many changes may be made during the editing stage.

Blue, white, red: liberty, equality, fraternity. It was Piesio's[1] idea that having tried to film the *Decalogue*, why shouldn't we try liberty, equality and fraternity? Why not try to make a film where the commanding dictums of the *Decalogue* are understood in a wider context? Why not try to see how the Ten Commandments function today, what our attitude to them is and how the three words liberty, equality and fraternity function today? – on a very human, intimate and personal plane and not a philosophical let alone a political or social one. The West has implemented these three concepts on a political or social plane, but it's an entirely different matter on the personal plane. And that's why we thought of these films.

Blue is liberty. Of course it's equality too. And it can just as easily be fraternity. But the film *Blue* is about liberty, the imperfections of human liberty. How far are we really free?

For all its tragedy and drama, it's hard to imagine a more luxurious situation than the one Julie finds herself in. She's completely free at the beginning because her husband and daughter die, she loses her family and all her obligations. She is perfectly provided for, has masses of money and no responsibilities. She doesn't have to do anything any more. And here the question arises: is a person in such a situation really free?

Julie thinks she is. Because she's not strong enough to do away with herself and follow her family into the next world, or maybe because she thinks she mustn't do so – we'll never know her reasons – she tries to live a different life. She tries to free herself of everything to do with the past. In this sort of film there ought to be many scenes with her visiting the cemetery or looking at old photographs and so on. There aren't any shots like this at all. There's no past. She's decided to cross it out. If the past comes back it does so only in the music. But it appears that you can't free yourself entirely from everything that's been. You can't, because at a certain moment something like simple fear arises, or a feeling of loneliness or, for example, as Julie experiences at a certain moment, the feeling of having been deceived. This feeling changes Julie so much that she realizes she can't live the way she wanted to.

That's the sphere of personal freedom. How far are we free from feelings? Is love a prison? Or is it freedom? Is the cult of television a prison or is it freedom? Theoretically it's freedom because, if you've got a satellite, you can watch channels from all over the world. But in fact you immediately have to buy all sorts of gadgets to go with the television. And if it breaks down you have to take it to be repaired or get an engineer to come and do it for you. You get pissed off with what's being said or shown on television. In other words, while theoretically giving yourself the freedom of watching various things you're also falling into a trap with this gadget.

Or you buy yourself a car. Theoretically, you're free. You can leave whenever you want. You don't have to reserve a ticket. You don't have to buy anything. You don't have to phone anywhere. You simply fill up with petrol and go. But, in practice, problems crop up straight away. Because someone might steal the car or smash the windscreen and take the radio, you install a radio which you can remove from the car. Of course this doesn't change anything because you keep thinking that someone's going to steal it anyway. So you go and get it numbered. But, of course, you think that that's not going to change anything because somebody's going to pinch it anyway. So you get yourself connected up to a computer system which, with the help of a satellite, allows you to locate the car should it get stolen. Apart from getting it stolen you might get it scratched, which you don't want because it's new. So you try and park it in such a way as not to get it scratched and you start looking for a garage which, in a city, is extremely difficult. There aren't any garages. There aren't any parking lots. You've got nowhere to park. So theoretically you're free but in practice you're a prisoner of your car.

85   Krzysztof Kieślowski with Krzysztof Piesiewicz.

Well, that's freedom and the lack of freedom as regards objects. The same applies to emotions. To love is a beautiful emotion but in loving you immediately make yourself dependent on the person you love. You do what he likes, although you might not like it yourself, because you want to make him happy. So, while having these beautiful feelings of love and having a person you love, you start doing a lot of things which go against your own grain. That's how we've understood freedom in these three films. On the personal level.

In *Blue* the prison is created by both emotions and memory. Julie probably wants to stop loving her husband because it would make it far easier for her to live. That's why she doesn't think about him. That's why she's forgotten. That's why she doesn't visit the cemetery and never looks through old photographs. When someone brings her old photographs, she says she doesn't want to see them. We don't actually show this in the film but it becomes clear later on that she's refused them. She wants to forget all this. But is it really possible to forget? There comes a moment when she starts to feel fine. She starts to function normally, smile, go for walks. So it is possible to forget. Or at least to try to forget. But suddenly there's jealousy and she can't get rid of it. She becomes a prisoner of a jealousy which is absurd because it concerns somebody who's been dead and buried for at least six months. There's nothing she can do for or against him. She can't define herself in relation to him. She can't say 'I love you' or 'I hate you'. There's nothing she can do yet the jealousy torments her as if he were still alive. She tries to fight it off and she does so in an absurd way. She suddenly becomes so good that she's too good. But she can't get out of the trap. She puts it quite clearly at a certain moment in the film, that all this is a trap: love, pity, friendship.

In a way, Julie's in a static situation. She's constantly waiting for something, waiting that something will change. She's extremely neurasthenic – because that's what she's decided to be – and the film, in a sense, has to follow her, follow her way of life and her behaviour. Of course this doesn't mean that if a film's about boredom it has to be boring itself.

There are various fade-outs. There's the typical elliptical fade-out: time passes. A scene ends, there's a fade-out and a new scene begins. And there are four fade-outs which bring us back to exactly the same moment. The idea is to convey an extremely subjective point of view. That is, that time really does pass but for Julie, at a certain moment, it stands still. A journalist comes to visit her on the hospital terrace, says 'Hello' and Julie replies 'Hello'. That's the way the fade-out starts the first time we see it. Two seconds go by between one 'hello' and the other. What I want to show is that for Julie time has stopped. Not only does the music come back to her but time stands still for a moment.

The same applies when the young stripper/neighbour approaches her in the swimming pool. The girl says: 'Are you crying?' And time stands still for Julie. Because she really is crying. Another example – Antoine says: 'Don't you want to know anything? I got to the car a couple of seconds after ...' And Julie replies: 'No.' And suddenly time stands still for her. She doesn't once visit the grave, which means she doesn't want to think about the accident or her husband. But the boy reminds her of it. By his very appearance he causes it all to come back to her.

Antoine is an important character – not for Julie but for us. He's somebody who's seen something, knows something. He tells us a lot about her husband, for example. What do we know about Julie's husband? Very little. All we know is what we find out from Antoine. We learn that he was one of those people who repeats a joke twice. And we find out a lot about Julie – that she noticed this in her husband and was able to mention it to the young man. Apart from that, Antoine brings something else, something which we haven't seen before. Julie laughs only once in the film and it's here, when she's with him. She keeps walking around with a long face but when she's with Antoine we see that she used to laugh.

Antoine's there for other reasons, too. I like observing fragments of life and I like films where I glimpse a bit of life without knowing how it began or how it ends. The way Antoine does.

All the three films are about people who have some sort of intuition or sensibility, who have gut feelings. This isn't necessarily expressed in dialogue. Things are very rarely said straight out in my films. Very often everything that's most important takes place behind the scenes, you don't see it. Either it's there in the actors' play, or it isn't. Either you feel it, or you don't.

White is also about a very sensitive person. Of course, he has very different reasons for this sensitivity from Julie, but the film is about a very sensitive man.

It'll be a very different film from *Blue*. That's how it was written and that's how it was made. It's supposed to be a comedy but I don't think it's going to be all that funny. I've cut out most of what was supposed to be funny but didn't turn out that way.

White is about equality understood as a contradiction. We understand the concept of 'equality', that we all want to be equal. But I think this is absolutely not true. I don't think anybody really wants to be equal. Everybody wants to be more equal. There's a saying in Polish: There are those who are equal and those who are more equal. That's what used to be said during Communism and I think it's still being said.

This is what the film's about. At the beginning, Karol is humiliated, trampled into the ground. He wants to get out of this situation, both literally and metaphorically. Of course, to a certain extent he's to blame, but that's the way things stand. He isn't having any success sleeping with his wife. Nobody knows why he's suddenly impotent. Once he could and now suddenly he just can't get it up. He says that maybe it's his work, wine at lunch or whatever, but we don't really know. And because he can't get it up he is extremely humiliated both as a man and as a human being. Everything he ever had is taken away from him and his love is rejected. Consequently, he wants to show that not just is he not as low as he's fallen, not just is he on a level with everybody else, but that he's higher, that he's better.

So he does everything he can to prove to himself and to the woman who, to put it mildly, has spurned him, that he's better than she thinks. And he does. Therefore he becomes more equal. Except that, while becoming more equal, he falls into the trap which he's set his wife because it turns out that he loves her – something he didn't know. He thought he no longer loved her. His aim was to get even with her. Whereas with this revenge it suddenly appears that love has returned. Both to him and to her.

You see them both on the ferry but you have to see the third film, *Red*, to know that *White* has a happy ending.

I've got an increasingly strong feeling that all we really care about is ourselves. Even when we notice other people we're still thinking of ourselves. That's one of the subjects of the third film, *Red* – fraternity.

Valentine wants to think of others but she keeps thinking about others from her own point of view. She simply can't have any other. The same way as you or I don't have any other way of looking at things. That's how it is. Now the question arises: even when we give of ourselves, aren't we doing so because we want to have a better opinion of ourselves? It's something to which we'll never know the answer. Philosophers haven't found it in 2,000 years and nobody will.

There's something beautiful in the fact that we can give something of ourselves. But if it turns out that while giving of ourselves we are doing so in order to have a better opinion of ourselves then immediately there's a blemish on this beauty. Is this beauty pure? Or is it always a little marred? That's the question the film asks. We don't know the answer, nor do we want to know it. We're simply reflecting on the question once again.

But *Red* is really about whether people aren't, by chance, sometimes born at the wrong time.

What interested me about *Véronique* were the parallels, the fact that one Véronique senses the other, that one has the feeling that she isn't alone in the world. And this idea is repeated very often in *Véronique*. Each of them says that she has a feeling that she isn't alone, or one of them says that she has a feeling that someone is next to her or that she's lost someone who's very important although she has no idea who that person is. Auguste in *Red* hasn't any feeling that a judge exists. The judge, of course, knows that Auguste exists. But we'll never be sure whether Auguste really does exist or whether he's only a variation of the judge's life forty years later.

The theme of *Red* is the conditional mood – what would have happened if the judge had been born forty years later. Everything that happens to Auguste happened to the judge although, perhaps, slightly differently. At one point in the film, the judge says that he saw a white mirror with the reflection of his fiancée's legs spread out and a man between them. Auguste doesn't see any white mirror. Auguste sees it differently but the situation's the same. He sees the legs spread out and a man between them. So, does Auguste really exist or doesn't he? Is Auguste repeating exactly the judge's life? Is it possible to repeat somebody's life after some time or not? But the essential question the film asks is: is it possible to repair a mistake which was committed somewhere high above? Somebody brought someone to life at the wrong moment. Valentine should

86–7 *Blue, Red*: liberty, fraternity.

have been called to life forty years earlier or the judge forty years later and then they'd have constituted a good pair. These people would probably have been very happy together. They probably suit each other very well. That's the theory of the two halves of an apple. If you cut one apple in half and cut another identical one, the half of the one apple will never fit with the half of the other. You have to put together the halves of the same apple to make the apple whole. The whole apple is comprised of a matching pair and it's the same with people. The question is: has a mistake been committed somewhere? And if it has then is there anybody in a position to rectify it?

Blue, *White* and *Red* are three individual films, three separate films. Of course they were made to be shown in this order but that doesn't mean that you can't watch them the other way round. There were a lot of connections between the films of the *Decalogue*. There are far fewer connections here and they're far less important.

It wasn't possible for me to manoeuvre the shooting schedule, nor did I want to. There's a very different kind of production set-up here. The *Decalogue* was shot in one city so there was the possibility of manoeuvring with the various films. We did this chiefly because of the actors, the cameramen's schedules and so on. But here we're making three films in three different countries with three different crews and three completely different sets of actors, so it's impossible to overlap like that. There's only one scene here where we could overlap. We shot a scene in Paris, in the Palace of Justice, which is in the film *Blue* and where you glimpse Zamachowski and Julie Delpy for a second, while in the film *White* Binoche briefly appears. That was an overlap where we simply had one or two shooting days during which half of the time was devoted to *Blue* and the other half to *White*.

First we shot the whole of *Blue*, then immediately the next day we started shooting that part of *White* which takes place in France. We had ten or twelve shooting days on *White* in Paris and then we went to Poland where everything was different, a new crew, new electricians. But a lot of people also came from France. The continuity girl was the same. So was the soundman, Jean-Claude Laureux.

After the memorable experience of having fourteen sound

engineers recording *Véronique*, I now only have one. One of the basic conditions with which I confronted production at the very start was that I have the same soundman from the beginning of the shoot to the finished copy. Of course, a different sound engineer comes along for the mixing because these are two different professions here. In Poland it's not like that. In Poland the soundman mixes his own film. He can't do that here, in the West, because mixing is so specialized and computerized. A soundman, if he's any good, can't know all about it because he hasn't got the time to learn. So Jean-Claude is with us to the end. I think he's pleased, although he's got an enormous amount of work. It's his creation. He's got his own sound path which he's creating. He's got some specialized equipment – I think it's the second time this system's being used in France for recording sound – and he's editing all the sound effects on a computer. He enters them onto the computer and edits. The computer belongs to him. He hires it out with himself and does all the work. He doesn't even use a cutting table, only his computer. Of course this is nothing new as far as music or mixing are concerned, but it is new in the case of effects.

I think I made a good choice with the lighting cameramen. First, I chose the ones with whom I wanted to work. *Three Colours* were a pretty good opportunity for them because this is a large and serious production. Although there are a number of Polish cameramen working abroad, most of them generally work for small productions or for television. Consequently, I thought it would be right to employ those lighting cameramen who had helped me on the *Decalogue* and with whom I'd enjoyed working. To be honest, I enjoyed working with all of them on the *Decalogue* but there were some whom I'd felt had done a better job or who'd put more into it. *Decalogue* was a very difficult film to make. Very hard for the cameramen, too. Very difficult conditions and little money. So I thought they simply deserved some sort of friendly gratitude.

I had to choose lighting cameramen who knew how things work in the West. Firstly, they had to know the language. And secondly, they had to know how production works. It's too great a responsibility, too complicated to have somebody who didn't know how a production works in any country other than Poland or who doesn't know any language other than Polish. So this choice was in itself limited.

I think they're well chosen for the style. Each one of them has a different world, sets up different lighting, uses the camera differently. When I decided to work with them, I bore in mind the needs of the films, their dramaturgy, their structure and so on. Of course, one could imagine Sławek Idziak lighting *Red* and Piotrek Sobociński lighting *Blue*, but Sławek clearly wanted to work on *Blue*. He had a certain amount of freedom – he's the lighting cameraman I've worked with the most. Apart from that I thought that *Blue* required his way of looking at the world, his way of thinking, above all.

All in all, I'm happy with the way *Blue* looks. There are a few impressive shots but there aren't too many effects as such. I cut out a great number of effects. We wanted to convey Julie's state of mind. When you wake up on an operating table what you see first is the lamp, the lamp becomes a great white haze and then it becomes clearer and clearer. After the accident, Julie can't see the man who brings her the television set clearly. She opens her eyes and, for a while, she sees a blur. This isn't accidental. It's typical of her mental state of absolute introversion, of focussing in on herself.

Piotrek Sobociński photographed *Red* very well indeed. Perhaps he restricts the actors a bit too much at times but that's how it is when a lighting cameraman really does follow strictly and consistently what he wants to do.

The vital components of *Red* are red, the filters aren't. Red clothes or a red dog's leash, for example. A red background to something. The colour is not decorative, it plays a dramaturgic role: the colour means something. For example, when Valentine sleeps with her fiancé's red jacket, the red signifies memories, the need of somebody. *Red* is very complex in its construction. I don't know whether we'll manage to get my idea across on the screen. We had all we needed. We had very good actors, because both Irène Jacob and Jean-Louis Trintignant were very good. The photography's very good and the conditions were good. We had excellent interiors. The locations in Geneva weren't badly chosen. So I've got everything I need to put across what I want to say, which really is quite complicated. Therefore, if the idea I've got in mind doesn't come across, it means that either film is too primitive a medium to support such a construction or that all of us put together haven't got enough talent for it.

*

It's different over here, in France. In Poland, it's the designer who generally looks for locations but here it's the director's assistant. I tell my assistant what I'm looking for, he searches, searches, searches and then the lighting cameraman and myself decide. The designer only comes later, to change what needs to be changed, to build walls, paint the right colours and so on. But I don't categorize so strictly. I don't want to bureaucratize the work. If the grip, for example, suddenly has a good idea for a location, then I go and see it – it might be very good.

Of course, *Blue* could take place anywhere in Europe. However, it's very French because the district Julie goes to live in is very Parisian in character. It's a very well-known part of Paris called rue Mouffetard. It took us a good two weeks to find it and we chose it because of the possibilities it offered for shooting. We found a place on rue Mouffetard where we could set the camera up on four sides and we shot from all four sides although you can hardly see that. The district's a bit too touristy and postcard-like for me but all places with a market tend to be like that. And we wanted a market and lots of people. The idea was that Julie should feel that she could lose herself very easily, that when she goes there nobody will find her, she'll drown.

Initially, Julie and her husband were to live in a villa in Paris and she was to move to the suburbs, but we decided that they'd have a house some 30 kilometres from Paris and Julie moves to the centre, to a district where she can lose herself in a crowd. You can find complete anonymity in a big city among people. To be honest, it's also partly to do with the fact that we couldn't find a good suburb.

You can never find what you really want. Geneva, where the action of *Red* takes place, is exceptionally unphotogenic. There's nothing there you can photograph. There's nothing to catch the eye. The architecture isn't uniform. The whole of Geneva has been hacked to pieces. Houses have been pulled down and the gaps filled with modern buildings dating from the 1960s, 70s or 80s. It irritates me immensely. Geneva is spread out and lacks character. Of course, in a wide shot showing the fountain, you know it's Geneva, but apart from that there's nothing characteristic.

We needed houses in Geneva which topographically fit in with each other. We must have gone through the whole of Geneva, which isn't large, and found two places like that. Of course, it isn't all that important that the action takes place in Geneva but if you're in a city you do want to convey some sort of character of the place.

I don't know anything about music. I know more about atmosphere than music as such. I know what sort of atmosphere I want to have in my films but I don't know what music would help achieve it or how to write that music. Zbyszek Preisner is somebody I can work together with, rather than just ask him to come up with a given effect. I often want to put music in where he says it would sound absurd, and there are scenes which I don't imagine having music but which he thinks should have music, so we put the music in. He is definitely more sensitive in this area than I am. I think in a more traditional way whereas his thinking is more modern, full of surprises. That is, it surprises me where he wants music.

Music is important in *Blue*. Musical notes often appear on the screen, so in this sense the film's about music, about the writing of music, about working on music. For some people Julie is the author of the music we hear. At one stage the journalist asks Julie: 'Did you write your husband's music?' And Julie slams the door on her. So this possibility does exist. Then the copyist says: 'There are a lot of corrections.' There had always been a lot of corrections. Did Julie only do the corrections? Maybe she's one of those people who aren't able to write a single sheet of music but is wonderful in correcting a sheet which has already been written. She sees everything, has an excellent analytical mind and has a great talent for improving things. The written sheet of music isn't bad but when she's improved it it is excellent. But it's not all that important whether she's the author or co-author, whether she corrects or creates. Even if she only does do the corrections she's still the author or co-author because what has been corrected is better than it was before. The music is cited all through the film and then at the end we hear it in its entirety, solemn and grand. So we're led to think that she's played a part in its creation. In this sense the film's about music.

As yet I haven't got any ideas for the music in *White*, the Polish film about equality, apart from the fact that Karol plays 'The last Sunday, tomorrow we'll part'[2] on a comb two or three times. It'll probably have a certain simplicity characteristic of music written for silent films, but it won't be played on a piano. It'll be a bit more complicated musically. I suspect that it'll be inspired, to a certain extent, by Polish folk music such as the mazurka, for example, music which is a bit coarse yet at the same time romantic.

Preisner has written a long bolero for the last film, Red. A bolero is always made up of two motifs which interweave with one another. We're going to use the two motifs and then, at the end, they'll combine into a bolero. Or maybe we'll use the bolero at the beginning and then divide it into the two motifs which we'll use in the film. We'll see how things go.

In each of the three films we cite Van der Budenmajer. We already used him in *Véronique* and in the *Decalogue*. He's our favourite Dutch composer from the end of the nineteenth century. He doesn't exist. We invented him a long time ago. Van der Budenmajer is really Preisner, of course. Preisner is now taking his old works and saying that they were written by Van der Budenmajer. Van der Budenmajer has even got a date of birth and a date of death. All his works are catalogued and the catalogue numbers used for recordings.

There were four versions of the script for each of the films. Then there was another, so-called amended fourth version which only dealt with dialogue. A dialogue writer was to join us initially but the producer and I managed to persuade Marcin Latałło to translate our dialogue properly, finding all the correct idioms.

I generally dedicate a whole day only to changes in dialogue. The actors sit around and for the whole day we hack it out to see whether anything could be put in a better way, more concisely or even left out. Then we change it on set another ten times, of course.

I don't rehearse actors. I never have, not even in Poland. And I don't use stand-ins. Except, perhaps, when somebody's got to get punched in the nose and the actor doesn't want to get punched, then I use a stuntman. We did, however, use a stand-in for Jean-Louis Trintignant who had difficulty walking because of an accident and had to use a walking stick. But that was only in rehearsal. Because, despite what I've just said, I did have to rehearse certain very long scenes in *Red*, scenes with actors which last some ten minutes. That's extremely long and everything has to be prepared very accurately. We rehearsed these scenes with the lighting cameraman for two or three days in the proper interiors, to decide exactly where each actor was to sit, where we could put the lights and so on and so on.

I try to make what I do interesting for people. Just as I want the audience to be interested, so I want the crew to be interested, too. I think that as soon as they see where I'm putting the camera, where the cameraman is arranging the lights, how the soundman is preparing himself and what the actors are doing, they realize very quickly what sort of a world we're in. Besides, they are experienced people who have already worked on a large number of films.

Of course I try to get as much out of everyone as I can. I'm always expecting people to tell me something simply because I think that they often know better than I do. I expect it from actors, cameramen, soundmen, editors, electricians, assistants, everyone. As soon as I start carrying boxes around, which I most willingly do, they stop thinking that they're allotted to a certain box and realize they, too, can belong to a different box. They immediately sense that I'm open to their ideas.

I can't complain about producers. Up until now I've always worked without a producer because there weren't any producers as such in Poland. My friends and colleagues, without putting a penny into any of my films, were like producers to me. They'd look on from the side at everything I did and express their opinions. And that, in fact, is what I look for in a producer in the West. I look for two things really. I expect a certain amount of freedom to do what I believe is right. And I expect partnership.

Freedom, of course, is tied up with many things. Money, for example. I wouldn't like to work with a producer for whom I'd have to find the money. I prefer to work with someone who will ensure that I have the necessary amount of money. I'm over fifty and I'm not young or fresh enough to play at film school. I can't do that. I have to have my requirements guaranteed. I keep repeating that I want to make low budget films but that doesn't mean I'm going to look for my own hotel, for example, when I'm on location. And I'm not going to ask my friends to play the main roles or to do the make-up and costumes. I prefer everything to be done professionally. So I expect peace from the production side, so to speak.

This peace is intrinsically tied up with the possibility of my having a certain freedom to maneouvre. While discussing the script with the producer and coming to an agreement with him about the budget and working conditions – and I try hard to keep to these conditions very strictly – I expect him to give me the possibility of manoeuvring. That, for example, I'll be able to shoot a scene which isn't in the script, or that he'll allow me to cut a very expensive one out if that scene turns out not to be necessary.

On the other hand, I expect the producer to be a partner. That is, I expect him to have an opinion, to know something about films and the film market. That's why it's extremely important for the producer to have contacts with distributors, or to be one himself.

The producer of *Véronique*, who was a very good partner to me and created very good working conditions, turned out not to be a producer at all, because he didn't tell me the truth about how the film was being financed and that led to numerous misunderstandings. But he was a real partner. He had his tastes, his opinions, and ensured that I got what I wanted, that is, freedom within the production.

In *Three Colours*, which I'm making now, I've also got this freedom. Maybe even to a greater degree, because I've got a decidedly better executive producer. Yvon Crenn is far more experienced than my previous executive producer. He is far better in managing the money and creates better working conditions. An executive producer, someone who directly supervises the set and spends the money on a daily basis, is an extremely important person.

On the other hand, Karmitz, of course, is far more experienced than my previous producer and therefore has far more pronounced opinions. Yet he's always ready to talk, discuss and find a way which will suit us both. He's helped me resolve a good many artistic problems. That's another thing I expect of a producer, of course. That, in a sense, he'll be an arbitrator, somebody I can turn to in difficult moments. I don't think there are many producers like that in the world.

As to whether I'm going to make any more films, that's another question altogether, and one which I can't answer at the moment. I probably won't.

Notes

Chapter 1

1 Kieślowski's country house, which he built himself in north-east Poland.

2 When the map of Europe was redrawn and agreed upon by Stalin, Roosevelt and Churchill at the Yalta Conference and at Potsdam in 1945, the Polish borders shifted west. In compensation for the eastern lands that were lost to the Soviet Union, Poland was given some land in the west which used to belong to Germany. These are known as the Regained Territories because, during the medieval era, Poland ruled over some of them.

3 At the age of seven children started 'first school', which was compulsory and where they remained for seven years. At the end of each year reports were issued and if a child didn't achieve the required standard he or she had to repeat a year. 'Middle school', which lasted four years, followed. It could be general or professional. General schools prepared children for exams which could then qualify them for higher education such as university; professional schools did not. All schooling was State funded.

4 Joseph Stalin died in 1953.

5 During Communism, each citizen had to register with the local authorities. In some large cities, Warsaw for example, the number of inhabitants was officially limited in order to prevent uncontrolled migration.

6 A north-western district of Warsaw.

7 Full-time students were partly exempt from compulsory full-time military service. They only had to put in one day a week.

8 *W Pustyni i w Puszczy* (1911) (*In the Desert and Wilderness*) (Eng. trans. 1912). A Polish children's classic by Henryk Sienkiewicz (1846–1916) who was awarded the Nobel prize for literature in 1905.

9 Agnieszka Holland (b. 1948). Director of feature films, now living in Paris. Films include: *The Fever* (*Gorączka*) (1980), *The Lonely Woman* (*Kobieta Samotna*) (1981), *Europa, Europa* (1991), *Olivier, Olivier* (1992).

10 Prior to 1970, the Polish Film-makers' Association was similar to a trade union, and like most other institutions was financed and therefore controlled by the Party. But in the mid-1970s, a certain degree of liberalization was introduced, though no structural changes were made. Thanks firstly to documentaries and then features, it became a centre which gently supported the

reform movement. In August 1980, at the time of the strikes, the Film-makers' Association headed the opposition movement among Polish artistic unions but after the introduction of martial law in December 1981, it turned out to be the most open to compromise due to its dependence on State money. The fact that General Jaruzelski didn't dissolve the Film-makers' Association whereas he did dissolve both the Writers' and the Actors' Associations, was taken as evidence of this.

11 Just after the Second World War, Władysław Gomułka was a member of the Communist government in Poland and Minister for the Regained Territories. Imprisoned in 1951 by Bolesław Bierut, the Soviet-imposed Stalinist Polish President, for having revisionist tendencies, he was released three years later, after Stalin's death. As a result of the Polish October, he was triumphantly brought to power in 1956 as Party Secretary. After a time, he acquired all the worst vices of his predecessors and was toppled in 1970 when workers rose in strike against price rises.

12 General Mieczysław Moczar, Minister of the Interior, led the anti-Semitic campaign and purge in 1968 with the aim of taking power.

13 Andrzej Wajda (b. 1926). Director and writer of feature films and theatre director. After the independence of Poland in 1990, he became a senator. Films include: *A Generation (Pokolenie)* (1954), *Canal (Kanał)* (1956), *Ashes and Diamonds (Popiół i Diament)* (1958), *Man of Marble (Człowiek z Marmuru)* (1977), *Man of Iron (Człowiek z Żelaza)* (1981), *Danton* (1982).

14 Jerzy Skolimowski (b. 1938). Director of feature films, now living in the United States. Films include: *The Barrier (Bariera)* (1966), *The Departure (Le Départ)*, (1967), *Deep End* (1970), *The Shout* (1978), *Moonlighting* (1982), *The Lighthouse* (1985), *Ferdydurke* (1991).

15 Krzysztof Zanussi (b. 1939). Director of feature films. Head of Tor Produc-tion House. Films include: *The Crystal Structure (Struktura Kryształu)* (1969), *Illumination (Iluminacja)* (1973), *The Constant Factor (Konstans)* (1980), *Camouflage (Barwy Ochronne)* (1976), *Life for Life (Życie za Życie)* (1991), *The Touch (Dotknięcie)* (1992).

16 Edward Żebrowski (b. 1935). Director of feature films and scriptwriter. He has written many scripts both for and with K. Zanussi. Films include: *Salvation (Ocalenie)* (1972), *Transfiguration Hospital (Szpital Przemienienia)* (1978), *In Broad Daylight (W Biały Dzień)* (1981).

17 Antoni Krauze (b. 1940). Director of documentary and feature films. Films include: *Finger of God (Palec Boży)* (1973), *Weather Forecast (Prognoza Pogody)* (1982).

18 Andrzej Titkow (b. 1948). Director, mainly of documentaries, and poet.

19 Tomasz Zygadło (b. 1948). Director of feature and documentary films and theatre director. Films include: *Workers '71 (Robotnicy '71)* (1972 – co-director K. Kieślowski), *Rebus* (1977), *The Moth (Ćma)* (1980).

20 Krzysztof Wojciechowski (b. 1939). Director of feature and documentary films. Films include: *The Family (Rodzina)* (1976), *Antiques (Antyki)* (1978), *The Charge (Szarża)* (1981).

21 Piotr Wojciechowski finished Łódź Film School and became a novelist.

22 Kazimierz Karabasz (b. 1930). Director of documentary films. Former professor of Łódź Film School. Films include: *Where the Devil says goodnight (Gdzie Diabeł mówi dobranoc)* (1956), *Men from the Desert Zone (Ludzie z pustego obszaru)* (1957), *The Musicians (Muzykańci)* (1960).

23 Janusz Kijowski (b. 1948). Director of feature films. Films include *Kung-Fu* (1979) and *Voices (Głosy)* (1980).

24 Grzegorz Królikiewicz (b. 1939). Director of feature and documentary films. Feature films include: *Through and Through (Na Wylot)* (1972).

25 Andrzej Jurga (b. 1936). Director of documentary films.

26 Janusz 'Kuba' Morgenstern (b. 1922). Director of feature films. He taught at Łódź Film School. Films include: *The Colombuses (Kolumbowie)* (1970), and the TV serial *Polish Ways (Polskie Drogi)* (1977).

27 Jerzy Kawalerowicz (b. 1922). Director of feature films. President of the Polish Film-makers' Association 1966–78. Films include: *Mother Joan of the Angels (Matka Joanna od Aniołów)* (1961), *Pharoah (Faraon)* (1965), *Death of a President (Śmierć Prezydenta)* (1977).

28 Bohdan Kosiński (b. 1922). Director of documentary films.

Chapter 2

1 Marek Piwowski (b. 1935). Director of documentary and feature films. Documentaries include: *Fly-swat (Muchołuk)* (1967), *Psychodrama* (1969), *Corkscrew (Korkociąg)* (1971). Feature films include: *The Cruise (Rejs)* (1970), *Excuse me, do they beat you up here? (Przepraszam, czy tu biją?)* (1973).

2 During the Communist era, the entire film industry, including television, was State owned and State financed. Money from the State Treasury would be allocated to the production houses for feature films – the main studios being in Łódź and Wrocław – to documentary film studios – the main studio being the Wytwórnia Filmów Dokumentalnych (WFD) (State Documentary Film Studios) in Warsaw – and to Television. Television used this money not only on films and programmes made in its own studios but also to commission TV drama films from the Production Houses. In this book, Television with a capital 'T' is used to denote Television as a production company. Television, on the whole, was stricter in its censorship and rulings than the production houses which, depending on their heads, tended to give directors a freer hand.

3 Stanisław Niedbalski. Distinguished documentary cameraman. One of the

founders of the critical documentary film movement in the 1960s. In the 1980s he lost an eye in a domestic accident but still continues to work.

4 *Trybuna Ludu* was an official Party daily newspaper.

5 On 13 December 1970 Party Secretary Władysław Gomułka announced a thirty per cent rise in basic food prices. Shipyard workers came out on strike in protest. There were violent confrontations with the police. These events were swiftly followed by an emergency session of the Politburo that brought in Edward Gierek to office as Party Secretary.

6 Edward Gierek, brought to power on the wave of strikes in 1970, later fell from power during the strikes of 1980.

7 Witold Stok, BSc, 'Tolo' (b. 1946). Polish lighting cameraman of feature and documentary films. Now lives in London. Documentaries include: *From a Night Porter's Point of View, Seven Women of Different Ages, Personnel, Station* with Kieślowski. Features include *In Broad Daylight* (*W Biały Dzień*), *Hidden City* (1988), *Close my Eyes* (1991), *A Dangerous Man* (1991), *Century* (1992).

8 Wojciech Wiszniewski, 'Szajbus' (Madman) (1946–80). Director of documentaries. Died of heart failure.

9 Stefan Olszowski. Contender for power during the Gierek era.

10 Radio Free Europe is a broadcasting station based in Munich. Opposed to Communism, it transmits uncensored information to eastern Europe, and was covertly listened to by many people in Poland.

11 The Party Control Committee was a Communist organization. Party members who were believed to have deviated from the Party's way of thinking stood trial before local Party Boards of Control. The trials were informal, that is, sentences ranged from reprimands to withdrawal of Party membership.

12 Filip Bajon (b. 1947). Director of feature films and novelist. Films include: *Aria for an Athlete* (*Aria dla Atlety*) (1979).

13 Teatr Stary (Old Theatre) in Kraków is one of the greatest theatres in Poland. It has housed numerous memorable productions including Polish classics directed by Konrad Swinarski, and Adam Mickiewicz's *Forefather's Eve* (*Dziady*) directed by Andrzej Wajda.

14 Jerzy Stuhr. Repertory actor with Teatr Stary and screen actor. He has appeared in many of Kieślowski's films including *The Scar, The Calm* , the *Decalogue* and *White*.

15 Jerzy Trela. A repertory actor with Teatr Stary, and film actor. He has played many lead roles in Polish classics.

16 Konrad Swinarski. Legendary theatre director in post-war Poland. Died at an early age in a plane crash.

17 *See* note 5, Chapter 1.

18 Michał Żarnecki recorded sound on several of Kieślowski's films.

19 Małgorzata Jaworska. One of the leading sound recordists in Poland.

20 Jacek Petrycki (b. 1948). Lighting cameraman on both feature and documentary films. He has worked on numerous films with Kieślowski including *Camera Buff, The Calm, Blind Chance,* as well as documentaries.

21 Krzysztof Wierzbicki, 'Dziób' (Beak). First assistant director on a large number of Kieślowski's films – both documentaries and features.

22 Ochota, a western suburb of Warsaw, to the town centre, Śródmieście.

23 Ewunia and Ewka are diminutive forms of Ewa, Polish for Eve.

24 *See* note 2, Chapter 2.

25 The years leading up to Solidarity were a little more liberal for the arts. After the strikes of August 1980, and the formation of Solidarity, millions of people handed in their Party membership cards and openly criticized the Party. The Round Table Talks also included a clause giving the free trade unions and the Catholic Church access to the media.

26 Confrontations (*Konfrontacje*): an annual film season where the best Polish and foreign films, prior to being released are shown in selected cinemas. Screenings are open to the public but books of tickets have to be bought in advance and are hard to come by because there is a limited number of performances.

27 Orwo-Colour was East German film stock known for the poor quality of its colour. Orwo exaggerated colours such that, for example, flesh-coloured skin tones would appear red.

Chapter 3

1 During the Communist era, a vice-minister from the Ministry of Arts and Culture was allocated specially to the film industry. The State, therefore, could intervene in every stage of film production and set down rules concerning who was considered qualified or suitable to make a first feature, and so on. Day-to-day details of production such as the length of shooting schedules, crewing, etc, were overseen by the Production Houses.

2 Sławomir Idziak. Lighting cameraman on many of Kieślowski's feature films including *The Scar, A Short Film about Killing, The Double Life of Véronique, Blue.*

3 Ireneusz Iredyński. Scriptwriter. Author of many radio plays.

4 Hanna Krall. Distinguished journalist.

5 Stanisław Różewicz (b. 1924). Brother of poet Tadeusz Różewicz. Director of

feature films. Artistic head of Tor Production House since the 1970s. Films include: *Westerplatte* (1967), *Leaves have fallen (Opadły Liście z Drzew)* (1975), *The Lynx (Ryś)* (1981).

6 Juliusz Machulski (b. 1955). Untrained actor and son of screen star Jan Machulski. Director of feature films. Films include *Va Bank* (1981) and *Sex Mission (Seksmisja)* (1983).

7 Wojciech Marczewski (b. 1944). Director of feature films. Films include *Nightmares (Zmory)* (1978), *Shivers (Dreszcze)* (1981).

8 Feliks Falk (b. 1941). Director of feature films. Films include: *Top Dog (Wodzirej)* (1977), *And there was Jazz (Był Jazz)* (1981).

9 Under Communism, the film industry was financed by the State. A sum of money would be allocated to each Production House by the State. The Production House, in turn, decided a set budget for each film in production.

10 Poland being predominantly a Catholic country, the Church is an extremely strong power. During the Communist years, people from all kinds of backgrounds turned to the Church as an antidote to Communism, identifying the Church with their struggle for freedom. Religion was – and to a large extent still is – a part of people's lives so that it influenced all walks of life, including film.

11 *See* note 2, Chapter 2.

12 *Top Dog (Wodzirej)* (1979), directed by Feliks Falk.

13 Sometimes when there's a special screening or season of films, local communities or film clubs invite directors and/or authors to take part, after the film, in a discussion with the audience.

14 Krzysztof Piesiewicz (b. 1945). Co-scripted *No End, Decalogue* and *Three Colours* with Kieślowski. He graduated in law from Warsaw University in 1970. Initially specializing in criminal law, he became more involved in political cases after the declaration of martial law in 1981. He was one of the prosecutors during the trial of the three security policemen accused of the murder of Father Jerzy Popiełuszko in 1985.

15 The UB (Urząd Bezpieczeństwa) was the Polish secret service, Poland's equivalent of Soviet Russia's NKGB.

16 The SB (Służba Bezpieczeństwa) were the secret security forces, the Polish equivalent of Soviet Russia's KGB.

17 In the Culture Department of the Central Committee of the Communist Party.

18 *See* Introduction *and* note 9, Chapter 3.

19 Tadeusz Konwicki (b. 1926). Novelist – first published in the 1950s – and film director. He was literary director of Kadr Production House. Films include: *The Last Day of Summer (Ostatni Dzień Lata)* (1958), *The*

Somersault (Salto) (1965), *All Souls' Day (Zaduszki)* (1961). But it is for his novels that he is best known. His novels include: *The Polish Complex (Kompleks Polski)* (1977), *A Minor Apocalypse (Mala Apokalipsa)* (1979).

20 Andrzej Szczypiorski (b. 1924). Novelist and journalist. Novels include: *Mass for the Town of Arras (Msza za Miasto Arras)* (1971), *And They Passed Emaus By (I omineli Emaus)* (1974), *Three in a Straight Line (Trzech w Linii Prostej)* (1981).

21 Jerzy Andrzejewski. Novelist. Works include *Ashes and Diamonds (Popiół i Diament)*, which was adapted for the screen, and directed by Andrzej Wajda.

22 General Wojciech Jaruzelski was head of the Polish Army during the rise of Solidarity in 1980. Three years after the opposition's victory in 1989, Jaruzelski was tried before the constitutional court and took the entire responsibility for martial law.

23 KOR (Komitet Obrony Robotników), the Workers' Defence Committee, was formed in September 1976 to offer arrested workers legal and financial support. The Committee later expanded to treat all cases of human rights violations.

24 KPN (Konfederacja Polski Niepodległej), the Confederation of Independent Poland, was one of the most extreme factions of the opposition movement in the 1970s and 1980s.

25 Czesław Kiszczak, the Minister of the Interior during martial law, was General Jaruzelski's right-hand man.

26 Klemens Szaniawski. A distinguished professor of philosophy.

27 *Man of Marble (Człowiek z Marmuru)* (1977), directed by Andrzej Wajda.

28 *Man of Iron (Człowiek z Żelaza)* (1981), directed by Andrzej Wajda.

29 *Workers '80 (Robotnicy '80)*, directed by Andrzej Chodakowski and Andrzej Zajączkowski, records the events of August 1980 in the Gdańsk Shipyard.

30 *See* note 4, Chapter 2.

31 Marcel Loźinski (b. 1940). Director of documentaries. Films include: *Microphone Test (Próba Mikrofonu)*, *Katyń Forest (Las Katyński)* (1990), *Seven Jews from My Class (Siedmiu Zydow z mojej Klasy)* (1992) and *89 Millimetres from Europe (89 Milimetrów od Europy)* (1993).

32 He came from a Jewish family.

33 Adam Michnik, of Jewish descent, was an active dissident in 1968 and during the 1970s and 1980s. He was interned numerous times. An important figure of the opposition during the Communist era, and founding member of the Workers' Defence Committee (KOR), he is now Editor-in-Chief of the best-selling Polish daily newspaper *Gazeta Wyborcza*.

34 Norman Davies, *God's Playground: A History of Poland* (2 vols), OUP, 1981.

35 When an Act is to be passed by Polish Parliament (the Seym), it is first passed on to the Senate (Senat), where it can be vetoed. The Senate itself is not empowered to pass an Act. During the Communist era the Senate ceased to exist, but it was reinstated with the fall of Communism.

36 Andrzej Mleczko, a satirical cartoonist.

37 Every production house has a literary manager who is responsible for commissioning and selecting scripts.

38 *See* note 4, Chapter 2.

Chapter 4

1 Jacek Kaczmarski sang dissident songs during the Solidarity era and martial law.

2 Józef Cyrankiewicz, a survivor of Auschwitz, was prime minister of Poland 1945–56.

Chapter 5

1 'Piesio': Krzysztof Piesiewicz.
2 'The Last Sunday' (*Ostatnia niedziela*) (Petersburski-Starski, Schlechter): a Polish song from the 1930s.

Filmography

1966

The Tram
(TRAMWAJ)

SHORT FEATURE

Night. A boy runs and jumps on a tram. There are very few passengers: a worker on his way to work, a pretty girl. The boy, attracted to the girl, tries to make her laugh, then watches her fall asleep. He gets off at his stop but has second thoughts and, as in the first sequence, runs after the same tram where the girl sleeps.

Director:	Krzysztof Kieślowski
Screenplay:	Krzysztof Kieślowski
Cinematography:	Zdzisław Kaczmarek
Production company:	Łódź Film School
Cast:	Jerzy Braszka, Maria Janiec

35 mm   black and white
5 mins 45 secs

The Office
(URZĄD)

DOCUMENTARY

The counter of a State-owned insurance office, a queue forms in front of the counter window and the employee repeats the question: 'What have you done in your lifetime?'. A satire on the impenetrability of bureaucracy.

Director:	Krzysztof Kieślowski
Screenplay:	Krzysztof Kieślowski
Cinematography:	Lechosław Trzęsowski
Production company:	Łódź Film School

35 mm   black and white
6 mins

1967

Concert of Requests
(KONCERT ŻYCZEŃ)

FEATURE
A coachful of rowdy youths stops by a lake. They drink, play football, generally fool around. One of the youths runs after the ball and sees a couple among the bushes. He stares, entranced by the girl, but the coach driver sounds his horn; it's time to go. The coach leaves. The couple pack their bags and overtake the coach on their motorbike. The girl, sitting on the back of the bike, drops her backpack. The coach driver stops, picks it up. The couple turn back for the bag. The driver won't hand them the bag unless the girl travels in the coach with the drunken youths. She's ready to do so but peace is restored as the girl goes back to her boyfriend. The youth with the football wistfully watches the couple ride away.

Director:	Krzysztof Kieślowski
Screenplay:	Krzysztof Kieślowski
Cinematography:	Lechosław Trzęsowski
Editor:	Janina Grosicka
Production company:	Łódź Film School

35 mm   black and white
17 mins

1968

The Photograph
(ZDJĘCIE)

DOCUMENTARY
An old photograph of two little boys, wearing soldiers' hats and holding rifles. The camera goes in search of these two boys, now grown men, and registers their emotion as they are confronted with the photograph.

Director:	Krzysztof Kieślowski
Cinematography:	Marek Jóźwiak
Editor:	Niusia Ciucka
Production company:	Polish Television

16 mm   black and white
32 mins

1969

From the City of Łódź
(Z MIASTA ŁODZI)

DOCUMENTARY

'A portrait of a town where some people work, others roam around in search of Lord knows what . . . A town which is full of eccentricities, full of all sorts of absurd statues and various contrasts . . . full of ruins, hovels, recesses.' (Krzysztof Kieślowski)

Director:	Krzysztof Kieślowski
Cinematography:	Janusz Kreczmański, Piotr Kwiatkowski, Stanisław Niedbalski
Editor:	Elżbieta Kurkowska, Lidia Zonn
Sound:	Krystyna Pohorecka
Production managers:	Stanisław Abrantowicz, Andrzej Cylwik
Production company:	WFD

35 mm   black and white
17 mins 21 secs

1970

I Was a Soldier
(BYŁEM ŻOLNIERZEM)

A documentary 'about men who had been soldiers and lost their sight in the Second World War . . . The soldiers just sit there, in front of the camera, throughout the film, and talk.' (Krzysztof Kieślowski)

Director:	Krzysztof Kieślowski
Screenplay:	Krzysztof Kieślowski, Ryszard Zgórecki
Cinematography:	Stanisław Niedbalski
Production company:	Czołówka

35 mm   black and white
16 mins

Factory
(FABRYKA)

DOCUMENTARY

A working day in the Ursus tractor factory. Shots of workers alternate with those of a management board meeting. The factory cannot meet its production quota because there is a shortage of equipment, parts, and so on. Papers are sent out, licences are applied for, numerous meetings held, but there seems to be no way out of the vicious network of misunderstandings and bureaucracy – the left hand doesn't know what the right is doing. As one of the board members says: 'the bureaucracy in this country hampers any solution'. Yet the workers still have to meet their quota.

Director:	Krzysztof Kieślowski
Cinematography:	Stanisław Niedbalski, Jacek Tworek
Editor:	Maria Leszczyńska
Sound:	Małgorzata Jaworska
Production manager:	Halina Kawecka
Production company:	WFD

35 mm   black and white
17 mins 14 secs

1971

Before the Rally
(PRZED RAJDEM)

DOCUMENTARY

Ten days of preparation for the Monte Carlo rally. The two Polish drivers battle with the technical shortcomings of the Polish Fiat 125. They did not finish the race. An allegory of the country's industrial and economic problems.

Director:	Krzysztof Kieślowski
Cinematography:	Piotr Kwiatkowski, Jacek Petrycki
Editor:	Lidia Zonn
Sound:	Małgorzata Jaworska
Production manager:	Waldemar Kowalski
Production company:	WFD

35 mm   black and white/colour
15 mins 9 secs

1972

Refrain
(REFREN)

Documentary about the bureaucracy involved in funerals. Grief and emotions are turned into numbers and a pile of paperwork. Then children are born. And so it goes on and on.

Director:	Krzysztof Kieślowski
Cinematography:	Witold Stok
Editor:	Maryla Czołnik
Sound:	Małgorzata Jaworska, Michał Żarnecki
Production manager:	Waldemar Kowalski
Production company:	WFD

35 mm   black and white
10 mins 19 secs

Between Wrocław and Zielona Góra
(MIĘDZY WROCŁAWIEM A ZIELONĄ GÓRĄ)

A commissioned film about the Lubin copper mine.

Director:	Krzysztof Kieślowski
Cinematography:	Jacek Petrycki
Editor:	Lidia Zonn
Sound:	Andrzej Bohdanowicz
Production manager:	Jerzy Herman
Production company:	WFD, commissioned by Lubin Copper Mine

35 mm   colour
10 mins 35 secs

The Principles of Safety and Hygiene in a Copper Mine
(PODSTAWY BHP W KOPALNI MIEDZI)

Commissioned film about the conditions of safety and hygiene in the Lubin copper mine.

Director:	Krzysztof Kieślowski
Cinematography:	Jacek Petrycki
Editor:	Lidia Zonn
Sound:	Andrzej Bohdanowicz
Production manager:	Jerzy Herman

Production company: WFD, commissioned by Lubin Copper Mine

35 mm   colour
20 mins 52 secs

Workers '71: nothing about us without us
(ROBOTNICY '71: NIC O NAS BEZ NAS)

DOCUMENTARY

Filmed after the strikes of December 1970 and the downfall of Gomułka, the film 'was intended to portray the workers' state of mind in 1971. We tried to draw a broad picture showing that the class which, theoretically at least, was said to be the ruling class, had somewhat different views from those which were printed on the front page of the *Trybuna Ludu*.' (Krzysztof Kieślowski) The film was later re-edited by Polish Television and shown, without credits, as *Masters* (*Gospodarze*).

Directors:	Krzysztof Kieślowski, Tomasz Zygadło, Wojciech Wiszniewski, Paweł Kędzierski, Tadeusz Walendowski
Cinematography:	Witold Stok, Stanisław Mroziuk, Jacek Petrycki
Sound:	Jacek Szymański, Alina Hojnacka
Editors:	Lidia Zonn, Maryla Czołnik, Joanna Dorożyńska, Daniela Cieplińska
Production managers:	Mirosław Podolski, Wojciech Szczęsny, Tomasz Gołębiewski
Production company:	WFD

16 mm   black and white
46 mins 39 secs

1973

Bricklayer
(MURARZ)

Documentary about a bricklayer who, during the Stalinist era, was encouraged by the Party to become an exemplary worker and further the Communist cause. A young activist, he was promoted and, he says, 'I became a jack-in-office, instead of an activist ... I got a desk job and gasped for breath, I had to let in fresh air through the window ... And then came the year 1956 and everything tumbled down all of a sudden. It was a little painful. The question was: What now? And in 1956 I asked them to relieve me and send me back to my job in production. I returned where I had come from.' The camera follows the bricklayer – a man whose life has been used up by ideological powers above him – during a May Day parade, alternating with scenes from his daily life.

Director:	Krzysztof Kieślowski
Cinematography:	Witold Stok
Editor:	Lidia Zonn
Sound:	Małgorzata Jaworska
Production manager:	Tomasz Gołębiewski
Production company:	WFD

35 mm   colour
17 mins 39 secs

Pedestrian Subway
(PRZEJŚCIE PODZIEMNE)

TV DRAMA
A woman has left her teaching job in a small town where she used to live and works as a shop decorator in a pedestrian subway in Warsaw. Her husband comes looking for her in the hope that she will return to him.

Director:	Krzysztof Kieślowski
Screenplay:	Ireneusz Iredyński, Krzysztof Kieślowski
Cinematography:	Sławomir Idziak
Sound:	Małgorzata Jaworska
Production company:	Polish Television
Cast:	Teresa Budzisz-Krzyżanowska, Andrzej Seweryn, Anna Jaraczówna, Zygmunt Maciejewski, Jan Orsza-Łukaszewicz, Janusz Skalski

35 mm   black and white
30 mins

1974

X-Ray
(PRZEŚWIETLENIE)

DOCUMENTARY
Patients suffering from tuberculosis speak of their fears and of their wishes to return to a normal life.

Director:	Krzysztof Kieślowski
Cinematography:	Jacek Petrycki
Editor:	Lidia Zonn
Sound:	Michał Żarnecki
Production manager:	Jerzy Tomaszewicz

35 mm   colour
12 mins 63 secs

First Love
(PIERWSZA MIŁOŚĆ)

TV DOCUMENTARY
The camera follows a young unmarried couple during the girl's pregnancy, through their wedding, and the delivery of the baby.

Director:	Krzysztof Kieślowski
Cinematography:	Jacek Petrycki
Editor:	Lidia Zonn
Sound:	Małgorzata Jaworska, Michał Żarnecki
Production company:	Polish Television

16mm   colour
30 mins

1975

Curriculum vitae
(ŻYCIORYS)

DRAMA DOCUMENTARY
A Party Control Committee cross-examines a Party member threatened with expulsion from the Party. The life-story of the accused is a fictional one – although the man playing the role had experienced something similar in his own life – while the Party Control Committee is real. As the meeting progresses, the Control Committee begins to believe in the authenticity of the case and gives the accused its professional inquisitorial treatment.

Director:	Krzysztof Kieślowski
Screenplay:	Janusz Fastyn, Krzysztof Kieślowski
Cinematography:	Jacek Petrycki, Tadeusz Rusinek
Editor:	Lidia Zonn
Sound:	Spas Christow
Production manager:	Marek Szopiński
Production company:	WFD

35 mm   black and white
45 mins 10 secs

Personnel
(PERSONEL)

TV DRAMA

Romek, a sensitive and forthright young man fascinated with the magic of art, comes to the opera to work as a tailor. Gradually, as he is confronted with the reality behind the scenes – the bickering, petty jealousies, vindictiveness and corruption – his illusions shatter. The film ends with Romek sitting in front of a blank sheet of paper on which he is to denounce his friend, a fellow tailor who was sacked through the maliciousness of one of the performers.

Director:	Krzysztof Kieślowski
Screenplay:	Krzysztof Kieślowski
Cinematography:	Witold Stok
Editor:	Lidia Zonn
Artistic director:	Tadeusz Kozarewicz
Costumes:	Izabella Konarzewska
Producer:	Zbigniew Stanek
Production company:	Polish Television and Tor Production House
Cast:	Juliusz Machulski (*Romek*), Irena Lorentowicz, Włodzimierz Boruński, Michał Tarkowski, Tomasz Lengren, Andrzej Siedlecki, Tomasz Zygadło, Janusz Skalski

16mm   colour
72 mins

1976

Hospital
(SZPITAL)

DOCUMENTARY

The camera follows orthopaedic surgeons on a 32-hour shift. Instruments fall apart in their hands, the electrical current keeps breaking, there are shortages of the most basic materials, but the doctors persevere hour after hour, and with humour.

Director:	Krzysztof Kieślowski
Cinematography:	Jacek Petrycki
Editor:	Lidia Zonn
Sound:	Michał Żarnecki
Production manager:	Ryszard Wrzesiński
Production company:	WFD

35 mm   black and white
21 mins 4 secs

Slate
(KLAPS)

A compilation of footage from *The Scar* not used in the final cut of the feature film.

Director:	Krzysztof Kieślowski
Cinematography:	Sławomir Idziak
Sound:	Michał Żarnecki

35 mm   colour
6 mins

The Scar
(BLIZNA)

FEATURE

1970. After discussions and dishonest negotiations, a decision is taken as to where a large new chemical factory is to be built and Bednarz, an honest Party man, is put in charge of the construction. He used to live in the small town where the factory is to be built, his wife used to be a Party activist there, and he has unpleasant memories of it. But he sets to the task in the belief that he will build a place where people will live and work well. His intentions and convictions, however, conflict with those of the townspeople who are primarily concerned with their short-term needs. Disillusioned, Bednarz gives up his post.

Director:	Krzysztof Kieślowski
Screenplay:	Krzysztof Kieślowski, based on a story by Romuald Karaś
Dialogue:	Romuald Karaś, Krzysztof Kieślowski
Cinematography:	Sławomir Idziak
Editor:	Krystyna Górnicka
Art director:	Andrzej Płocki
Sound:	Michał Żarnecki
Music:	Stanisław Radwan
Producer:	Zbigniew Stanek
Production company:	Tor
Cast:	Franciszek Pieczka (*Bednarz*), Mariusz Dmochowski, Jerzy Stuhr, Jan Skotnicki, Stanisław Igar, Stanisław Michalski, Michał Tarkowski, Halina Winiarska, Joanna Orzechowska, Agnieszka Holland, Małgorzata Leśniewska, Asia Lamtiugina

35 mm colour
104 mins

The Calm
(SPOKÓJ)

TV DRAMA

Antek Gralak has just been released from prison. He leaves his home town of Kraków and sets to work on a building site in Silesia. All he wants are the simple things in life: work, somewhere clean to sleep, something to eat, a wife, television and peace. Anxious to avoid conflicts and happy to be alive and free, he is friendly with his colleagues and open-hearted and grateful to his employer. He finds a girl, marries, but conflicts at work prove inevitable. Building materials disappear and Gralak's boss is involved in the theft. Thinking that he's found a potential accomplice in Gralak, the boss proposes to bring him in on the underhand deals. A strike breaks out among the builders. Torn between the two sides – his boss and his colleagues – and longing for peace, Gralak turns up for work. The builders believe he has grassed and beat him up as he mutters 'Calm ... calm.'

Director:	Krzysztof Kieślowski
Screenplay:	Krzysztof Kieślowski, based on a story by Lech Borski
Dialogue:	Krzysztof Kieślowski, Jerzy Stuhr
Cinematography:	Jacek Petrycki
Editor:	Maryla Szymańska
Art director:	Rafał Waltenberger
Sound:	Wiesław Jurgała
Music:	Piotr Figiel
Producer:	Zbigniew Romantowski
Production company:	Polish Television
Cast:	Jerzy Stuhr (*Antek Gralak*), Izabella Olszewska, Jerzy Trela, Michał Szulkiewicz, Danuta Ruksza, Jerzy Fedorowicz, Elżbieta Karkoszka

16 mm colour
44 mins

1977

From a Night Porter's Point of View
(Z PUNKTU WIDZENIA NOCNEGO PORTIERA)

DOCUMENTARY

Portrait of a factory porter, a fanatic of strict discipline, who extends his power even into his personal life as he tries to control everybody and everything in the belief that 'rules are more important than people . . . That means that when a man doesn't obey the rules,' he says, 'you could say he's a goner . . . Children also have to conform to the rules and adults who live on this earth, for whom this beautiful world has been created. I reckon you've got to have capital punishment . . . Simply hang him [the culprit]. Publicly. Tens, hundreds of people would see it.'

Director:	Krzysztof Kieślowski
Cinematography:	Witold Stok
Editor:	Lidia Zonn
Sound:	Wiesława Dembińska, Michał Żarnecki
Music:	Wojciech Kilar
Production manager:	Wojciech Kapczyński
Production company:	WFD

35 mm   colour
16 mins 52 secs

I Don't Know
(NIE WIEM)

DOCUMENTARY
'The confession of a man who was the director of a factory in Lower Silesia. He was a Party member but opposed the Mafia-like organization of Party members which was active in that factory or region. Those people were stealing and debiting the factory account. He didn't realize that people higher up were involved in the affair. And they finished him off.' (Krzysztof Kieślowski) 'Was I right? I don't know!' the man concludes.

Director:	Krzysztof Kieślowski
Cinematography:	Jacek Petrycki
Editor:	Lidia Zonn
Sound:	Michał Żarnecki
Production managers:	Ryszard Wrzesiński, Wojciech Kapczyński
Production company:	WFD

35 mm   black and white
46 mins 27 secs

1978

Seven Women of Different Ages
(SIEDEM KOBIET W RÓŻNYM WIEKU)

DOCUMENTARY

Episodes in which each day of the week shows a ballerina of classical dance at work or in rehearsal; but the ages of the dancers vary from the smallest child taking her first steps in ballet to the eldest ballerina who is now a ballet teacher.

Director:	Krzysztof Kieślowski
Cinematography:	Witold Stok
Editor:	Alina Siemińska, Lidia Zonn
Sound:	Michał Żarnecki
Production company:	WFD

35 mm   black and white
16 mins

1979

Camera Buff
(AMATOR)

FEATURE

Filip Mosz buys himself an 8 mm camera to record the first years of his new baby. He becomes fascinated with his new acquisition and his interests turn to filming subjects other than his family. In the factory where he works, his bosses seize the opportunity and appoint him their official chronicler. His films win prizes at amateur contests and as his creative talents develop so does his desire to record reality as it really is and not as it is officially reported to be. At his factory he is confronted with censorship and as a result of his films his immediate boss is sacked: the management believe a documentary portrait of a disabled worker to be a discredit to their factory even though the person concerned is a model worker. Meanwhile his wife, despising the time and commitment Mosz dedicates to his films, leaves him. Mosz opens his cans of film, exposing them to light. He turns the camera on himself.

Director:	Krzysztof Kieślowski
Screenplay:	Krzysztof Kieślowski
Dialogue:	Krzysztof Kieślowski, Jerzy Stuhr
Cinematography:	Jacek Petrycki
Editor:	Halina Nawrocka
Art director:	Rafał Waltenberger

Sound:	Michał Żarnecki
Music:	Krzysztof Knittel
Producer:	Wielisława Piotrowska
Production company:	Tor
Cast:	Jerzy Stuhr (*Filip Mosz*), Małgorzata Ząbkowska (*Irka Mosz*), Ewa Pokas (*Anna Włodarczyk*), Stefan Czyżewski (*Manager*), Jerzy Nowak (*Osuch*), Tadeusz Bradecki (*Witek*), Marek Litewka (*Piotrek Krawczyk*), Bogusław Sobczuk (*Television Editor*), Krzysztof Zanussi (*himself*)

35 mm   colour
112 mins

1980

Station
(DWORZEC)

DOCUMENTARY

Warsaw's Central Railway Station. 'Someone has fallen asleep, someone's waiting for somebody else. Maybe they'll come, maybe they won't. The film is about people like that, people looking for something.' (Krzysztof Kieślowski) Overhead video 'spy' cameras watch over the station.

Director:	Krzysztof Kieślowski
Cinematography:	Witold Stok
Editor:	Lidia Zonn
Sound:	Michał Żarnecki
Production manager:	Lech Grabiński
Production company:	WFD

35 mm   black and white
13 mins 23 secs

Talking Heads
(GADAJĄCE GŁOWY)

DOCUMENTARY

Seventy-nine Poles, aged seven to 100, answer three questions: When were you born? What are you? What would you like most?

Director:	Krzysztof Kieślowski
Cinematography:	Jacek Petrycki, Piotr Kwiatkowski

Editor:	Alina Siemińska
Sound:	Michał Żarnecki
Production manager:	Lech Grabiński
Production company:	WFD

35 mm black and white
15 mins 32 secs

1981

Blind Chance
(PRZYPADEK)

FEATURE

Witek runs after a train. Three variations follow on how such a seemingly banal incident could influence the rest of Witek's life. One: he catches the train, meets an honest Communist and himself becomes a Party activist. Two: while running for the train he bumps into a railway guard, is arrested, brought to trial and sent to unpaid labour in a park where he meets someone from the opposition. He, in turn, becomes a militant member of the opposition. Three: he simply misses the train, meets a girl from his studies, returns to his interrupted studies, marries the girl and leads a peaceful life as a doctor unwilling to get mixed up in politics. He is sent abroad with his work. In mid-air, the plane he is on explodes.

Director:	Krzysztof Kieślowski
Screenplay:	Krzysztof Kieślowski
Cinematography:	Krzysztof Pakulski
Editor:	Elżbieta Kurkowska
Art director:	Rafał Waltenberger
Sound:	Michał Żarnecki
Music:	Wojciech Kilar
Producer:	Jacek Szeligowski
Production company:	Tor
Cast:	*Episode 1:* Bogusław Linda (*Witek*), Tadeusz Łomnicki (*Werner*), Bogusława Pawelec (*Czuszka*), Zbigniew Zapasiewicz (*Adam*); *Episode 2:* Bogusław Linda (*Witek*), Jacek Borkowski (*Marek*), Adam Ferency (*Priest*), Jacek Sas-Uchrynowski (*Daniel*), Marzena Trybała (*Werka*); *Episode 3:* Bogusław Linda (*Witek*), Irena Burska (*Aunt*), Monika Goździk (*Olga*), Zbigniew Hübner (*Principal*).

35 mm colour
122 mins

Short Working Day
(KRÓTKI DZIEŃ PRACY)

FEATURE

'It's a critical film about a Party Secretary in a pretty large town 100 kilometres from Warsaw. Rebellions and strikes started up in 1976 because of price rises. A large protest broke out which ended with the people setting fire to the regional Party Committee headquarters. At almost the last moment, the Secretary fled the building. He tried to stay right up to the end but when the furniture started getting hot, the police, with help from their informers, somehow managed to get him out.' (Krzysztof Kieślowski)

Director:	Krzysztof Kieślowski
Screenplay:	Hanna Krall, Krzysztof Kieślowski, based on a report by Hanna Krall 'View from a First Floor Window' ('Widok z okna na pierwszym piętrze')
Cinematography:	Krzysztof Pakulski
Editor:	Elżbieta Kurkowska
Sound:	Michał Żarnecki
Music:	Jan Kanty Pawluśkiewicz
Producer:	Jacek Szeligowski
Production company:	Polish Television
Cast:	Wacław Ulewicz (*Party Secretary*)

35mm colour
79 mins 22 secs

1984

No End
(BEZ KOŃCA)

FEATURE

The ghost of a young lawyer observes the world as it is after martial law. Three motifs interweave. A worker accused of being an activist with the opposition and whom the young lawyer was to defend, is now being defended by an older, experienced colleague who is resigned to a degree of compromise. The lawyer's widow only realizes after her husband's death how much she loved him and tries to come to terms with her emptiness. And there's the metaphysical element, 'that is, the signs which emanate from the man who's not there anymore, towards all that he's left behind'. (Krzysztof Kieślowski)

Director:	Krzysztof Kieślowski
Screenplay:	Krzysztof Kieślowski, Krzysztof Piesiewicz
Cinematography:	Jacek Petrycki

Editor	Krystyna Rutkowska
Art director:	Allan Starski
Sound	Michał Żarnecki
Music:	Zbigniew Preisner
Producer:	Ryszard Chutkowski
Production company:	Tor
Cast:	Grażyna Szapołowska (*Urszula Zyro*), Maria Pakulnis (*Joanna*), Aleksander Bardini (*Labrador*), Jerzy Radziwiłłowicz (*Antoni Zyro*), Artur Barciś (*Dariusz*), Michał Bajor (*Apprentice Lawyer*), Marek Kondrat (*Tomek*), Tadeusz Bradecki (*Hypnotist*), Daniel Webb (*American*), Krzysztof Krzemiński, Marzena Tybała, Adam Ferency, Jerzy Kamas, Jan Tesarz

35 mm   colour
107 mins

1988

Seven Days a Week
(SIEDEM DNI W TYGODNIU)

DOCUMENTARY
One of a cycle of films made about cities by various directors. Warsaw. Monday to Saturday, each day shows a fragment of the life of a different person. Sunday all six are reunited at supper; they are all members of one family.

Director:	Krzysztof Kieślowski
Cinematography:	Jacek Petrycki
Editor:	Dorota Warduszkiewicz
Sound:	Michał Żarnecki
Music:	Fryderyk Chopin
Production manager:	Jacek Petrycki
Production company:	City Life, Rotterdam

35 mm   colour
18 mins

A Short Film about Killing
(KRÓTKI FILM O ZABIJANIU)

FEATURE
A youth randomly, and brutally, murders a taxi-driver. Piotr has just passed his law exams and been admitted to the bar. He is to defend Jacek, the young

murderer. There is no evidence for the defence and no apparent motive. Jacek is put on trial, found guilty and executed by hanging. Piotr, after his first case, is left with the bitter doubt – does the legal system, in the name of the people, have the right to kill in cold blood?

Director:	Krzysztof Kieślowski
Screenplay:	Krzysztof Kieślowski, Krzysztof Piesiewicz
Cinematography:	Sławomir Idziak
Editor:	Ewa Smal
Art director:	Halina Dobrowolska
Sound:	Małgorzata Jaworska
Music:	Zbigniew Preisner
Producer:	Ryszard Chutkowski
Production company:	Tor and Polish Television (for the television version, *Decalogue 5*)
Cast:	Mirosław Baka (*Jacek*), Krzysztof Globisz (*Piotr*), Jan Tesarz (*Taxi-driver*), Zbigniew Zapasiewicz (*Police Inspector*), Barbara Dziekan-Wajda (*Cashier*), Aleksander Bednarz, Jerzy Zass, Zdzisław Tobiasz, Artur Barciś, Krystyna Janda, Olgierd Łukaszewicz

35 mm   colour
85 mins

A Short Film about Love
(KRÓTKI FILM O MIŁOŚCI)

FEATURE

Tomek, a young post office worker, is obsessed with Magda, the promiscuous woman who lives in the tower block opposite. He spies on her through a telescope and finally declares his love. She initiates him into the basic fact of life – there is no love, only sex. Tomek, shattered, tries to commit suicide but doesn't succeed. When he returns from hospital, it is Magda who becomes obsessed with him.

Director:	Krzysztof Kieślowski
Screenplay:	Krzysztof Kieślowski, Krzysztof Piesiewicz
Cinematography:	Witold Adamek
Editor:	Ewa Smal
Art director:	Halina Dobrowolska
Sound:	Nikodem Wołk-Łaniewski
Music:	Zbigniew Preisner
Producer:	Ryszard Chutkowski
Production company:	Tor

Cast: Grażyna Szapołowska (*Magda*), Olaf Lubaszenko
(*Tomek*), Stefania Iwińska (*Godmother*), Artur Barciś
(*Young Man*), Stanisław Gawlik (*Postman*), Piotr
Machalica (*Roman*), Rafał Imbro (*Bearded Man*), Jan
Piechociński (*Blond Man*), Małgorzata Rożniatowska,
M. Chojnacka, T. Gradowski, K. Koperski,
J. Michalewska, E. Ziółkowska

35 mm   colour
87 mins

The Decalogue
(DEKALOG)

Ten television drama films, each one based on one of the Ten Commandments.

Decalogue 1 (Dekalog 1)

Krzysztof introduces his small son, Paweł, to the mysteries of the personal
computer, a machine which he believes to be infallible. It is winter. Paweł,
anxious to try out his new pair of skates, asks his father if he can go out to the
local pond which has just frozen over. They consult the computer; the ice will
hold the boy's weight; he can go. Paweł doesn't come home. There was a freak
local thaw; the computer was wrong; Paweł drowned. Krzysztof runs to the
church in protest and despair, falls against an altar. Candle wax splashes over the
face of the Black Madonna and dries on her cheeks as tears.

Director:	Krzysztof Kieślowski
Screenplay:	Krzysztof Kieślowski, Krzysztof Piesiewicz
Cinematography:	Wiesław Zdort
Editor:	Ewa Smal
Art director:	Halina Dobrowolska
Sound:	Małgorzata Jaworska
Music:	Zbigniew Preisner
Producer:	Ryszard Chutkowski
Production company:	Polish Television
Cast:	Henryk Baranowski (*Krzysztof*), Wojciech Klata (*Paweł*), Maja Komorowska (*Irena*), Artur Barciś (*Man in the sheepskin*), Maria Gładkowska (*Girl*), Ewa Kania (*Ewa Jezierska*), Aleksandra Kisielewska (*Woman*), Aleksandra Majsiuk (*Ola*), Magda Sroga-Mikołajczyk (*Journalist*), Anna Smal-Romańska, Maciej Sławinski, Piotr Wyrzykowski, Bożena Wróbel

35 mm   colour
53 mins

Decalogue 2 (Dekalog 2)

Dorota visits Andrzej, her dying husband, in hospital. She is pregnant – this might be the last chance for her to have a baby – but not by him. She asks the Consultant in charge of her husband's case, whether Andrzej will die. If he lives, she will have to have an abortion; if he dies, she can have the child. How can the doctor decide the life or death of an unborn child? How can he be certain whether his patient will die or miraculously recover? He tells Dorota that her husband doesn't have a chance; but Andrzej recovers. Dorota tells Andrzej that they are going to have a baby; he thinks it's his.

Director:	Krzysztof Kieślowski
Screenplay:	Krzysztof Kieślowski, Krzysztof Piesiewicz
Cinematography:	Edward Kłosiński
Editor:	Ewa Smal
Art director:	Halina Dobrowolska
Sound:	Małgorzata Jaworska
Music:	Zbigniew Preisner
Producer:	Ryszard Chutkowski
Production company:	Polish Television
Cast:	Krystyna Janda (*Dorota*), Aleksander Bardini (*Consultant*), Olgierd Łukaszewicz (*Andrzej*), Artur Barciś (*Young Man*), Stanisław Gawlik, Krzysztof Kumor, Maciej Szary, Krystyna Bigelmajer, Karol Dillenius, Ewa Ekwińska, Jerzy Fedorowicz, Piotr Siejka, Aleksander Trąbczyński

35 mm   colour
57 mins

Decalogue 3 (Dekalog 3)

Christmas Eve, a night when families are together and nobody wants to be alone. Ewa tricks Janusz, her ex-lover, away from his family and under various pretexts tries to keep him with her for the night. Janusz wants to go home but Ewa is determined. They part at dawn.

Director:	Krzysztof Kieślowski
Screenplay:	Krzysztof Kieślowski, Krzysztof Piesiewicz
Cinematography:	Piotr Sobociński
Editor:	Ewa Smal
Art director:	Halina Dobrowolska
Sound:	Nikodem Wołk-Łaniewski
Producer:	Ryszard Chutkowski
Production company:	Polish Television

Cast:	Daniel Olbrychski (*Janusz*), Maria Pakulnis (*Ewa*), Joanna Szczepkowska (*Janusz's wife*), Artur Barciś (*Tram-driver*), Krystyna Drochocka (*Aunt*), Krzysztof Kumor, Dorota Stalińska, Zygmunt Fok, Jacek Kalucki, Barbara Kołodziejska, Maria Krawczyk, Jerzy Zygmunt Nowak, Piotr Rzymszkiewicz, Włodzimierz Rzeczycki, Włodzimierz Musiał

35 mm   colour
56 mins

Decalogue 4 (*Dekalog 4*)

Anka is 20 years old. Her mother is dead and she lives with Michał, her father. They get on well together. Michał has to go on a trip abroad. While he is away, Anka finds an envelope in her father's room: 'Not to be opened before my death.' Within that envelope is another, addressed, in her mother's handwriting, to her. Anka meets her father on his return and quotes the letter where her mother reveals that Michał is not Anka's real father. A different relationship emerges between Anka and Michał as Anka subtly tries to seduce him. Michał resists; she might still be his daughter. As Michał leaves for another trip, Anka runs after him, confessing that she hasn't read the letter after all.

Director:	Krzysztof Kieślowski
Screenplay:	Krzysztof Kieślowski, Krzysztof Piesiewicz
Cinematography:	Krzysztof Pakulski
Editor:	Ewa Smal
Art director:	Halina Dobrowolska
Sound:	Małgorzata Jaworska
Music:	Zbigniew Preisner
Producer:	Ryszard Chutkowski
Production company:	Polish Television
Cast:	Adrianna Biedrzyńska (*Anka*), Janusz Gajos (*Michał*), Artur Barciś (*Young Man*), Adam Hanuszkiewicz (*Professor*), Jan Tesarz (*Taxi-driver*), Andrzej Blumenfeld (*Michał's friend*), Tomasz Kozłowicz (*Jarek*), Elżbieta Kilarska (*Jarek's mother*), Helena Norowicz (*Doctor*)

35 mm   colour
55 mins

Decalogue 5 (*Dekalog 5*)

Television version of *A Short Film about Killing* (see above).

35 mm   colour
57 mins

Decalogue 6 (Dekalog 6)
Television version of *A Short Film about Love* (see above).

35 mm   colour
58 mins

Decalogue 7 (Dekalog 7)
Six-year-old Ania is being brought up by Ewa in the belief that Majka, Ewa's daughter, is her sister, whereas Majka is really her mother. Tired of living this lie and desperate to have Ania love her as a mother, Majka 'kidnaps' Ania and runs away from her parents. She seeks refuge with Wojtek, Ania's father. Majka was just a schoolgirl when Wojtek, her teacher, got her pregnant. Ewa, jealous of Ania's love, looks for her everywhere, phones Wojtek. Majka seizes her little girl and continues to run; she will only return home if her mother allows her to bring up her own daughter in the recognition of the true relationship. Majka and Ania hide at a nearby station. Ewa asks the woman at the ticket office whether she has seen a young woman with a little girl. The ticket woman lies – yes, she did see them but they left some two hours ago. In the background, Ania wakes up and sees Ewa. 'Mummy,' she calls and runs to her. A train arrives, Majka jumps on, rejecting Ewa's pleas for her to come home.

Director:	Krzysztof Kieślowski
Screenplay:	Krzysztof Kieślowski, Krzysztof Piesiewicz
Cinematography:	Dariusz Kuc
Editor:	Ewa Smal
Art director:	Halina Dobrowolska
Sound:	Nikodem Wołk-Laniewski
Music:	Zbigniew Preisner
Producer:	Ryszard Chutkowski
Production company:	Polish Television
Cast:	Anna Polony (*Ewa*), Maja Barełkowska (*Majka*), Władysław Kowalski (*Stefan*), Bogusław Linda (*Wojtek*), Bożena Dykiel (*Ticket Woman*), Katarzyna Piwowarczyk (*Ania*), Stefania Błońska, Dariusz Jabłoński, Jan Mayzel, Mirosława Maludzińska, Ewa Radzikowska, Wanda Wróblewska

35 mm   colour
55 mins

Decalogue 8 (Dekalog 8)
Elżbieta, researching the fate of Jewish war survivors, is visiting from New York and sits in on lectures in ethics at the University of Warsaw. She approaches Zofia, the professor, and tells her that she is the little Jewish girl whom Zofia refused to shelter from the Nazis during the Occupation. As Zofia explains the reason for this apparent cowardice – someone had betrayed Zofia's husband who was active in the underground and any Jewish child would have fallen into the

hands of the Gestapo – her long-standing sense of guilt is cleared while Elżbieta's faith in humanity is restored.

Director:	Krzysztof Kieślowski
Screenplay:	Krzysztof Kieślowski, Krzysztof Piesiewicz
Cinematography:	Andrzej Jaroszewicz
Editor:	Ewa Smal
Art director:	Halina Dobrowolska
Sound:	Wiesława Dembińska
Music:	Zbigniew Preisner
Producer:	Ryszard Chutkowski
Production company:	Polish Television
Cast:	Maria Kościałkowska (*Zofia*), Teresa Marczewska (*Elżbieta*), Artur Barciś (*Young Man*), Tadeusz Łomnicki (*Tailor*), Marian Opania, Bronisław Pawlik, Wojciech Asiński, Marek Kępiński, Janusz Mond, Krzysztof Rojek, Wiktor Sanejko, Ewa Skibińska, Hanna Szczerkowska, Anna Zagórska

35 mm   colour
55 mins

Decalogue 9 (*Dekalog 9*)

Roman learns he's impotent. Recognizing his wife, Hanka's, sexual needs, he encourages her to take a lover. She is reluctant; she loves Roman, but does have an affair with Mariusz, a student. Roman, despite his own words, becomes excessively jealous and obsessed with the thought that Hanka might have followed his encouragement and taken a lover. He spies on her and learns of her relationship with Mariusz, unaware of the fact that Hanka has broken off the affair. Roman tries to commit suicide but survives. Hanka rushes to his side.

Director:	Krzysztof Kieślowski
Screenplay:	Krzysztof Kieślowski, Krzysztof Piesiewicz
Cinematography:	Piotr Sobociński
Editor:	Ewa Smal
Art director:	Halina Dobrowolska
Sound:	Nikodem Wołk-Łaniewski
Music:	Zbigniew Preisner
Producer:	Ryszard Chutkowski
Production company:	Polish Television
Cast:	Ewa Błaszczyk (*Hanka*), Piotr Machalica (*Roman*), Artur Barciś (*Young Man*), Jan Jankowski (*Mariusz*), Jolanta Piętek-Górecka (*Ola*), Katarzyna Piwowarczyk (*Ania*), Jerzy Trela (*Mikołaj*), Małgorzata Boratyńska, Renata Berger, Janusz Cywiński, Joanna Cichoń, Sławomir Kwiatkowski, Dariusz Przychoda

35 mm   colour
58 mins

Decalogue 10 (Dekalog 10)
A man dies leaving an extremely valuable stamp collection to his two sons, Jerzy
and Artur. Although they know very little about stamps, they are unwilling to
sell. They learn that one very rare stamp is needed to complete a valuable set. To
acquire the stamp Jerzy donates his kidney – the man in possession of the stamp is
in need of a kidney for his daughter. Returning from hospital, Jerzy and Artur
find that they have been burgled. The entire stamp collection is gone. Shamefully,
they confess that they suspected each other and are reconciled.

Director:	Krzysztof Kieślowski
Screenplay:	Krzysztof Kieślowski, Krzysztof Piesiewicz
Cinematography:	Jacek Bławut
Editor:	Ewa Smal
Art director:	Halina Dobrowolska
Sound:	Nikodem Wołk-Łaniewski
Music:	Zbigniew Preisner
Producer:	Ryszard Chutkowski
Production company:	Polish Television
Cast:	Jerzy Stuhr (*Jerzy*), Zbigniew Zamachowski (*Artur*), Henryk Bista (*Shopkeeper*), Olaf Lubaszenko (*Tomek*), Maciej Stuhr (*Piotrek*), Jerzy Turek, Anna Gronostaj, Henryk Majcherek, Elżbieta Panas, Dariusz Kozakiewicz, Grzegorz Warchoł, Cezary Harasimowicz

35 mm   colour
57 mins

1991

The Double Life of Véronique
(LA DOUBLE VIE DE VÉRONIQUE) (*Podwójne Życie Weroniki*)

FEATURE
Poland. Weronika, who sings beautifully, suffers from a heart condition. She has
to choose – continue singing with all the strain and stress which this involves and
risk her life, or give up her singing career to lead a normal life. She wins a singing
contest and chooses her career. During a concert she suffers a heart attack and
dies.

France. Véronique is Weronika's double. She, too, has a beautiful voice and a
heart condition. But without knowing it, she shares Weronikas's wisdom. When
Weronika suffers, Véronique senses that she must avoid the situation which leads
to the pain. Véronique rejects her singing career and teaches music at a primary

school. One day, Alexandre, a puppeteer and story writer, visits her school. She is entranced by him and reads the books he has written. Days later she receives mysterious messages – an empty cigar box, a shoe lace, a cassette recording of various sounds made in a station café. She finds the station café and sees Alexandre waiting for her. In the hotel room where they make love, Alexandre finds the photographs which Véronique took when she visited Poland. He sees Weronika, thinking it's Véronique. It is only now that Véronique realizes that she has – or had – a double. She feels that Alexandre is her fate but her illusion is shattered. Alexandre makes two puppets, one of Véronique, the other, an identical one, of Weronika; he wants to use Véronique's life and emotions for his own purposes. Véronique leaves and returns home to her father.

Director:	Krzysztof Kieślowski
Screenplay:	Krzysztof Kieślowski, Krzysztof Piesiewicz
Cinematography:	Sławomir Idziak
Editor:	Jacques Witta
Art director:	Patrice Mercier
Music:	Zbigniew Preisner
Executive producer:	Bernard-P. Guireman
Producer:	Leonardo de la Fuente
Production company:	Sidéral Productions/Tor Production/Le Studio Canal Plus
Cast:	Irène Jacob (*Weronika/Véronique*), Aleksander Bardini (*Orchestra Conductor*), Władysław Kowalski (*Weronika's Father*), Halina Gryglaszewska (*Weronika's Aunt*), Kalina Jędrusik (*Gaudy Woman*); Philippe Volter (*Alexandre*), Sandrine Dumas (*Catherine*), Louis Ducreux (*Professor*), Claude Duneton (*Véronique's Father*), Lorraine Evanoff (*Claude*), Guillaume de Tonquedec (*Serge*), Gilles Gaston-Dreyfus (*Jean-Pierre*), Alain Frerot, Youssef Hamid, Thierry de Carbonnières, Chantal Neuwirth, Nausicaa Rampony, Bogusława Schubert, Jacques Potin, Nicole Pinaud, Beata Malczewska, Barbara Szalapa, Lucyna Zabawa, Bernadetta Kus, Philippe Campos, Dominika Szady, Jacek Wójciki, Wanda Kruszewska, Pauline Monier

35 mm   colour
98 mins

1993/4

Three Colours: Blue, White, Red

Three feature films work separately and as a trilogy in which the present meanings of the three concepts Liberty, Equality and Fraternity are explored.

Blue (1993)
Julie loses her husband Patrice, a renowned composer, and their young daughter Anna in a car accident. She tries to forget, to cut herself off from all previous ties and begin a new life. She moves to an area in Paris where she believes no one will find her but she cannot avoid all the traps – feelings, ambitions and deceptions – which threaten her new freedom. Nor can she lose her husband's – or is it her own? – music. This is one aspect of her life which she cannot control.

Director:	Krzysztof Kieślowski
Screenplay:	Krzysztof Kieślowski, Krzysztof Piesiewicz
Cinematography:	Sławomir Idziak
Editor:	Jacques Witta
Art director:	Claude Lenoir
Sound:	Jean-Claude Laureux
Sound mixer:	William Flageollet
Music:	Zbigniew Preisner
Executive producer:	Yvon Crenn
Producer:	Marin Karmitz
Production companies:	MK2 SA/CED Productions/France 3 Cinema/CAB Productions/Tor Production
Cast:	Juliette Binoche (*Julie*), Benoit Regent (*Olivier*), Florence Pernel (*Sandrine*), Charlotte Very (*Lucille*), Helene Vincent (*The Journalist*), Philippe Volter (*Estate Agent*), Claude Duneton (*Patrice*), Emmanuelle Riva (*Mother*), Florence Vignon (*The Copyist*), Jacek Ostaszewski (*The Flautist*), Yann Tregouet (*Antoine*), Isabelle Sadoyan, Daniel Martin, Catherine Therouenne, Alain Ollivier, Pierre Forget, Philippe Manesse, Idit Cebula, Jacques Disses, Yves Penay, Arno Chevrier, Stanislas Nordey, Michel Lisowski, Philippe Morier-Genoud, Julie Delpy, Zbigniew Zamachowski, Alain Decaux

35 mm   colour
100 mins

White (1993)
Karol, a Polish hairdresser in Paris, is humiliated. He has become impotent and his wife throws him out on to the streets. He meets an equally forlorn fellow

countryman who helps smuggle him back into Poland. On home ground, Karol tries to be 'more equal' than others and plots revenge on his wife. No longer happy with the small-time hairdressing establishment which he ran with his brother, he tries his hand at making quick money. Through connivance and cunning, he makes himself a fortune, then feigns his own death. His wife appears at his 'funeral', and when Karol discloses himself to her, their love for each other is resurrected. But it is too late.

Director:	Krzysztof Kieślowski
Screenplay:	Krzysztof Kieślowski, Krzysztof Piesiewicz
Cinematography:	Edward Kłosiński
Editor:	Urszula Lesiak
Art director:	Claude Lenoir
Music:	Zbigniew Preisner
Sound:	Jean-Claude Laureux
Sound mixer:	William Flageollet
Executive producer:	Yvon Crenn
Producer:	Martin Karmitz
Production companies:	Tor Production/MK2 Productions SA/CED Productions/France 3 Cinema/CAB Productions
Cast:	Zbigniew Zamachowski (*Karol*), Julie Delpy (*The Wife*), Jerzy Stuhr (*Karol's Brother*)

35 mm colour
100 mins

Red (1994)
Valentine, a young model, knocks over a dog as she drives. She takes the bitch in, checks out her address and goes in search of her owner. She finds the villa and discovers an elderly gentleman, living in neglect and eavesdropping on telephone conversations. Initially indignant at what the man is doing, she is nevertheless drawn into a psychological relationship. A friendship grows as the Judge begins to confide in Valentine.

Director:	Krzysztof Kieślowski
Screenplay:	Krzysztof Kieślowski, Krzysztof Piesiewicz
Cinematography:	Piotr Sobociński
Editor:	Jacques Witta
Art director:	Claude Lenoir
Music:	Zbigniew Preisner
Sound:	Jean-Claude Laureux
Sound mixer:	William Flageollet
Executive producer:	Yvon Crenn
Producer:	Martin Karmitz
Production companies:	CAB Productions/MK2 Productions SA/Tor Production/CED Productions/France 3 Cinema

Cast: Irène Jacob (*Valentine*), Jean-Louis Trintignant (*The Judge*)

35 mm   colour
100 mins

Index

Adamek, Witek, 166, 171
America, 205–7; concept of family home
    in, 7–9; films in, 179, 209; television in,
    153, 154
Andrzejewski, Jerzy, 124
Army, 24–9
Atarax, 40
Au revoir les enfants, 175

Baca, Mirosław, 164–6
Bajon, Filip, 62
Balasz, Bela, 41
Barciś, Artur, 132
Bardini, Aleksander, 96
Battleship Potemkin, 32
Before the Rally (Przed Rajdem), 87
Bergman, Ingmar, 32, 33, 195; *Sawdust
    and Tinsel*, 33
*Between Wroclaw and Zielona Góra
    (Między Wroclawiem a Zieloną Górą)*,
    52
Blind Chance (Przypadek), 113–15, 116,
    119, 172, 174, 179, 208
Bricklayer (Murarz), 82
Britain, television in, 153
Budzisz-Krzyżanowska, Teresa, 94–5

Calm, The (Spokój), xviii, 60, 88, 91,
    106–10, 172, 174, 201
Camera Buff (Amator), xiii, 62, 110–12,
    145, 170, 172, 174, 194, 208, 210
Camus, Albert, 5, 194
Chodakowski, A., 136
Church, 136, 142, 189
Cinema of Moral Anxiety, xiii, 41, 104
Citizen Kane, 34, 154, 194
College for Theatre Technicians, xv, 17, 18,
    22, 29, 96
Concert of Requests (Koncert Życzeń), 87
Confederation of Independent Poland
    (KPN), 126
Confrontations, 75
Conscription Board, 24–9
Contemporary Theatre (Teatr
    Współczesny), 96–7
Conversation in The Cathedral, 194
Corbiau, Gerard: *The Music Teacher*, 175
Cortazar, Julio, 195

Crenn, Yvon, 227
Curriculum vitae (Życiorys) (film), xiv,
    xviii, 58–62
Curriculum vitae (Życiorys) (play), 62
Cyrankiewicz, Józef, 208
Czechoslovakia, invasion of, 43
Czołówka, 54

Dante Alighieri, 179
Davies, Norman, 141
Decalogue (Dekalog), xiii, 110, 131,
    143–60, 174, 194, 212, 218, 221, 225;
    film 1 of, 147, 198; film 5 of, 157, 162;
    film 6 of, 170; film 9 of, 148, 177
Dostoevsky, Fyodor, 5, 34, 194
*Double Life of Véronique, The (Podwójne
    Życie Weroniki)*, 172–91, 194, 196–7,
    202, 210–11, 227; 'Antek' in, 60, 62;
    ending of, 7, 188–9
Dziewoński, E., 96
'Dziób' (Krzysztof Wierzbicki), 65–6, 78

Eisenstein, Sergei: *Battleship Potemkin*, 32
Ewa Ewunia, 67–8

Falk, Feliks, 104
Fanfan la Tulipe, 13, 15
Faulkner, William, 194
Fellini, Federico, xxii, 32, 33, 51, 195; *La
    Strada*, 33
Filipski (actor), 119
Firemen's Training College, xv, 16, 18, 25,
    95
First Love (Pierwsza Miłość), 63–8, 90
Flying University, xvii
Fly-swat (Muchołluk), 51
Forefathers' Eve (Dziady), xv
From the City of Łódź (Z Miasta Łodzi),
    44–51, 89
*From a Night Porter's Point of View (Z
    Punktu Widzenia Mocnego Portiera)*,
    xviii, 75–9, 179

Gdansk, xvi, xix
Geneva, 221–2
Gierek, Edward, xvi, xix, 55
Gomułka, Wadysław, xv–xvi, 38, 208
Gorbachev, Mikhail, xxi

Gorczyce, 6, 9
Grotowski, Jerzy, xvii

Henson, Jim, 180
Hitler, Adolf, 36
Holland, Agnieszka, 37–8, 41, 104, 138,
    139
Hospital (Szpital), 68–73

I Don't Know (Nie Wiem), 73–4
I Was a Soldier (Byłem Żołnierzem), 54
Idziak, Sławek, 93, 139, 158, 162, 185,
    186, 222
Illumination (Illuminacja), 178
Iredyński, Irek, 93–4
Irzykowski Studio, 41–3

Jacob, Irène, 175, 180, 182, 183, 184, 185,
    187, 222
Jadzia (in First Love), 63–8
Jaruzelski, General Wojciech, xix-xx, 125
Jaworska, Małgosia, 65
John Paul II, Pope, xix
Jurga, Andrzej, 42, 43

Kaczmarski, Jacek, 208
Kafka, Franz, 34, 194
Kantor, Tadeusz, xvii
Karabasz, Kazimierz, 40
Karaś (journalist), 99
Katowice Film School, 43
Kawalerowicz, Jerzy, 42
Kes, 32, 195
Khrushchev, Nikita, xv
Kieślowski, Marysia (wife), 49, 50, 64–5,
    121, 173
Kieślowski, Marta (daughter), 21, 22, 45,
    64–5, 173
Kieślowski, (father), xiv, 2, 3, 5, 9, 13, 14,
    16, 18, 20, 22, 95, 134–5
Kieślowski, (grandmother), 10, 13
Kieślowski, (mother), xiv, 2, 4, 5, 6, 13, 18,
    19, 20, 22, 23, 26
Kieślowski, (sister), xiv, 4, 5, 9–10, 12, 13,
    14, 20
Kijowski, Janusz, 41, 43, 104
Kilar, Wojciech, 178
Kiszczak, Czesław, 128–9
Kobek, Mieczysław, 97
Koczek, 2
Konwicki, Tadeusz, 124
Kosiński, Bohdan, 42
Kraków, Old Theatre in, 62
Kraków Film Festival, 58–9, 75, 140
Kraków School of History, 141
Krall, Hania, 93, 115, 126
Krauze, Antek, 40, 62
Królikiewicz, Grześ, 42

Kurón, Jacek, xviii

Latałło, Marcin, 187
Laureux, Jean-Claude, 220–21
Lengren, Tomasz, 97
Lenin Shipyard (Gdansk), xvi, xix
Libération, xxii
Liberum Veto, 141
Londe, Boguslaw, 114
Loach, Ken, 32; Kes, 32, 195
Łódź, 44–51
Łódź Film School, xiii, xv, 23, 29–32, 34,
    36–8, 39–40, 44–5, 51, 105
Łomnicki, Tadeusz, 96
Lorentowicz, Irena, 97
Loziński, Marcel, 138
Lower Silesia, 15, 74
Lubaszenko, Olaf, 167, 168, 169
Ludowa Spółdzielnia Wydawnicza (The
    People's Publishing Co-operative), 78

MacDowell, Andie, 174–5
Mach, Wilhelm, 159
Machulski, Julek, 97
Malle, Louis: Au revoir les enfants, 175
Man of Iron, 134
Man of Marble, 134
Marceau, Marcel, 176
Marczewski, Wojtek, 104
Michnik, Adam, xviii, 140
Mickiewicz, Adam: Forefather's Eve
    (Dziady), xv
Military Service, 24–9
Ministry for Arts and Culture, xvii–xvii,
    42, 74, 153
Miramax, 7
Mleczko, Andrzej, 152
Moczar, Mieczyław, xv, xvi, 38, 208
Moretti, Nanni, 175
Morgenstern, Kuba, 42
Music Teacher, The (Le Maître de
    Musique), 175

New York, 206–7
New York Film Festival, 7, 206–7
Niedbalski, Staś, 54
No End (Bez Końca), xiii, 92, 130–7, 142,
    169, 174, 179, 194, 206

Odyssey, The, 7
Olszowski, Stefan, 55, 57
Osuch, Marian, 75, 76–7, 78–9

Painter (Malarz), 125–6
Party see PZPR
Party Control Committee/Party Board of
    Control, 59–60, 62
Paskulski, Krzysztof, 92

Pedestrian Subway (Przejście Podziemne),
   93–5
Personnel (Personel), xiii, 60, 95–8, 174,
   210
Petrycki, Jacek, 65, 87, 90
Philipe, Gérard, 13
Piesiewicz, Krzysztof, 104, 110, 126–7,
   128, 130, 143, 145, 170, 180, 212, 214
Piwowski, Marek: *Fly-swat (Muchotłuk)*,
   51
Poland, 1–2, 141–3, 160–2, 205; concept
   of family home in, 7–9; critics in,
   189–91; film-making in, xiii, xvii-xviii,
   xx-xxi, 104–5, 152–3, 196, 198–9, 223,
   226; martial law in, 119–21, 123,
   125–30, 137, 144; political and
   economic events in, xiii-xxi, 38–9, 55,
   58, 99, 137–8; reactions to Communist
   past in, 115–16, 118–19, 122–5
Polański, Roman, xiii
Polish Film-makers' Association, 37–8, 39
Pope John Paul II, xix
Preisner, Zbigniew, 176, 178, 179, 224–5
*Principles of Safety and Hygiene in a
   Copper Mine (Podstawy BHP w Kopalni
   Miedzy)*, 51, 53, 54
Production Houses (*Zespól*), xvii-xviii,
   123–4, 144
PZPR (Polish United Workers' Party; 'The
   Party'), xv-xvi, xix-xx, 13, 42–3, 58, 74,
   116, 118, 119, 140; and *Curriculum
   vitae*, 58–60; and *Workers '71*, 55, 57

Radio Free Europe, 57, 130
Radziwiłłowicz, Jurek, 131, 134
Refrain (Refren), 85
Regained Territories, 6, 9, 15
Romek (in *First Love*), 63–8
Round Table talks (1989), xxi
Różewicz, Staś, 95

Sawdust and Tinsel, 33
Scar, The (Blizna), 99–102, 174, 208
Schwartz, Bruce, 180–83
Second World War, 9–10, 36
*Seven Women of Different Ages (Siedem
   Kobiet w Różnym Wieku)*, 83
Seweryn, Andrzej, 94–5
Shakespeare, William, 34, 173, 194
*Short Film about Killing, A (Krótki Film O
   Zabijaniu)*, 159–66, 186, 189, 210
*Short Film about Love, A (Krótki Film O
   Miłości)*, 166–72, 210
Short Working Day (Krótki Dzień Pracy),
   92, 93, 102, 115–19, 121, 209
Sienkiewicz, Henryk: *W Pustyni i w Puszcy*,
   28–9
Silesia, 10, 13, 15, 74

Skolimowski, Jerzy, xiii, 39
Sobociński, Piotr, 222
Socio-realism, 99
Sokołowsko, 15–16
Solidarity, xix, xx, xxi, 39, 55, 120
Spółdzielnia Woreczek ('Money-bag
   Co-op'), 51
Stalin, Joseph, 36, 124; death of, 13
State Documentary Film Studios *see* WFD
Station (Dworzec), 68, 79–81, 86, 112
Stok, Witold ('Tolo'), 55, 79, 90
Strada, La, 33
Strzemieszycre, 10, 13, 15
Stuhr, Jurek, 62, 106, 107, 108, 110, 111,
   201
*Sunday in the Country (Un Dimanche à la
   Campagne)*, 177
Swinarski, Konrad, 62
Świrgoń, Waldemar, 123–4, 129
Szapołowska, Grażyna, 131, 132, 133, 167,
   168, 169–71
Szczypiorski, Andrzej, 124

Talking Heads (Gadające Głowqy), 55
Tarkovsky, Andrei, 33–4, 195
Tavernier, Bertrand: *A Sunday in the
   Country*, 177
Teatr Stary (Krakow), 62
Teatr Współczesny, 96–7
Television (production company), 54, 67–8,
   74, 108, 110, 119, 126, 128, 144, 153
Terminator 2, 192
Theatre Technicians' College, xv, 17, 18,
   22, 29, 96
Three Colours (Trzy Kolory), 104, 157, 174,
   179, 192, 194, 212–27
Titkow, Andrzej, 49; *Atarax*, 40
'Tolo' (Witold Stok), 55, 79, 90
Top Dog (Wodzirek), 110
Tor Production House, 144
Trela, Jurek, 62
Trintignant, Jean-Louis, 222, 225
Trybuna Luda, 55, 137, 191

UB (Urząd Bezpieczeństwa), 122
United States of America, 205–7; concept
   of family home in, 7–9; films in, 179,
   209; television in, 153, 154
Upper Silesia, 13

Vargas Llosa, Mario: *Conversation in The
   Cathedral*, 194
Volter, Philippe, 175, 183

W Pustyni i w Puszczy, 28–9
Wajda, Andrzej, xiii, 39, 41, 42, 62, 104,
   129, 138, 142, 151; *Man of Iron*, 134;
   Man of Marble, 134

Walentynowicz, Anna, xix
Wałęsa, Lech, xix
Warsaw, 1, 18–20, 141, 142; in *A Short
    Film about Killing*, 161, 186
Welles, Orson, 32, 193, 194; *Citizen Kane*,
    34, 154, 194
WFD (Wytwórnia Filmów
    Dokumentalnych; State Documentary
    Film Studios), xviii, 42, 44, 51, 54, 78,
    81, 125, 128, 208
Wierzbicki, Krzysztof ('Dziób'), 65–6, 78
Wisznieswki, Wojtek, 55
Witta, Jacques, 187
Wojciechowski, Krzyś, 40, 42
Wojciechowski, Piotr, 40
Wojtyła, Cardinal, xix
Workers '71 (Robotnicy '71), xiii, 54–7,
    81, 90, 91, 136, 197, 208
Workers '80 (Robotnicy '80), 136

Workers' Defence Committee (KOR), xviii-
    xix, 126
WRON (Wojskowa Rada Ocalenia
    Narodowego), 125

X-ray (*Prześwietlenie*), 84

Zajączkowski, A., 136
Zalewski, Witek, 158–9
Zanussi, Krzysztof, xiii, 39–40, 41, 42, 43,
    104, 110, 138, 144, 151; *Illumination
    (Illuminacja)*, 179
Zapasiewicz, Zbyszek, 96
Żarnecki, Misio, 65
Żebrowski,Edek, 39–40, 41, 43, 104, 138,
    139
Zespól (Production Houses), xvii-xviii,
    123–4, 144
Zygadło, Tomek, 55, 57, 97

"The best of European cinema... Outstanding"

Derek Malcolm, The Guardian

MARIN KARMITZ PRESENTS

IRÈNE JACOB
JEAN-LOUIS TRINTIGNANT

THREE COLOURS

RED ⑮

A FILM BY
KRZYSZTOF KIESLOWSKI

TROIS COULEURS ROUGE with JEAN-PIERRE LORIT - FREDERIQUE FEDER screenplay KRZYSZTOF PIESIEWICZ and KRZYSZTOF KIESLOWSKI original music ZBIGNIEW PREISNER director of photography PIOTR SOBOCINSKI set design CLAUDE LENOIR editor JACQUES WITTA second JEAN-CLAUDE LAUREUX costume designer CORINNE JORRY assistant director EMMANUEL FINKIEL executive producer YVON CRENN director of production for CAB PRODUCTIONS SA GERARD RUEY a MK2 PRODUCTIONS SA - FRANCE 3 CINEMA - CAB PRODUCTIONS SA - 'TOR' PRODUCTION co-production with the participation of CANAL + and of TELEVISION SUISSE ROMANDE and with the support of FONDS EURIMAGES DU CONSEIL DE L'EUROPE and L'OFFICE FEDERAL DE LA CULTURE BERNE
Original soundtrack available on ⓔ records   English Subtitles   *An Artificial Eye Release*

FROM FRIDAY 11 NOVEMBER 1994

 ST MARTINS LANE WC2 PHONE 071.379 3014 & 071. 836 0691   206 KING'S ROAD 071.351 3742   **RENOIR** BRUNSWICK SQ.WC1 RUSSELL SQUARE TUBE PHONE 071.837 8402

The Screen on the Hill
203 Haverstock Hill, NW3. ☎ 435 3366   **GATE** C·I·N·E·M·A NOTTING HILL GATE TEL 071-727 4043 PHONE BOOKINGS   **RICHMOND FILMHOUSE** 081-332 0030

OUT ON VIDEO IN 1995

From the director of 'THE DOUBLE LIFE OF VERONIQUE'

"The most highly acclaimed and
truly European director"
Derek Malcolm THE GUARDIAN

MARIN KARMITZ PRESENTS

JULIETTE BINOCHE

THREE COLOURS
BLUE 15

A FILM BY
KRZYSZTOF KIESLOWSKI

with **BENOIT RÉGENT** · HÉLÈNE VINCENT · FLORENCE PERNEL · CHARLOTTE VERY and EMMANUELLE RIVA screenplay by KRZYSZTOF
KIESLOWSKI and KRZYSZTOF PIESIEWICZ original music ZBIGNIEW PREISNER photography SLAWOMIR IDZIAK art director CLAUDE LENOIR editor JACQUES WITTA
sound JEAN-CLAUDE LAUREUX director of production YVON CRENN assistant director EMMANUEL FINKIEL for MK2 PRODUCTIONS SA · CED PRODUCTIONS ·
FRANCE 3 CINEMA · CAB PRODUCTIONS · "TOR" STUDIO PRODUCTION co-production with the participation of CANAL+ and with the support of FONDS EURIMAGES
Original soundtrack available ⊕ records · English Subtitles · An Artificial Eye Release

OUT NOW ON VIDEO

KIESLOWSKI ON VIDEO

Dekalog 1-5

'Each film is a miniature jewel'
The Sunday Times

Dekalog 6-10

'A work of classic stature'
The Times

Kieślowski's British Academy Award-winning masterpiece is one of the landmarks of 1980s cinema. The ten hour-long films are all set around the same Warsaw apartment block and deal with the universal themes of love, marriage, infidelity, faith and compassion.

Dekalog confirms Kieślowski as a master director at the height of his powers.

The Films of Krzysztof Kieślowski on Video

From acclaimed director Krzysztof Kieślowski the haunting and disquieting romantic mystery **"The Double Life of Veronique"** starring Irene Jacob winner of the Cannes 1991 Best Actress Award, now available to buy from Tartan Video.
In addition look out for the video premiere of the full theatrical versions of Kieślowski's **"A Short Film About Killing"** and **"A Short Film About Love"**.

Tartan Video offers you the finest in independent and world cinema. Films of distinction and enduring quality digitally remastered for superior quality and presented with extensive liner notes.
An outstanding collection of classic films by some of the world's greatest directors including Ingmar Bergman's celebrated **"The Seventh Seal"**, Pedro Almodovar's sleek and sensual **"Matador"**, Jean Luc-Godard's groundbreaking **"A Bout De Souffle"**, Bigas Luna's outrageous sex farce **"Jamon Jamon"**, Patrice Leconte's dazzling **"The Hairdresser's Husband"**, Gillo Pontecorvo's stunning **"The Battle of Algiers"**, the hit black comedy **"Man Bites Dog"** and for the very first time in its original widescreen format, Giuseppe Tornatore's heart-warming **"Cinema Paradiso"**.
These and many others are now available to buy on both high quality VHS and Laserdisc in their original widescreen format.

Cinema Paradiso

The Double Life of Veronique

A Bout De Souffle

Tartan Video, the art in art house.

For further information on how to order these titles

please write to Tartan Video,

79 Wardour Street, London W1V 3TH or call 071 494 1400